In the Light of the Menorah
Story of a Symbol

Edited by Yael Israeli

The Israel Museum, Jerusalem

English edition published with the Jewish Publication Society, Philadelphia

The Israel Museum, Jerusalem

In the Light of the Menorah: Story of a Symbol
Weisbord Exhibition Pavilion
Spring – Summer 1998

This book is a translation of the original Hebrew catalogue that accompanied the exhibition "In the Light of the Menorah: Story of a Symbol," presented at the Israel Museum in 1998 on the occasion of the 50th Anniversary of the State of Israel. Certain minor adjustments have been made in the English version with the authors' permission.

Chief curator: Iris Fishof
Curator-in-charge: Daisy Raccah-Djivre
Curators: Lihi Habas, Yael Israeli, Daphna Lapidot, David Mevorah, Rachel Sarfaty, Judith Spitzer
Assistants to the curators: Miriam Apfeldorf, Irit Carmon-Popper, Osnat Sirkin, Hila Zahavi

Exhibition design: Elisheva Yarhi
Restoration: Ruth Yekutiel, David Bigelajzen, Andre Vainer, Adaya Meshorer, Connie Kestenbaum Green, Paolo Recanati
Technical staff: Pesach Ruder, Menachem Amin, Morris Lasry

Editor of the original Hebrew edition: Efrat Carmon
Editor of the English edition: Nancy Benovitz
Editorial support: Rachel Sarfaty
Copyediting: Aloma Halter
Photographic editor: Irène Lewitt
Translations: Anna Barber (pp. 87–91); Nancy Benovitz (pp. 17–23, 180–185, as well as all introductions and captions); Jonathan Chipman (pp. 143–146); Carl Ebert (pp. 43–49, 71–75, 76–80); Malka Jagendorf (pp. 175–179); David Louvish (pp. 50–53, 117–121, 126–131, 147–151, 205–209); David Maisel (pp. 122–125); Lindsey Taylor-Guthartz – Sagir International Translations Ltd. (pp. 39–42, 109–112)
The translations of the biblical passages are, in most cases, taken from *Tanakh, The Holy Scriptures, The New JPS Translation According to the Traditional Hebrew Text* (Philadelphia: The Jewish Publication Society, 1988).

Catalogue design: Tirtsa Barri, Masha Pozina, Nirit Zur
Design adaptation (English edition): Stephanie and Ruti Design, Jerusalem
Color separations: Kal Press Ltd., Tel Aviv
Production: Achsa Benaya-Gamlieli, Israel Museum Products Ltd.
Printed in China

Catalogue no. 425
ISBN: 965 278 237

The Museum's exhibition program in celebration of the 50th Anniversary of the State of Israel has been made possible through the generous support of the donors to its 50th Anniversary Fund:

Judy and Michael Steinhardt, New York
Nash Family Foundation, New York
Audrey and Martin Gruss, New York
Melva Bucksbaum, New York
Maureen and Marshall Cogan, New York
Ruth and Leon Davidoff, Paris and Mexico City
Sylvia Olnick Golber, New York
Marion and David Khalili, London
Lisbet and Joseph Koerner and
Anne and Marty Peretz, Cambridge, MA
Barbara and Richard S. Lane, New York
Denise Lévy, Paris
Phyllis and William Mack, New York
Sondra and David S. Mack, New York
Marcia Riklis, New York
The Michael Sacher Charitable Trust, London
Blanche and Romie Shapiro, New York
Uzi Zucker, New York and Tel Aviv

The exhibition was also supported by the Israel Ministry of Education, Culture, and Sport, the Central Office of Information.

Contents

List of Contributors

Rachel Arbel, Beth Hatefutsoth, The Nahum Goldmann Museum of the Jewish Diaspora, Tel Aviv

Prof. Dan Barag, The Hebrew University of Jerusalem

Dr. Iris Fishof, The Israel Museum, Jerusalem

Lihi Habas, The Hebrew University of Jerusalem

Prof. Rachel Hachlili, University of Haifa

Nogah Hareuveni, Neot Kedumim

Prof. Moshe Idel, The Hebrew University of Jerusalem

Esther Juhasz, The Hebrew University of Jerusalem

Prof. Bianca Kühnel, The Hebrew University of Jerusalem

Daphna Lapidot, The Israel Museum, Jerusalem

Prof. Lee I. Levine, The Hebrew University of Jerusalem

Rivka Merhav, The Israel Museum, Jerusalem

Dr. Alec Meshori, The Open University of Israel

Prof. Bezalel Narkiss, The Hebrew University of Jerusalem

Prof. Elisheva Revel-Neher, The Hebrew University of Jerusalem

Prof. Avraham Ronen, Tel Aviv University

Rachel Sarfaty, The Israel Museum, Jerusalem

Prof. Daniel Sperber, Bar-Ilan University

Shlomit Steinberg, The Israel Museum, Jerusalem

Foreword

While the menorah is a well-known symbol for Jews and non-Jews alike, its story has always been veiled in mystery. After the destruction of the Second Temple in 70 CE, the golden menorah of the Temple was carried off to Rome, and the Jewish historian Josephus wrote that it was placed there in the Temple of Peace built by the Emperor Vespasian. According to one Christian tradition, it was transferred to Carthage when Rome was conquered by the Germanic peoples and from there to Constantinople. The Byzantine historian Procopius wrote that a Jew warned Justinian about the danger of keeping the menorah, since both Rome and Carthage had been destroyed, and told him that it should be removed from the city. The Emperor acceded, and the Temple menorah was transported to a church in Jerusalem, from which it disappeared. Other traditions have claimed that the menorah is in Ethiopia, buried in various places in Europe, or hidden in the cellars of the Vatican.

Even if the Temple menorah no longer exists, its presence remains strong as an idea and as a message for the State of Israel and for Jews everywhere. It was therefore a special challenge, on the occasion of the 50th Anniversary of the State of Israel, for the Israel Museum to prepare a comprehensive exhibition and book on a subject which is so familiar and commonplace at the same time that it is so complex. The menorah bears both personal and public meanings for each of us, and articulating this full range of expression has been a monumental undertaking. Because the subject is also connected substantively with every curatorial wing and nearly every curatorial department of the Museum, the staff which joined together to prepare this book and the exhibition which it accompanied did so responsibly and enthusiastically. Their work in assessing the menorah from earliest archaeology through contemporary design has made great strides in illustrating its history and its intrinsic beauty.

As with the Museum's other exhibitions in celebration of Israel's 50th Anniversary, it is a pleasure for me to thank the donors to our 50th Anniversary Fund, listed elsewhere in this publication, for the generous support which made possible this important undertaking. For the exhibition, we were deeply indebted to Daisy Raccah-Djivre, Curator of Judaica, and to Iris Fishof, Chief Curator of Judaica and Ethnography, for their leadership as curator and curator-in-charge respectively for the project. For this accompanying publication, we especially thank Yael Israeli, Chief Curator of Archaeology, and Rachel Sarfaty, coordinating editor. They were ably joined in this undertaking by an interdepartmental team, representing each of the Museum's curatorial wings, and by the Publications Department, Exhibition Design Department, and Museum Laboratories, and by other staff members throughout the Museum, who lovingly brought this project to fruition.

Today, as the State of Israel is well into its 52nd year, we are pleased to present the English edition of the original Hebrew catalogue, in order to afford readers worldwide the opportunity to explore the remarkable story of the menorah.

James S. Snyder
Anne and Jerome Fisher Director
August 1999

Introduction

The idea of mounting an exhibition on the menorah that would encompass the Museum's different wings was raised several times over the course of the Museum's history, but never pursued. About a year ago, it was proposed again as a fitting exhibition for Israel's 50th Anniversary, and today, this proposal has finally been realized.

The menorah is practically the only visual symbol to have accompanied the Jewish people throughout its history, from its earliest days in the land of Israel through its wanderings in the Diaspora. It started out as a cultic object, serving as the bearer of light and holiness in the Temple in Jerusalem for approximately one thousand years. Yet already in the time of the Second Temple, it began to convey additional messages: In the vision of the biblical prophet Zechariah, which dates from the time of the Return to Zion, it represents rebirth and redemption, against the background of the hardships encountered by the exiles returning from Babylonia. On the coins of Mattathias Antigonus, the last Hasmonaean king, it appears to convey a national message, related to the struggle against Roman rule. After the menorah was, for all intents and purposes, lost forever following the destruction of the Temple almost two thousand years ago, it evolved into a symbol bearing an ever-growing body of messages, from the most abstract, conceptual spheres to concrete, personal protection in the form of amulets. Its symmetrical shape and uplifted branches conveyed both balance and energy, perfection and exaltation, its design a formal expression charged with meaning until this very day.

Despite its important role in both religious and state contexts, no detailed, comprehensive research has been done on the menorah, whether out of respect for its sanctity or because of its ubiquity (even though the original menorah itself has been lost). This, however, is far from the case when it comes to concrete manifestations of the menorah: in the Museum's collections, there are menorahs and menorah designs of different sizes, materials, and purposes from all periods of Jewish history and from all parts of the Jewish Diaspora.

Shortly after it was decided to hold the menorah exhibition, it became clear that in order to demonstrate the continuity and the complexity of this symbol, it would be necessary to avoid presenting an inventory of menorahs, or arranging them systematically, according to chronology or type. We realized that despite the fact that the basic structure of the menorah has remained unchanged for centuries, different nuances of form have emerged that express the menorah's different layers of meaning, and the similarities and parallels between them are fascinating, at times even quite remarkable. For this reason, it seemed more appropriate to place the emphasis on the associative links, both formal and conceptual, between the different incarnations of the menorah. Not surprisingly, most variation on the menorah motif has occurred over the past century, during which the menorah became a symbol of the return to the land of Israel and the fulfillment of the Zionist dream and was used much more frequently for everyday, secular purposes. These modern expressions of the menorah have barely been studied, and are discussed even less than those from ancient or medieval times. For this reason, as well, the exhibition is a mixture of old and new, presenting objects from different fields and periods of time alongside one another.

The aim of this book is to examine the menorah from a variety of perspectives. The eighteen articles appearing here were written by scholars and experts in their fields: some were composed especially for the book, and some were adapted from previously published articles for this purpose. Each article discusses a specific topic, though the list is by no means comprehensive. The articles are brief, but further references are provided for those who wish to learn more on each topic. The book opens with an essay on the selection of the national emblem of the State of Israel. The next group of articles relates to the sources of the menorah's form. This is followed by a discussion of the messianic message inherent in the menorah. A large section deals with the role of the menorah in liturgical contexts and on ritual objects from ancient times through the modern era, including a discussion of the menorah in Christianity. Also included is the story of the menorah in Kabbalah and mysticism, followed by articles on the role of the menorah in contemporary art and applied graphics. The book concludes with a discussion of the relationship between the menorah and the Magen David, a symbol that has accompanied the menorah since the late Middle Ages, sometimes even taking its place.

The plates have been organized according to the various symbolic meanings of the menorah; here as well, the arrangement is intentionally non-chronological, relying, instead, on conceptual and associative ties. The groups deal with the form and sources of the menorah; its messianic message; its role in houses of worship and on ceremonial objects; its magical significance; its use as a symbol of national identity and of destruction and redemption; and its popularity as a modern graphic motif. Each group is prefaced by a brief introduction, in which we have attempted to allude to these meanings, as opposed to actually spelling them out in too restrictive terms. It should be borne in mind that it is often difficult to express the precise meaning or symbolism of any given menorah, for each menorah has several layers, both symbolic and formal. Several possible distinctions in meaning have been proposed here, but these are by no means the only ones, and everyone is entitled to organize the material as he or she sees fit.

We wish to thank the contributors to this book, who willingly agreed to our request for material, despite the short notice, and the entire staff, whose combined efforts made this book possible.

Yael Israeli
Tamar and Teddy Kollek Chief Curator for Archaeology

Designing a National Emblem

Immediately after the establishment of the State of Israel, it became necessary to create an official flag and emblem that would represent the new sovereign nation among the countries of the world. The Provisional State Council deliberated over which formal elements to include so as best to reflect the spirit and character of Israel, and even appointed a special committee to supervise the search.

In a small announcement published in the newspaper, the public was invited to submit proposals for the design of an emblem to represent the State of Israel. The following guidelines were listed: "Colors of the emblem: light blue and white, as well as any additional color, at the designer's discretion. Body of the emblem: the seven-branched menorah with seven six-pointed stars. Other proposals will also be considered."

Hundreds of people from all over the country and all walks of life responded to the announcement. Unfortunately, only a few of their proposals have been preserved for posterity in the State Archives. The participants included well-known graphic designers (such as Ote Valish and V. Strosky), prominent artists (including Ze'ev Raban), and many ordinary citizens. There were entries by a twelve-year-old boy, military personnel, kibbutz members, and city-dwellers, all of whom appear to have grasped the importance of this historic moment.

Many of the participants in the competition not only incorporated the menorah, seven stars (a motif based on Herzl's writings), and the Magen David, but also added other symbols from Jewish and Zionist contexts: two doves, the Lion of Judah, the Tablets of the Law, sheaves of wheat, olive branches, the *sabra* (cactus) plant, a tree stump with a menorah-like branch growing from it, and so on. Some of the proposals included Hebrew words or phrases, such as "State of Israel," "Israel," "Peace on Israel," and "The People of Israel Lives." The emblems were designed according to different formats, though most resemble European coats of arms.

The proposals appearing on pages 9–14 are courtesy of the State Archives, Jerusalem.

מדינת ישראל

י ש ר א ל

ישראל
הצעת סמל המדינה
ג.גפל, ת״א, רח׳ ריינס 46

הצעה:
סמל מדינת ישראל
מ.קפלן
ת. רופין 28, ת.א.

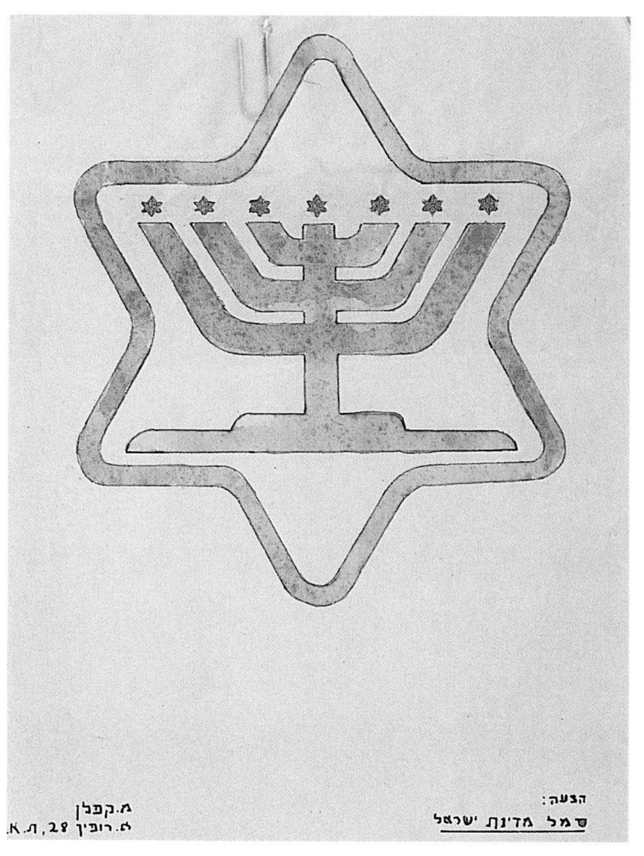

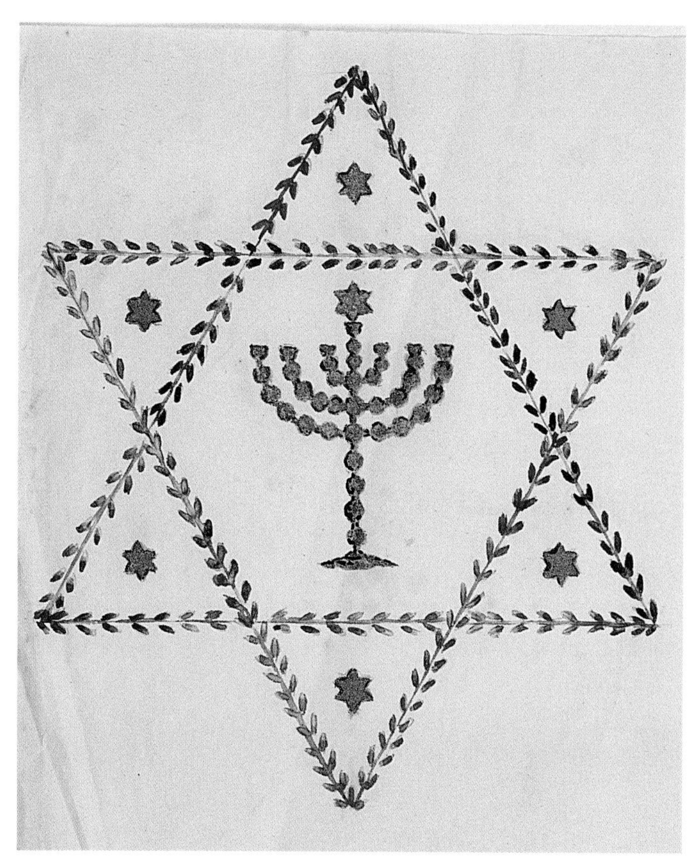

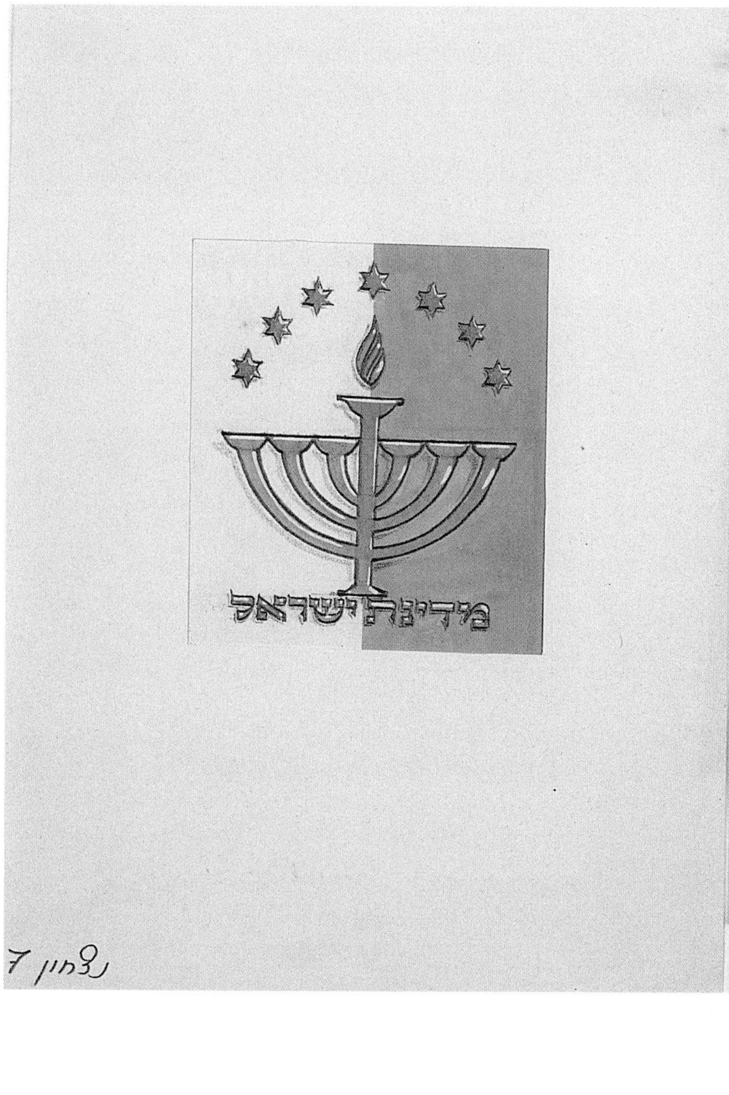

מדינת ישראל
נצחון 7

נצחון 7

לתשומת לבך!

סקיצות מהירות אלה מוצעות מהחצית.
הן נעשו ללא כל מכשיר מתאים - ללא שולחן.
משום כך לא היה באפשרותי למסור עבודה
מעובדת ונקיה, והוצאה לפועל מדויקת!
מחוסר זמן לא שלחתי את ההצעות
גם בשחור לבן.
כל אחד מהתרשימים המצורפים ניתן להקטנה
ובקלות אפשר להעבירו לשחור לבן, לטכניקה של
גלופת קו (שטריך קלישה), בצבע אחד.

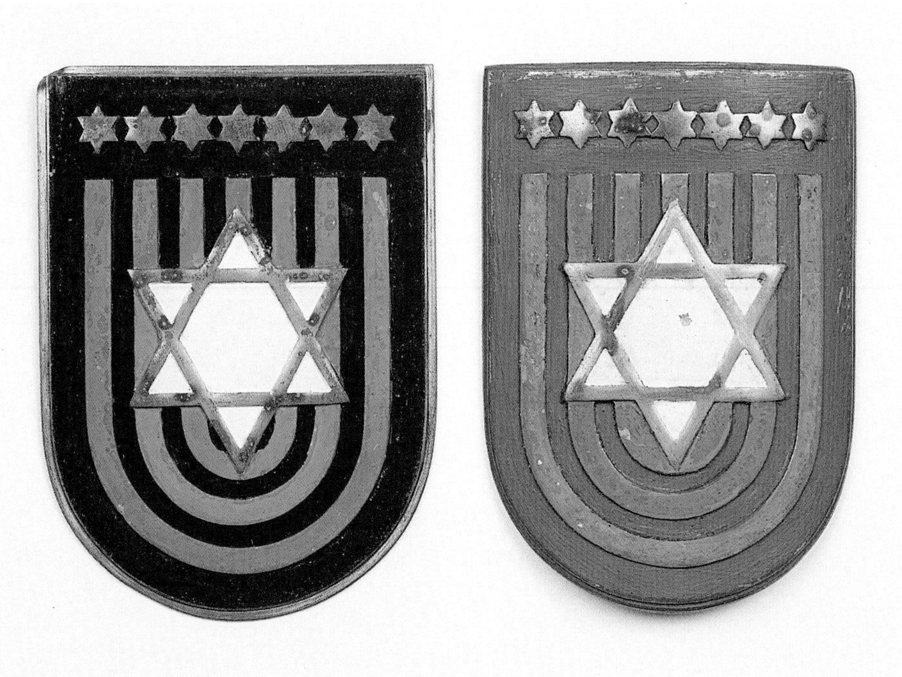

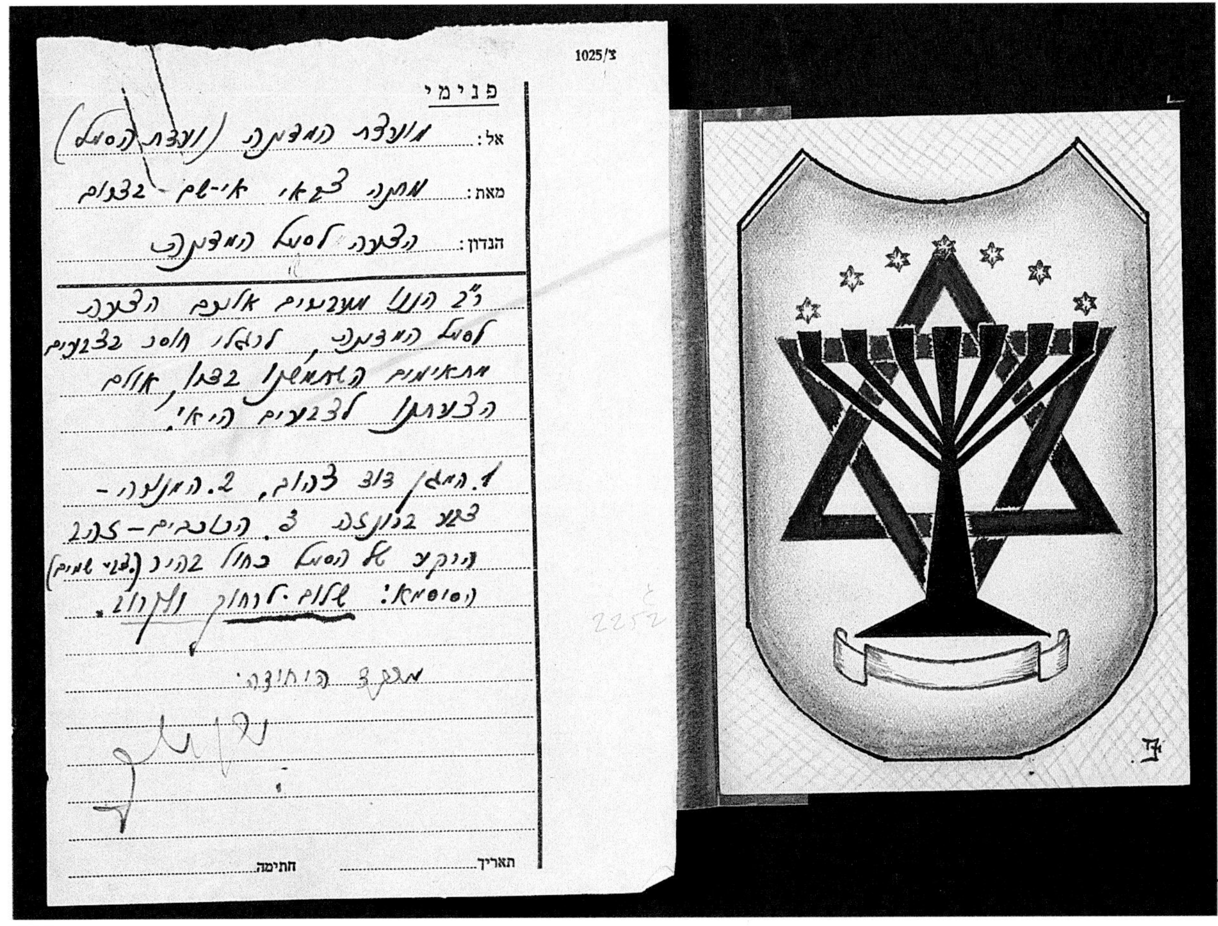

1025/צ

פנימי

אל: מועצת המדינה (ועדת הסמל)

מאת: מחנה צבאי אי-שם בצפון

הנדון: הצעה לסמל המדינה

תאריך .... חתימה ....

כי בצדקה יכון כסא
מדינת
ישראל

הצעה לסמל המדינה
׳נחשון׳

ישראל

עמ' 404 עתון רשמי מס' 50 י"ב בשבט תש"ט, 11.2.1949

מועצת־המדינה הזמנית

הכרזה על סמל מדינת ישראל

מועצת־המדינה הזמנית מכריזה ומודיעה כי סמל מדינת ישראל הוא כמצוייר בזה:

י"א בשבט תש"ט (10 בפברואר 1949)

מועצת־המדינה הזמנית
יוסף שפרינצק
יושב ראש

1
Proclamation of the official emblem of the State of Israel

Alec Meshori

Menorah and Olive Branches

The Design Process of the National Emblem of the State of Israel*

With the establishment of the State of Israel and in preparation for its entry into the United Nations, it became necessary to create an official flag and emblem that would represent the new sovereign nation among the nations of the world. On February 11, 1949, the "Proclamation of the Emblem of the State of Israel" was published in the official gazette of the Provisional Government (fig. 1).[1] This declaration represented the culmination of a process that had begun some ten months earlier.

On July 15, 1948, approximately two months after the establishment of the State, the Provisional State Council convened for its tenth session; on the agenda was the selection of the national flag and emblem. Foreign Minister Moshe Shertock delivered a report and passed out copies of the proposed designs, which had been prepared by graphic artists Ote Valish and V. Strosky. Their proposals had been selected from 450 others, which had been submitted by 164 participants in the competition for the design of the national flag and emblem that had been announced somewhat earlier (fig. 2 and pp. 9–14).[2]

Great significance was attached to the design of the national emblem, for it was meant to represent the realization of the Zionist dream. While the flag was conceived in the Diaspora by those dreaming to return to Zion, the emblem was created on Israeli soil by those who had made the dream come true. The emblem thus had to include carefully chosen symbolic elements. The sense of mission and responsibility was tremendous, and for this reason, the selection process was long and arduous, fraught with much deliberation and searching (see R. Arbel's article in this volume).[3]

מדינת ישראל
הממשלה הזמנית

הזמנה
מתבקשות הצעות
לדגל ולסמל המדינה

הנתונים הם:

הדגל: הצבעים — תכלת ולבן.
בגוף הדגל — מגן־דוד, או שבעה כוכבים (זהב או צבע אחר).

הסמל: הצבעים — תכלת ולבן וכל צבע נוסף, לפי טעמו של הצייר.
בגוף הסמל — מנורה בעלת שבעה קנים ושבעה כוכבים (בני ששה קצוות).

תתקבל לעיון גם כל הצעה אחרת, או רעיון אחר. אין הממשלה מתחייבת לקבל כל הצעה שהיא מן המוגשות.

את ההצעות יש למסור במעטפה סגורה ולרשום עליה:
מזכירות הממשלה הזמנית, ועדת הסמלים.

המעטפה תשא סימן היכר ולא שם מפורש, או משהו, המעיד על זהותו של מגיש ההצעה. במעטפה שניה יפורש שמו של בעל הסימן ותנאיו. המועד האחרון להגשת ההצעה הוא יום ב׳, ז׳ לסיון תש״ח, (14 ביוני 1948), שעה 12.00 בצהרים, לפי שעון ישראל.

2
Publication of the competition for the design of the national flag and emblem

Nine months passed from time of the founding of the State until the final form was selected for the emblem that would represent Israel on its official documents, on the presidential standard, and on government buildings both in Israel and abroad. By the time the emblem had reached its present form, it had undergone numerous changes. The design process was accompanied by various ideas and suggestions, each of which aspired to incorporate the symbolic elements worthy of representing the Jewish people in its land.

The three visual components of the emblem as it is known today are the menorah, olive branches, and the legend "Israel" written in Hebrew. Two virtually diametrically opposed forces attempted to dictate the emphasis that the emblem would have – "religious-ritual" values versus "secular" values. Over the course of the design process, the emphasis shifted from camp to camp, until the present form of the emblem was adopted.

Initial Ideas

Valish and Strosky's initial proposal (fig. 3) features the menorah, which would continue to figure in all later proposals, including the one that was ultimately adopted. The Temple menorah is undoubtedly the oldest Jewish symbol that can be positively identified; it is unique in the world of heraldry in that a

* This article is an abbreviated version of an article previously published in *Cathedra* 46 (1987): 169–187 (Hebrew).

3
Valish and Strosky's proposal for the national emblem
State Archives, Jerusalem

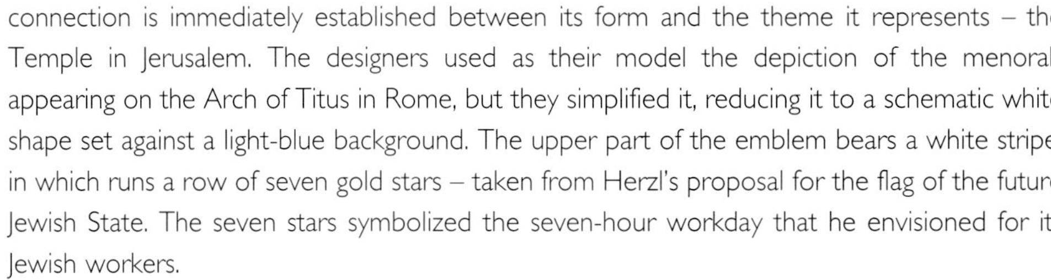

connection is immediately established between its form and the theme it represents – the Temple in Jerusalem. The designers used as their model the depiction of the menorah appearing on the Arch of Titus in Rome, but they simplified it, reducing it to a schematic white shape set against a light-blue background. The upper part of the emblem bears a white stripe, in which runs a row of seven gold stars – taken from Herzl's proposal for the flag of the future Jewish State. The seven stars symbolized the seven-hour workday that he envisioned for its Jewish workers.

The Provisional State Council was not quick to adopt this proposal and postponed the vote on it. Prime Minister David Ben-Gurion summed up the session with the words "One doesn't choose a national emblem and flag everyday."[4] The decision was thus made to appoint a special committee – the Emblem and Flag Committee – which would be responsible for examining new proposals. Beba Idelson was nominated chairperson of the committee, which consisted of government ministers and members of Knesset (Parliament).[5]

The committee convened on July 28, 1948 and decided to reject Valish and Strosky's proposal. No one denied that the menorah should remain one of the components of the emblem, but new visual elements were also proposed. At the same time, the committee clearly strove to use as few visual elements as possible and to find "something that speaks to the heart of the Jew, that warms it and evokes moral conduct . . ."[6]

4
David and Schechter's proposal for the national emblem without the *shofar* and *lulav* (engraving)
State Archives, Jerusalem

On August 16, 1948, the committee reconvened. This time, experts in various fields were present: architect Aba Elhanani, archaeologist Eleazar L. Sukenik, artist Reuven Rubin, and artist-architect Leopold Krakauer. One of their suggestions was that the design of the emblem emphasize the traditional element, that it be taken from an "ancient tradition," and that the use of "modern symbolism" be avoided. Prof. Sukenik, who had recently unearthed a mosaic floor from a 6th-century synagogue in Jericho, proposed that the menorah not be the only component of the emblem, since "in many instances [the menorah appears] together with additional symbols, such as the *shofar* (ram's horn) and palm branches." He further added that the Magen David (Star of David) is not a Jewish symbol and suggested that the committee avoid "the inclusion of this dubious symbol in the national emblem." At the close of the session, the committee decided to approach several designers – Itamar David, Francesca Baruch, and Yerahmiel Schechter, as well as Ote Valish – and ask them to come up with new suggestions. The sum of 300 Israeli pounds was budgeted for this purpose.

Further Proposals

On September 28, 1948, the committee convened for the fifth time. Beba Idelson presented the proposals of David and Schechter, which contained the following elements: the menorah; *lulav* (palm branch), *etrog* (citron), *shofar*, the Hebrew inscription "Peace on Israel"; and Herzl's seven stars (fig. 4). These components sparked heated arguments among the Knesset members and members of the committee regarding the relative emphasis on the two aspects – the secular and the religious – in the emblem.

In ancient times, the menorah was one of the primary symbols of the Temple, appearing on coins and on glass plaques, in wall paintings in catacombs and synagogues, and on synagogue pavements (pp. 62, 67, 97). In such depictions, the menorah rarely stands alone; it is usually portrayed along with other Temple implements, namely, the incense shovels and the *shofar*, as well as additional symbols, such as the *lulav* and *etrog*, which are associated with Sukkot – the Feast of Tabernacles – which was the main Temple festival. The menorah from the mosaic floor of the synagogue in Jericho, which is flanked by a *shofar* and a *lulav* and has beneath it the Hebrew inscription "Peace on Israel" (fig. 5), or a similar menorah, served as the model for the new proposals.

David and Schechter made several slight alterations in the design of the menorah from the Jericho synagogue: they replaced the circle around the menorah, *lulav*, *shofar*, and inscription with an ellipse, in imitation of the shape of ancient seals. They also included a greater number of components than had appeared in Valish's former proposal, thus creating a more complex message. The menorah in David and Schechter's proposal, being a visual quotation from the floor of an ancient synagogue, established a clear connection to the Jewish people's glorious past, since the ancient synagogue was perceived as a substitute for the Temple – a symbolic remnant of the Temple in its glory. The connotations that such a visual quotation lent to the emblem were therefore of a religious-ritual nature. This was reinforced by the use of the phrase "Peace on Israel" from Psalms 125:5, which apart from expressing the peaceful intentions of the State of Israel, implied that the glory of the Jewish people is bestowed by divine providence. The use of a border in the shape of an ancient Hebrew seal, suggestive of the monarchy in the days of the First Commonwealth, added a political dimension to the emblem, and the combination of this shape with the inscription alluded to a union of the spiritual and the political, which characterized the monarchy in ancient times. Herzl's seven gold stars represented the emblem's secular message: besides its link to the glorious past of the Jewish people in its land, the new state would be based on the secular-modern-liberal teachings of the visionary who inspired its creation.

David and Schechter's proposal juxtaposed the religious-ritual aspect, which relates to the past, with the secular-modern aspect, which looks toward the future. The struggle concerning the relative emphasis that each of these aspects would receive in the emblem was expressed by the submission of an additional proposal. The latter was actually a variation of the first proposal; it included, at the request of the committee members, all the components appearing in the previous proposal except for the *shofar* and *lulav* (some members claimed that there were more than enough elements in the emblem, and that the *shofar* and *lulav* were unnecessary). The space that these had occupied was filled with the golden stars.

The committee decided to present both proposals to the members of the Provisional State Council, certain that one of them would be adopted. Believing that the role of the Emblem and Flag Committee had ended, Beba Idelson closed the meeting by thanking the participants for a job well done. She suggested that they invite the team of experts who had assisted them to the meeting of the Provisional State Council, at which the proposals would be submitted for final approval. Two weeks later, the proposals were presented to the Provisional State Council, at its twenty-third session, and in a vote of eleven to five, it was decided to postpone the decision of the national emblem until a later date.

The Shamir Brothers' Proposal

The Emblem and Flag Committee subsequently decided to place another notice in the paper, in which it once again requested new ideas for the national emblem. This time, 131 people responded, most of whom included the menorah motif in their proposals. As in the first instance, the committee determined the emblem's components. Graphic artists Gabriel and Maxim Shamir (whose proposal was ultimately adopted, as we shall see below), related that "[the committee members] requested that the emblem include a menorah, seven stars, and an additional element or form to be determined by the artist." The committee retained, therefore, two of the components that had previously been included in the emblem (the menorah and the seven stars), but no longer stipulated that the emblem contain an inscription. At their sixth meeting on December 28, 1948, the committee decided that the Shamir Brothers' proposal was worthy of being selected, but that several changes had to be introduced. They requested that the designers prepare three additional designs: the menorah alone; the menorah with seven stars; and a more elongated version featuring the menorah with seven stars, two olive branches, and the legend "Israel" beneath the menorah. The committee thus expressed its desire for a more "secular" emblem, for this time as well, no inscription was required apart from the word "Israel." The Shamir Brothers' first proposal was indeed in keeping with this aim (fig. 6).

5
Section of the mosaic floor from the synagogue at Jericho
6th century CE

6
First proposal of the Shamir Brothers State Archives, Jerusalem

The proposal was based upon an heraldic format (which also can be seen in Valish's first proposal); within this format, the menorah appears, surmounted by seven stars and flanked by two stylized olive branches. Regarding the design of the emblem, Gabriel Shamir relates as follows: "After we decided to use the menorah, we looked for an additional element and reached the conclusion that olive branches are the finest expression of the Jewish people's love of peace. These leaves also constitute a highly decorative element. At this point, we were faced with the question: Which menorah should we depict? . . . We decided on a stylized menorah, as opposed to the ancient form. We intended to create a modern emblem and to forego the traditional aspect. We said to ourselves that the menorah is an ancient symbol in its own right, and that its very presence in the emblem was a traditional element. But its form should be modern."[7]

Indeed, the menorah they designed is a modern one, for it is not based on any specific ancient source. In most depictions of the menorah known from wall paintings in catacombs, from the mosaic floors of ancient synagogues, and even from the relief on the Arch of Titus, the branches consist of three rounded arches that traverse the vertical central stem. The Shamir Brothers' menorah, on the other hand, has six, right-angled branches. The right angle deviates sharply from the familiar curve of the ancient menorahs. The base that they employed, which is small and lacks the requisite strength to bear the weight of the branches, is also new. Thus, the modernism that the Shamir Brothers had attained reflects an intentional dissociation from traditional Jewish symbols.

The innovation in this proposal is the olive branches, the addition of which represents a visual metamorphosis of the concept of peace, which had already been proposed by David and Schechter by means of the inscription "Peace on Israel." The written word was replaced by a visual element in the form of olive branches, and thus, the idea of peace was retained in the emblem. Had this proposal been accepted, Israel's national emblem would have conveyed a message similar to that expressed by the Valish and Strosky proposal, which emphasized the connection between the Jewish people and its glorious past in the land of Israel, as well as the rebirth of the past in the light of Herzl's liberal, progressive ideas. However, the Shamir Brothers' proposal also expressed the striving for peace (which was not included in the first proposal), by means of the olive branches.

When the members of the Emblem and Flag Committee convened for the seventh time on January 10, 1949 and had the opportunity to view the Shamir Brothers' proposal, they began to have second thoughts about the "modernism" that they themselves had demanded in the emblem. They were dissatisfied with the design of the menorah, and the idea arose once again to refer to an ancient source, but this time in a different manner: Instead of using the menorah depicted on the floors of ancient synagogues in Israel, the suggestion was to quote directly from an archaeological artifact of no less consequence – the menorah relief from the Arch of Titus in Rome (pp. 190–191). The idea was apparently raised by David Remez, who sought to convey in the emblem the concept of the rebirth of the Jewish people.[8] As a visual expression of this concept, he wished to express the "homecoming" of the menorah – the source of light – after its long period of exile. He also wished to add a trowel as a symbol of manual labor. The committee members accepted Remez's ideas, and agreed that Beba Idelson would ask the Shamir Brothers for an additional design using the menorah from the Arch of Titus.

The menorah from the Arch of Titus had already appeared in Valish and Strosky's initial proposal, which had been rejected by the members of the Provisional State Council. This being the case, why did Remez propose using precisely this motif as one of the main components of the emblem? Unlike the menorah from the floor of the ancient synagogue at Jericho (used in David and Schechter's design), which symbolized the glory of the past (the present was represented by Herzl's golden stars), the decision to quote from the Arch of Titus endowed the menorah motif with an additional symbolic layer, which did not exist in any of the previous proposals: it expressed the idea that the menorah was not just a symbol of former glory, but also of the present and perhaps even the future. It was a visual metaphor of a concept that was popular at that time: Just as the fall of the Jewish state and the beginning of exile in 70 CE found visual expression in the relief depicting Titus' triumphal procession on the arch that was constructed in Rome in his honor, so would the rebirth of the Jewish state and the termination of exile be symbolized by the return of the menorah to its homeland, if not to the Temple, then to the State of Israel that had just been established. The menorah was being removed from the arch, where it served as a symbol of defeat and degradation, and placed in the most honored spot of all – in the emblem of the State of Israel, whose very establishment attests to the triumph of the Jewish people. Past, present, and future were thus joined together in a single, symbolic motif. The visual quotation from the Arch of Titus was also meant to add to the Shamir Brothers' proposal yet another dimension that did not exist in their previous work – the dimension of popular symbolism, which extends beyond the abstract idea.

The revised Shamir Brothers' proposal (which was designed in accordance with the committee's guidelines) was submitted to the committee in two versions during its final meeting on February 7, 1949. One of the versions included "the Titus menorah with two olive branches," while the other consisted of "the Titus menorah with two olive branches and seven stars." The committee members resolved to 1. adopt proposal A, namely: the Titus menorah with two olive branches, with the legend "Israel" beneath the menorah and 2. present this proposal alone to the members of the Provisional State Council for approval.[9]

With this, the committee had fulfilled its task. At the fortieth session of the Provisional State Council on February 10, 1949, Beba Idelson submitted the Shamir Brothers' proposal. A vote was held (and a second one), and the proposal was unanimously accepted.

Menorah and Olive Branches: A Whole Greater Than the Sum of Its Parts

The new national emblem, which was accepted by the members of the Provisional State Council, employs some of the ideas that had appeared in earlier proposals (and leaves out one of them): the olive branches indicate the country's hopes for peace; the menorah attests to the connection with the Jewish people's glorious past in its land and to the restoration of the people's former glory; "Israel" was the new name of the country, but also part of the phrase "Peace on Israel" that had appeared in earlier proposals. Herzl's stars, however, were omitted.[10]

On the surface, the version of the emblem that was adopted appears to indicate that in the struggle between the "secular camp," which emphasized the socialistic and democratic present and future of the nation, and the "religious camp," which stressed the connection to past glory and the God of Israel, victory had fallen to the former. But this interpretation is imprecise. The menorah and olive branches have been described here until now as two separate motifs, which were brought together in order to convey the complex message of the State of Israel as the realization of the Zionist dream – presumably the exclusive design of the Shamir Brothers. However, the combination of these two elements in a single metaphorical symbol already had graphic precedents in the Jewish tradition. It is based upon a well-known textual source – one of the visions of the biblical prophet Zechariah: "The angel who talked with me came back and woke me . . . He said to me, "What do you see?" And I answered, "I see a lampstand all of gold, with a bowl above it. The lamps on it are seven in number, and the lamps above it have seven pipes; and by it are two olive trees, one on the right side of the bowl and one on its left" . . . "And what," I asked him, "are those two olive trees, one on the right and one on the left of the lampstand?" . . . Then he explained, "They are the two anointed dignitaries who attend the Lord of all the earth" (Zechariah 4: 2–4).

Zechariah's vision is apparently based upon a tangible source: he had presumably seen the menorah that had been crafted along with the other ritual objects for the Second Temple, which was completed in 521 BCE. At that time, the Temple cult was reinstated, after a hiatus of more than fifty years.

Zechariah's description is the first detailed description of the menorah that stood in the Temple erected by Zerubbabel ben Sha'altiel. This was the very menorah that was captured by Titus some five hundred years later and carried off to Rome. The symbol of the menorah thus also embodies the concept of continuity: it signifies both destruction and exile, and, at the same time, the hope for redemption. The motifs of the menorah and the Temple appurtenances, with all their connotations, have been familiar to all educated Jews since the time of the Temple's destruction. They served as symbols of the coming of the Messiah and the rebuilding of the Temple in which the menorah, along with the other ritual objects, would serve as a sacred sign of the restored splendor of Jerusalem.

The menorah from Zechariah's vision is depicted on a carpet page from the Cervera Bible of the 14th century (p. 51). The combination of the menorah and olive branches is eschatological in nature and points to the artist's identification of the rebuilding of the Temple in Jerusalem with the coming of the Messiah (see R. Sarfaty's article in this volume). This graphic portrayal of Zechariah's vision was produced more than six hundred years before the emblem of the State of Israel was designed, but both were inspired by the same textual source. In the earlier depiction, the messianic-religious content is stressed, whereas the national emblem of the modern state expresses the idea of the realization of the vision by secular, more complex means. The use of Zechariah's dream in the national emblem thus conveyed the Zionist belief that the establishment of the State of Israel was parallel to the rebuilding of the Temple in the days of the Return to Zion. The two olive branches apparently occupied an important role in the conception of the new state, in which religion and state ("the two anointed" in the words of the prophet – high priest and secular ruler) exist side by side.

Public reaction to the new national emblem was swift. Only two days after its announcement, Gershon Schocken, editor of the *Ha'aretz* newspaper, published this scathing attack: "This proposal, which following the hasty decision of the State Council has become the national emblem of the State of Israel, is nothing but a horror from an aesthetic standpoint, and if this emblem, in a few days, is to be seen flying over the Constituent Assembly and within a short time over the embassies of Israel throughout the world, this will be tantamount to a worldwide declaration of the poor taste and utter lack of aesthetic culture of the State of Israel and its legislators . . . The execution is so vulgar and amateurish, that no self-respecting commercial firm would even consider selecting it as its trademark . . . The olive branches that were meant to serve as the frame are so large and crude that they overshadow the menorah, which was supposed to be the dominating motif in the emblem. The menorah, which is relatively small, is constricted by the two tremendous olive branches, whose leaves look more like swords than the leaves of the tree that symbolizes peace. The empty space above the menorah is very ugly, and attests to the utter helplessness of emblem's designer. The word "Israel" is written in letters that attest to the total ignorance of the artist with regard to Hebrew typography. All this is squeezed into the shape of a plaque, similar to those awarded to the winners of sports competitions.[11]

There was also a religious response. Rabbi Isaac Halevi Herzog, Israel's Chief Rabbi, wrote, among other things: "What our government has done today is wrong; now that we once again have been privileged to receive the light of Zion that is symbolized by the menorah, it has copied the depiction of the menorah of the Arch of Titus, which was apparently the work of foreigners, and is not entirely in accordance with the sacred prescriptions . . ."[12]

The design of the emblem of the State of Israel, which began with a proposal that had a rather simple message, one that emphasized the Jewish people's glorious past alongside Herzl's ideas of social progress, ultimately evolved into a far more complex emblem, which expresses a sophisticated, multilayered message based upon both verbal metaphors and visual and textual quotations. All this is accomplished by only three components, which faithfully convey the message articulated by the emblem's designers – among the first to realize the Zionist dream – in the most concise and direct manner possible.

1 *Iton Rishmi* 50 (11 February 1949): 404 (Hebrew).

2 *Rashumot,* "The Provisional State Council," 10th session, 15 July 1948, 10 (Hebrew).

3 See M. Avi-Yonah, "The State Emblem in Historical Perspective," *Moladeti* 13–15 (1950): 96–97 (Hebrew).

4 *Rashumot* (above, n. 2), 12.

5 The committee members included B. Idelson, A. Altman, Y. Harari, Z. Warhaftig, R. Cohen, D. R. Cohanovitz, S. Kobashi, R. Louvich, M. D. Levenstein, Z. Luria, B. Mintz, A. Zeisling, P. Rosenblitt (Rosen), D. Remez, Z. Chelouche, M. Shapira, and M. Shertock (Sharett). The report of its activities (State Archives, RG 78, Box 395, File 1/1005) as published in *Rashumot,* 40th session, 10 February 1949, 20 (Hebrew). The quotations from the committee's discussions mentioned below were taken from this report. I wish to thank Gilead Livneh from the State Archives for his dedicated assistance with locating material for this article.

6 Quoted from Beba Idelson at a meeting of The Provisional State Council, *Rashumot,* 23rd session, 14 October 1948, 44.

7 Based on "The Birth of the Emblem of the State of Israel" (an interview with the Shamir brothers), *Ma'ariv,* 16 February 1949 (Hebrew).

8 S. Z. Cahana claimed that he suggested using the menorah from the Arch of Titus as a model for the menorah in the national emblem. He requested that this be mentioned in a letter he wrote to the Emblem and Flag Committee on 20 January 1949, State Archives, (above, n. 5).

9 Protocol of the committee from 7 February 1949, State Archives, (above, n. 5).

10 Aaron Remez related that his father, David Remez, claimed that the stars would represent too great a connection to Herzl's *Der Altneuland.* But not all that is written in this work conformed to the ideas of the Israeli political parties of that time, and for this reason, the stars were removed from the emblem.

11 G. Schocken, "State Emblem or *Testimonium Paupertatis,*" *Ha'aretz,* 13 February 1949 (Hebrew).

12 I. Herzog, "The Shape of the Menorah in the Arch of Titus," in *Solomon S. Meyer Memorial Volume: Collection of Essays on the History of the Jews of Italy* (Milan-Jerusalem, 1956), 95–98 (Hebrew).

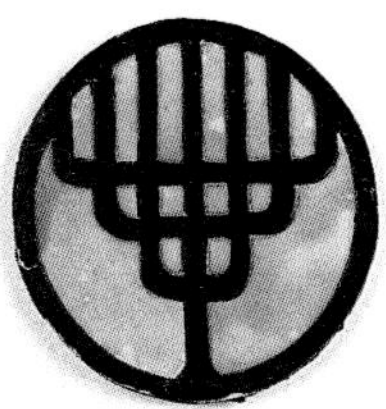

"And This Was the Workmanship of the Lampstand"

Despite the detailed description of the menorah that appears in the Bible, it is impossible to derive a clear picture of the menorah's form from the biblical text alone. Moreover, no illustration of the menorah predating the 1st century BCE has come down to us, a phenomenon that might be explained by a reluctance to reproduce this sacred ritual object. The question of the form of the menorah has thus been left to the imaginations of artists and scholars for generations. One of the interpretations proposed here is entirely different from the familiar model; it is, rather, much closer to the cultic lamps of the ancient world. There is also a clear formal resemblance between the menorah and the Tree of Life motif, prevalent in the art of the Ancient Near East. Today, it is widely accepted that the menorah's various details were inspired by the floral world. Consequently, many of the enigmatic terms used in the Bible in conjunction with the menorah were translated on the basis of a familiarity with local plant life, such as "calyx and petals," "cups shaped like almond-blossoms," and "branches." In fact, already in the early days of research on the flora and fauna of the land of Israel, it was proposed that the menorah's form was based on the local plant, the Jerusalem moriah.

Rashi and Maimonides were among the many individuals who grappled with the textual sources on the menorah, offering their own interpretations of its form. Their descriptions would greatly influence the illuminators of Hebrew manuscripts in the late Middle Ages. In his classic work on Jewish law, the *Mishneh Torah,* Maimonides even included his own sketches of the menorah. A manuscript of this work from 1460 contains illustrations that are believed to be quite similar to Maimonides' originals; the most striking feature of these drawings is their tree-like appearance.

Our notion of the menorah's basic form has remained virtually unchanged over the past two thousand years, since the end of the Second Temple period. Yet even in the 20th century, this symbol has continued to fire the imaginations of artists, who have dealt with it using the characteristic styles of this century, from the Jugendstil of the Bezalel School to the contemporary approaches of artists today.

Previous page:
Decorative pattern based on menorah motif (detail), by a Bezalel student, early years of the school,
Israel Museum Collection

Opposite:
The menorah, incense altar, and shewbread table. Graffito on plaster, found in a private house in the Upper City of Jerusalem (today the Jewish Quarter).
1st century BCE
H 20 cm
Israel Antiquities Authority Collection
It is possible that this image was drawn by someone who had actually seen the objects in the Temple.

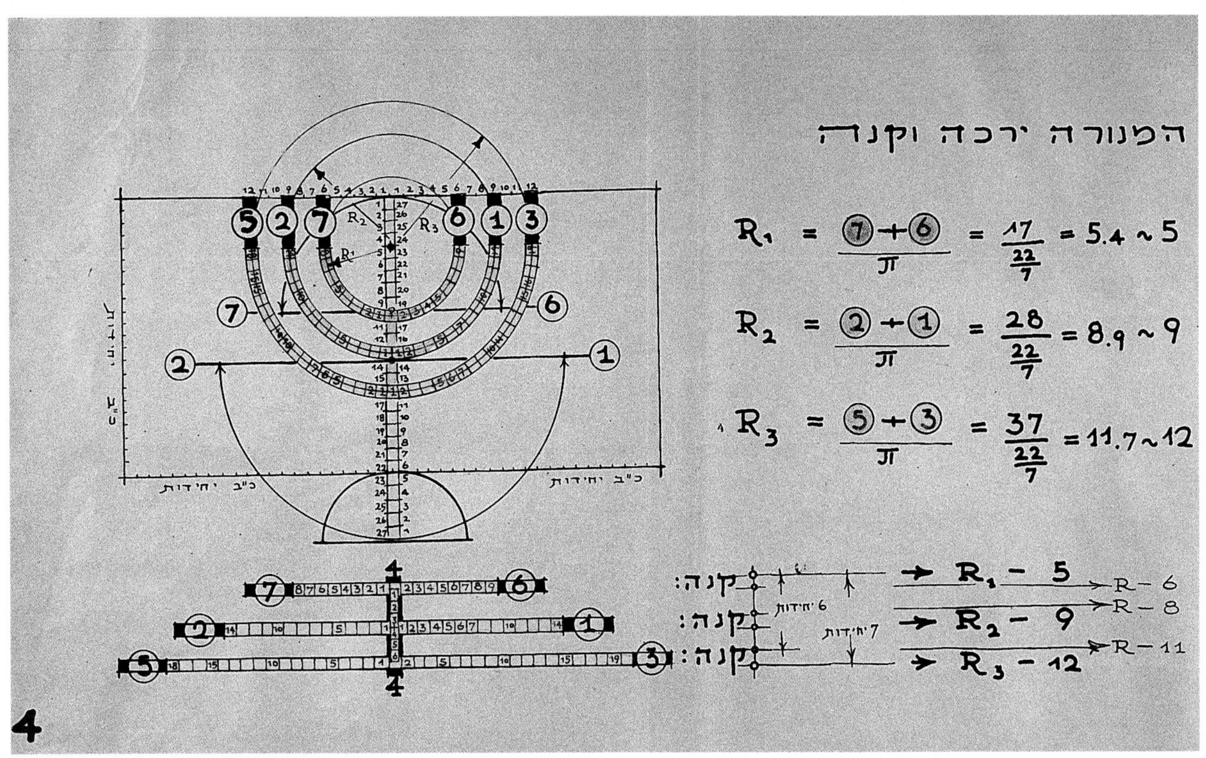

Pages from the booklet by Meir Ben-Uri (architect), *And This Was the Workmanship of the Lampstand,* 1956
Institute for Jewish Art, Haifa
25 x 42 cm
Collection of Alain Roth, Herzliya

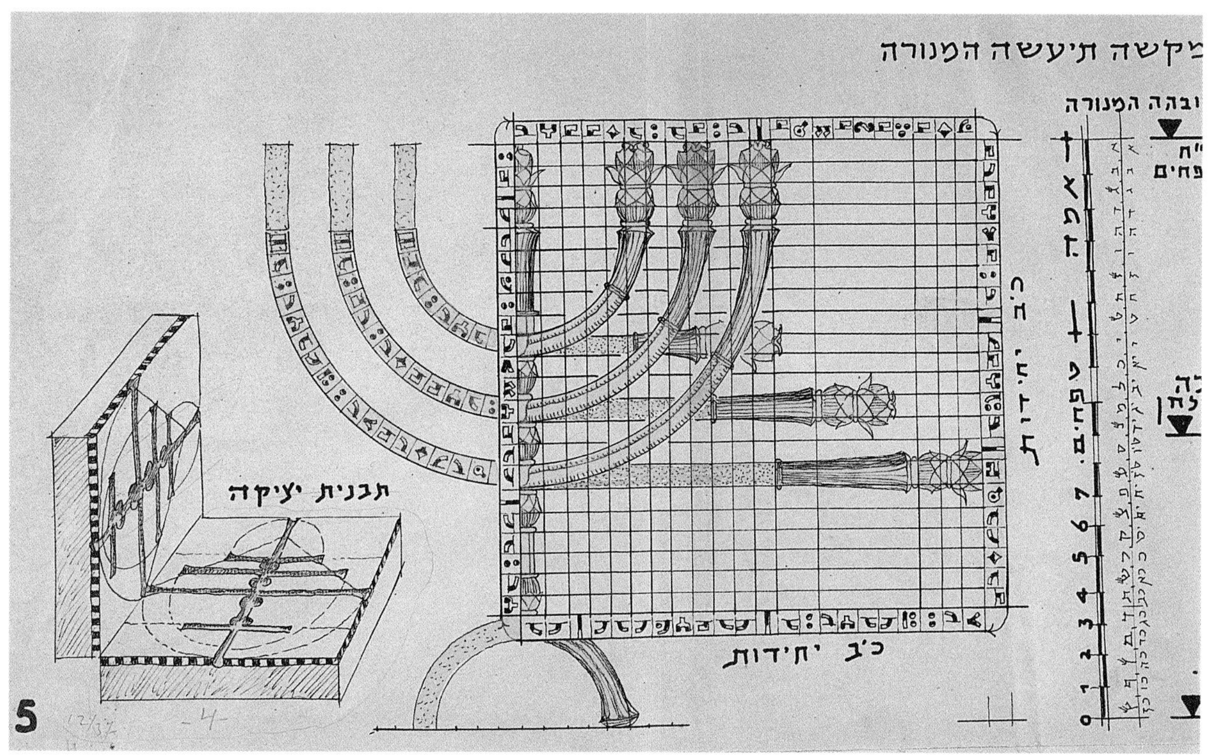
מקשה תיעשה המנורה
תבנית יציקה
כ״ב יחידות
5

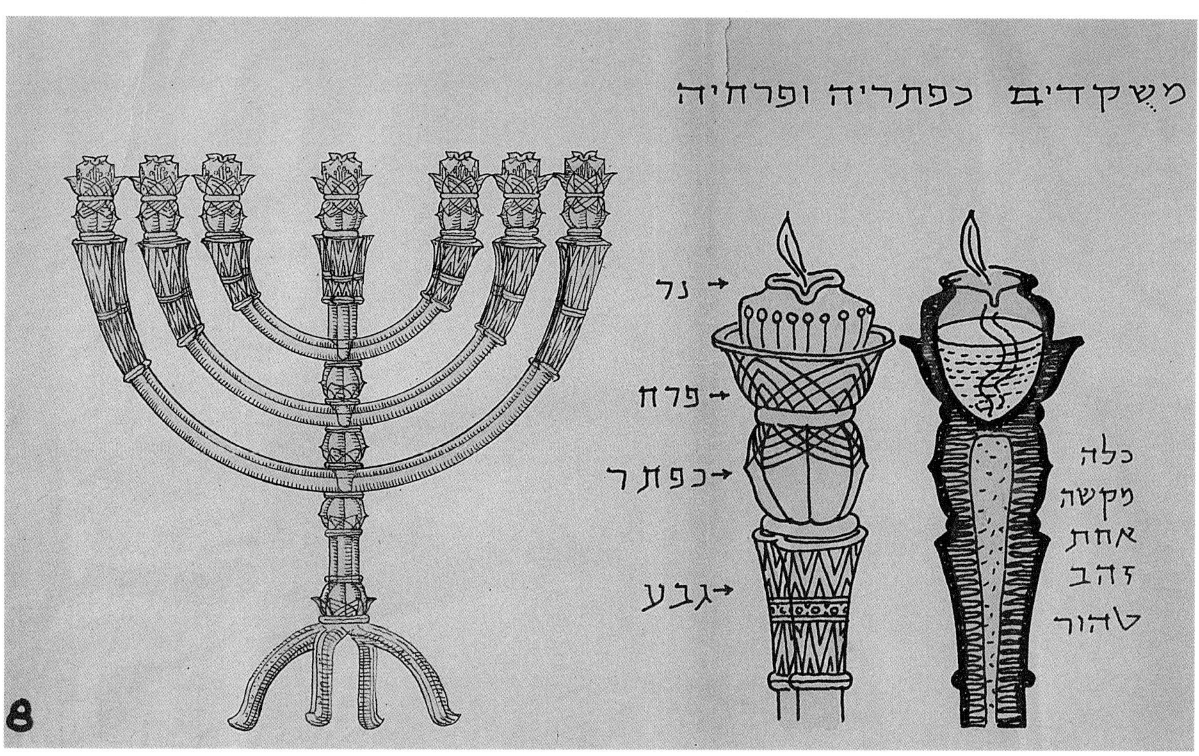
משקדים כפתריה ופרחיה
נר
פרח
כפתר
גבע
כלה
מקשה
אחת
זהב
טהור
8

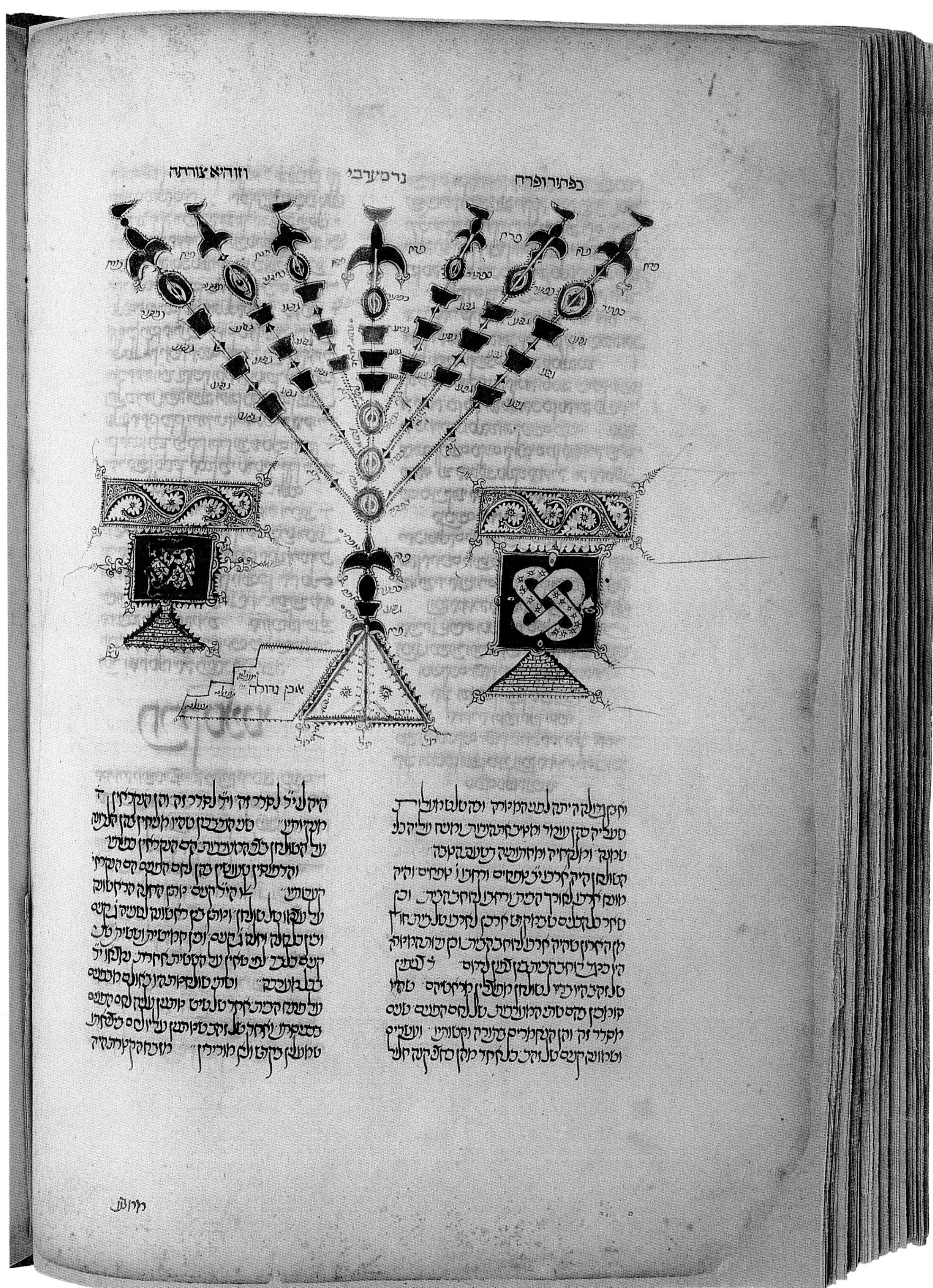
וזוהיא צורתה
נר מערבי
כפתור ופרח

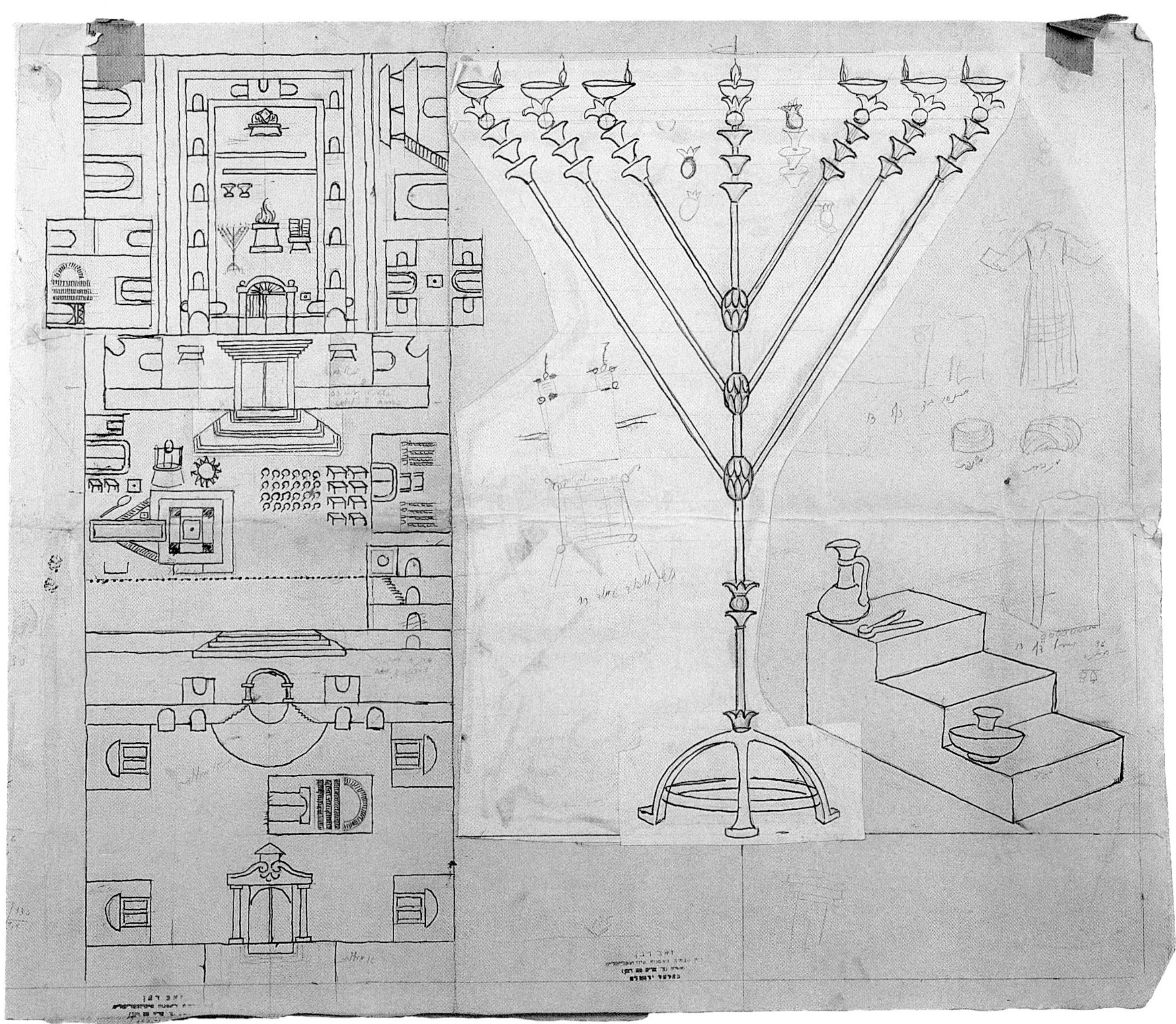

Sketch of the Tabernacle and its appurtenances, with the menorah in the center
Ze'ev Raban, 1890–1970
India ink, pencil, and collage on paper
56 x 47 cm
Collection of Itzhak Einhorn, Tel Aviv

Opposite:
Illuminated page from Maimonides' *Mishneh Torah*
Spain, c. 1460
Handwritten and illustrated in ink on paper, 41.5 x 29 cm
The Jewish National and University Library, Jerusalem
Apparently, the menorah was designed in accordance with Maimonides' original sketches.

Candelabrum from the Kingdom of Urartu (present-day Armenia) with a votive inscription of King Menua (810–786 BCE)
Bronze
H 178 cm
Israel Museum Collection

Opposite:
Olive-picking and oil pressing for the Temple menorah
Micrograph illustration in a Pentateuch
Scribe: Solomon Hacohen,
German Switzerland, 1294–1295
Handwritten in ink on parchment
53.5 x 37.5 cm
Bibliothèque Nationale de France, Paris

"Tower of David" carpet with two half-menorahs in its corners
Early years of the Bezalel School
Wool, 83 x 142 cm
Israel Museum Collection, the Recanati Fund for the Acquisition of Israeli Art

Opposite:
Book decorations based on the menorah motif
Early years of the Bezalel School,
Photograph, 2 pages, each 10 x 15 cm
Israel Museum Collection

Logo designs
Dan Reisenger, b. 1934

From right to left and top to bottom:

Habima National Theater, 1968

"Productive Zionism," 1982

Africa-Israel Investments, Inc., 1981

Institute for National Insurance, 1968

America House (Office for Israel America Commerce) Ltd., 1969

Prestenberg-Gronstein – Diamond Polishing, 1975

The Wolf Israel Fund for the Promotion of Science and Art for the Sake of Humanity, 1982

Botanical Gardens, Jerusalem, 1987

Dan Reisenger, winner of the Israel Prize for Graphic Design in 1998 – Israel's Jubilee year – is one of Israel's veteran graphic designers.

Many of the logos he has designed for companies, institutions, and organizations are based on the form of the seven-branched candelabrum. However, Reisenger, reduces this shape to its formal essence, and in doing so, adjusts it to the topic or product the logo is meant to represent, not always adhering to the traditional number of branches.

In his logos, Reisenger creates the form of the menorah from the company or institution's initials. He does this by integrating, doubling, and reversing the letters so that they form geometric shapes reminiscent of the shape of the menorah. These logos, based on geometric lines and symmetry, exhibit a clean, minimalistic style. His particular touch transforms the seven-branched candelabrum into a modern graphic image, related to the Israel of today, but clearly alluding to the past.

Above:

Chancel screen engraved and decorated in relief, synagogue at Susiya, southern Hebron hill region
Byzantine period, 5th–7th century CE
Marble, W 71.5 cm.
Courtesy of the Staff Officer for Archaeology, Judea and Samaria

Below:

Two menorahs, 1985
Achille Castiglioni, Italian, b. 1918
Makrolon, metal, molded rubber, H 40.5 cm
Produced in cooperation with Alessi SpA, Crusinallo di Omegna, Italy
Israel Museum Collection, gift of the artist

Jerusalem moriah on the Hill of the Menorah at Ne'ot Kedumim
Photo: Nogah Hareuveni

Nogah Hareuveni, Neot Kedumim

"Knob and Flower" in the Design of the Menorah

He [Bezalel] made the menorah of pure gold. He made the menorah – its base and its shaft of hammered work; its calyxes, knobs (kaftorim), *and flowers were of one piece with it. There were six branches stemming from its sides: three branches of the menorah stemmed from one side, and three branches from the other side. There were also three almond-shaped calyxes with a knob and flower on the first branch . . . and similarly for all six branches stemming from the menorah. On the main stem of the menorah there were four almond-shaped calyxes, its knobs and its flowers: a knob under two of its branches, . . . knobs under the six branches which stemmed from the menorah. The knobs and the branches were of one piece with it, all a single piece of beaten work of pure gold.* (Exodus 37: 17–23)*

1
Gallnut of the *Salvia triloba,* an example of a "knob and flower" of the Cretan apple type. Photo: Nogah Hareuveni

At first glance, it seems that this description of the menorah conceals more than it reveals, in spite of the numerous details it provides. Branches, flowers, almond-shaped calyxes, and perhaps even *kaftorim* (translated above as knobs) are all familiar concepts from the plant world, and our knowledge of them has been of great assistance in interpreting the enigmatic aspects of the biblical account. The emphasis on these concepts in the biblical description of the menorah inspired my parents, the late Dr. Ephraim and Hannah Hareuveni (among the first to study the natural environment of Israel in light of our ancient sources), to search throughout the land for the plant or plants that would help them understand these verses.

The first clue in their search came, strangely enough, from the Babylonian Talmud. In the context of a description of the Temple menorah, Samuel says: "What do the knobs (*kaftorim*) resemble? A sort of Cretan apple." (Menahot 28b). Thus writes Ephraim Hareuveni in 1928:[1]

> I started to trace this tradition and search for the Cretan apples in order to learn what they were like. I looked for a plant that produced apples and that grew mainly in Crete, and the only plant I found bore apples that were exactly what we were looking for. This plant is a member of the *Salvia* (sage) family and produces "apples." These are actually gallnuts (made by the aulax insect). They are about the size of a cherry or a nut, and are apple-shaped. When young, they are edible. Linnaeus gave the scientific name of *Salvia pommifera* (apple-bearing sage) to this plant. Several natural scientists [here Dr. Hareuveni lists a number of botanists of international reputation] have also compared its "fruits" to apples. Since the main area of distribution of this "fruit" is the island of Crete,[2] and it is considered a delicacy by the Cretans (its juice is tart and fragrant, and sweetened with sugar, it appeals to the oriental taste), this clearly indicates that these fruits must have been renowned throughout the Ancient Near East. . . . What connection did our sages see between the shape of this fruit and the knobs of the menorah? These apples grow directly out of the branch, as though they are "of one piece with it." Moreover, the plant continues growing above the top of the apples (several small leaves continue to grow there), just like the knobs of the menorah, for the branch enters them from below and passes upward through them. The leaves above the Cretan apples resemble the petals above the knobs of the menorah. . . . And perhaps the biblical name of the island [of Crete] – Caphtor – and its inhabitants is based on these *kaftorim,* since we often find

* This translation of the biblical passage has been provided by the author

that the ancients named countries after one of their characteristic plants. Such is the case with the Land of Moriah; similarly, Egypt was sometimes known as the Land of the Sycamore; perhaps this was true of the Land (or Island) of Caphtor.

This explanation of the origin of the "Cretan apples" in the Babylonian Talmud led Ephraim and Hannah Hareuveni to examine other plants of the *Salvia* family that grow in Israel and throughout Sinai. They hoped that the thorough study of these plants would clarify further aspects of the description of the menorah and its component parts. These field studies also included meetings with desert nomads in Sinai and the Negev and with villagers from both sides of the Jordan River, as well as Syria and Lebanon. At the same time, they assembled all that had been written on these plants from classical times to the beginning of the 20th century, encompassing both botanical and linguistic sources. Their conclusions, which extend far beyond the scope of this discussion, have been published in scientific journals in Israel and abroad. Only a brief summary of the conclusions pertaining to the topic at hand can be presented here:

A. The description of the menorah as a pillar, or as a central stem, with pairs of opposing "branches" issuing from it clearly reflects the structure of several types of *Salvia* growing in Israel and Sinai.

B. Although this structure of pairs of branches emerging from a central stem appears in many other species of the *Labiatae* family, the resemblance to the menorah is particularly pronounced in those species of *Salvia* that are closest to the type that grows in Crete and bears the Cretan apples described above.

2
A moriah plant blossoming in southern Sinai
Photo: Nogah Hareuveni

C. Among the common names for these species of *Salvia* in our area – both in ancient and modern lexicographic literature and in everyday usage (in ancient Syriac and in the various dialects of Arabic) – are many that contain the element *mr*, such as *marva, marmiya, marimiya, maro,* and *marmahon.*

D. The plants bearing these names characteristically exude the aromas of essential oils from their stems, leaves, and/or flowers – especially in the hot seasons when the sun is at its zenith.

E. All of the above seem to point to the biblical terms for myrrh (*mor*) and oil of myrrh, as well as the names "the Land of Moriah" and "Mount Moriah."

The Biblical commentator, Onkelos translates "the Land of Moriah" (Genesis 22:2) as *ar'a pulhana* (the Land of the Ritual), and Rashi comments: "because of the ritual of the incense which contained myrrh, nard, and other spices." Indeed, Aaron the High Priest was commanded to offer the incense when he kindled the lamps of the menorah at dusk and when he trimmed them "every morning" (Exodus 30:7–8). This commandment can be seen as a symbolic expression of what our ancestors experienced in the mountains and fields of the land of Israel as they made the pilgrimage to Jerusalem during the warm days of the festival of Shavuot. The natural phenomenon of fragrant plants whose aroma becomes stronger with increased light and heat was also expressed in the words of Rabbi Joshua ben Levi: "[At] each commandment [of the Ten Commandments, which according to tradition were given on Shavuot] which issued from the mouth of the Holy One, blessed be He, the entire world was filled with perfume" (Babylonian Talmud, Shabbat 88b).

These facts led Hannah and Ephraim Hareuveni to the conclusion that the fragrant plants of the *Salvia* species that grow in our region were known to our ancestors as *moriah* (which is composed of the elements *mor* [myrrh] and *Yah*, one of God's names), and that a clear link can be seen between the form of the menorah described in the Book of Exodus in terms derived from the plant world and these moriah plants, growing in the mountains of Sinai and common to the Judean hills (fig. 2 and p. 38).

Continuing Ephraim and Hannah Hareuveni's research, I attempted to investigate the meaning of the phrase "knob and flower" (kaftor vaferah) used in conjunction with the almond-shaped calyxes in the biblical description of the menorah. I have approached this problem from three different angles:

A. Observations of the development of almond blossoms;

B. The Babylonian Talmud on the hidden symbolism of the location of the menorah in the Tabernacle and the Temple;

C. The symbolic significance of the almond tree.

Several conclusions have emerged, which supplement the conclusions that have already been reached:[3]

A. There is a stage in the development of the almond in which neither the sepals nor the petals have fallen from the top of the developing fruit. This stage resembles a cup, or goblet: the lower part consists of the "knob" of the young fruit, while the rim is formed by the remains of the flower – indeed, an almond-shaped calyx with "knob and flower" (*kaftor vaferah*).

B. The Babylonian Talmud gives a clear explanation for the location of the menorah in the Tabernacle and the Temple: "A north wind is good for wheat when it has reached a third of its ripening [when it is still green and the kernels have not yet filled with starch] and bad for olives at the time when their flowers have opened. A south wind is bad for wheat when it has reached a third of its ripening and good for olives when their flowers have opened, and the sign of this is: The [shewbread] table in the north [side of the Tabernacle and the Temple] and the menorah in the south. Each calls forth its own [wind]" (Baba Batra 147a, and elsewhere).

The subject of this passage is the spell of erratic weather that passes over the country every year during the period of the Counting of the Omer, between Passover and Shavuot. The unpredictable weather during this period can determine the fate of the wheat and olives. This passage from the Talmud explains the symbolism of the location of the shewbread table in the north side of the Tabernacle sanctuary and the menorah in the south, as described in the Book of Exodus: "Place . . . the menorah by the south wall of the Tabernacle, opposite the table, which is to be placed by the north wall" (Exodus 26:35).

The shewbread *(lehem hapanim)* placed on the table represented the wheat and barley, and was turned toward the "north wind," while the menorah, in which olive oil was burnt, was turned toward the "south wind," which favored the growth of olives. Together they symbolized, according to the sages, the request that the Creator bring every wind at its proper time, as if to say: May it be Your will that the north wind blow during the first weeks after Passover, in order to give the barley and wheat time to mature and their kernels to fill with starch. The olive buds will wait to open their flowers, and may the south wind come only after the grain has ripened and the ears have hardened. In this manner, "each calls forth its own [wind]."

C. It seems that the symbolism expressed in the location of the menorah in the sanctuary, as explained in the Talmud, was also expressed in the design of the menorah, as described in Exodus. The design of the calyxes, in the shape of the young almond with traces of its flower still visible, was not dictated by aesthetic considerations only, but was also meant to express the plea that the olive flowers not be damaged by the winds and rains before the fruit has time to form.

When the prophet Jeremiah declares, "I see a branch of an almond tree [Hebrew: *shaked*]," he receives the answer, "You have seen right, for I am watchful [Hebrew: *shoked*] to bring my word to pass" (Jeremiah 1:11–12). The almond tree still displays its qualities of diligence, consistency, and daily watchfulness. It does indeed "watch" every day during the rainy season in order to make use of every spell of warmth and light between the waves of cold and rain to open its flowers and form its fruit. This very stage of the formation of the fruit before the petals and buds have fallen conveys this tree's special characteristic of watchfulness.

In light of all this, the significance of the decoration of the menorah – almond-shaped calyxes with knobs and flowers, the shape of the almond blossom at the time of fruit formation – is clear: This is an artistic way of expressing the symbolism of the placement of the menorah to the south, to stand on guard every day, as a kind of parallel to the days of the Counting of the Omer between Passover and Shavuot, the period of the alternating hot, dry south wind and the "north wind [that] produces rain" (Proverbs 25:23) weather that has our modern forecasters completely baffled.

3
Almond-shaped calyx. The fruit has already grown, but the sepals and stamens have not yet fallen off. Photo: Nogah Hareuveni

We now return to the Cretan apples. If the knobs of the menorah were indeed modeled after the shape of ripening almonds, why did Samuel cite the model of the Cretan apples? In order to understand this, it must be borne in mind that Samuel gave this example to his fellow Jews in Babylonia, who were removed from agricultural labor, and thus had no opportunity of observing the rapid transitions in the flowering of the almond tree. On the other hand, the Cretan apples, whose shape is reminiscent of the "knob and flower" (*kaftor vaferah*) of the menorah's calyxes, probably appeared on their tables frequently.

In summary, it is appears that the biblical description of the structure and artistic design of the menorah, rich with terms deriving from the plant world, embodied symbolic values, which reflect one of the major difficulties encountered by the ancient farmer in the land of Israel.

1 E. Hareuveni, "The Knobs of the Menorah and the Cretan Apples," *Leshonenu Quarterly* 1 (1928).

2 Years later, Dr. Ephraim Hareuveni discovered similar gallnuts, also with "knob and flower" – the gallnuts of the *Salvia triloba* . (see fig. 1).

3 My conclusions were published in N. Hareuveni, *Nature in Our Biblical Heritage* (Neot Kedumim, 1980), and idem, *The Emblem of the State of Israel: Its Roots in the Nature and Heritage of Israel* (Neot Kedumim, 1996).

Rachel Hachlili and Rivka Merhav

The Menorah of the First and Second Temple Periods in Light of Literary Sources and Archaeological Finds*

The menorah has occupied the attention of various scholars, who have considered both its morphological and conceptual aspects. The basic assumption is that the seven-branched menorah described in the Book of Exodus refers to the period of the desert wanderings, and that it is the earliest menorah connected to the Israelite cult. This conviction, however, which corresponds to the more general attitude in biblical studies concerning the antiquity of Pentateuchal literature, is not supported by the concrete finds discovered hitherto, which indicate instead that the seven-branched menorah does not antedate the Second Temple period.

The Description of the Tabernacle Menorah

The fullest account of the menorah in the Bible is found in Exodus 25:31–40 and 37:17–24. These verses discuss the material, weight, and shape of the menorah and its accessories. Chapter 25 contains a description of the Tabernacle, together with its furnishings, as conveyed to Moses on Mount Sinai. Chapter 37 describes the Tabernacle's construction by Bezalel ben Uri and his assistants.

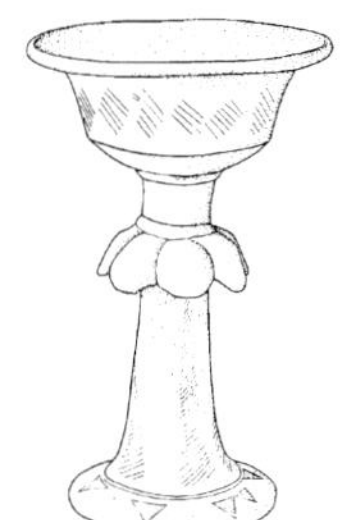

1
Pottery incense burner from Tel Safi

This issue deserves to be reexamined: do these passages, in fact, describe the seven-branched candelabrum, the earliest cultic menorah, or did, perhaps, the menorah undergo a transformation from a relatively simple lampstand to the elaborate seven-branched type which received currency during the Second Temple period? In our opinion, the description of the menorah in Exodus comprises two elements: the first – a lampstand, which is called a "menorah" in the opening verse; and the second – a more elaborate menorah, to which six branches[1] were added in Second Temple times and which was attributed to the Tabernacle. Our point of departure for this discussion stems from the biblical sources and their reconsideration in the light of archaeological finds from Israel and neighboring lands.

The menorah was made of gold, the noblest of metals, which appears at the head of the list of the materials collected as contributions for the erection of the Tabernacle: "And these are the gifts that you shall accept from them: gold, silver, and copper" (Exodus 25:3; see also 35:5). The preference for gold is expressed in its choice for the Tabernacle interior, that is to say, the structure itself and the ritual objects, whereas silver and copper, less valuable metals, sufficed for the courtyard and its furnishings (Exodus 27:9–19; 38:9–20). The gold of the menorah is defined as "pure gold." This definition is reserved for the Tabernacle ritual objects alone (ark, shewbread table, and menorah; Exodus 26:11, 17; 25:31) in contrast to the ordinary gold that plated the Tabernacle's planks and pillars (Exodus 26:6, 29, 37). It follows that there was a clear distinction between "pure gold," intended for the ritual objects and their accessories – the most sacred items – and "gold" that was not pure, intended for the less sacred articles. The menorah is also the only Tabernacle item termed "pure" (Exodus 31:8; 39:37), possibly pointing to symbolic meaning.

Only the weight of the menorah is specified in the description, not its dimensions: "He made it and all its furnishings out of a talent of pure gold" (Exodus 25:39; 37:24.)[2] This is in distinction to the other cultic furnishings – the ark, the table, and the altar – whose descriptions are accompanied by dimensions, but do not specify the amount of gold required for their manufacture. The difference may be explained by the latter's being made of wood overlaid with beaten gold, and thus the quantity of gold required was

* This article is an abridged and revised version of one that was published in *Eretz-Israel* 18 (1985): 256–267 (Hebrew).

determined by the object's size; the menorah, however, was made solely of gold, so that its weight was the basic datum that determined its dimensions.

As stated, a talent of gold was allotted to the menorah and its accessories – this out of a total of 29 talents and 730 (sacred) shekels contributed toward the Tabernacle's erection. In order to obtain pure gold, a greater amount of regular gold, which had to be refined, was needed. If one adds to this the quantity of pure gold required for the preparation of the remaining furnishings and utensils, it is clear that the total amount of pure gold that was required was considerable indeed. It is doubtful, however, that the amount of pure gold stipulated by the biblical description would have been available in the early period to which the Bible refers.

2
Complex incense burner from Megiddo

The Early Menorah – A Lampstand

The opening verse: "You shall make a lampstand of pure gold; the lampstand shall be made of hammered work *(miqsha)*; its base *(yarekh)* and its shaft *(kaneh)*, its cups *(gevi'im)*, calyxes *(kaftorim)*, and petals *(perahim)* shall be of one piece" (Exodus 25:31–3) describes the central section of the seven-branched candelabrum; it comprises a flaring base and a shaft with floral decoration at the top. Since the English translations do not fully coincide with the Hebrew text we offer here our interpretation and understanding of the terms included in the above text: *yarekh*, literally meaning thigh, loin, refers to a broadening base; *kaneh*, literally reed, is meant to describe a hollow shaft. As for *miqsha*, in our view it is not meant to describe a technique, but rather the form of the central unit – the base and the shaft combined into one piece. This section, which does not yet include the six branches, is termed in itself a "menorah." The Tabernacle menorah cited in Numbers 8:4 is described as made of a *miqsha* of gold from base to petal, namely, a menorah comprising a base and shaft and crowned with a floral element,[3] with no mention of seven branches. This shape was common in the Ancient Near East for incense burners and lampstands of cultic use; such objects were often surmounted by a bowl or an oil lamp (fig. 1). They were also sometimes fashioned from two or more units (fig. 2), which is possibly why the biblical text points out that the various parts of its menorah – the base, the shaft, and the floral decoration – be *miqsha*, namely, combined into one piece.

This type, henceforth to be called a "lampstand," is the basis of the more elaborate menorah to which six branches *(kanim)* were added. The fact that seven branches are not mentioned in Numbers 8:4, nor in connection with Solomon's Temple (see below), strengthens the assumption, in our view, that the early cultic menorah consisted solely of a lampstand. Furthermore, in I Samuel 3:3 it is written: "The lamp of God had not yet gone out, and Samuel was sleeping in the temple of the Lord, where the Ark of God was." It follows from this verse that the lighting device used in the sanctuary at Shiloh had a single lamp.

3
Pottery vessel with seven containers from Carthage 6th century BCE

The *Menorot*** of Solomon's Temple

Ten *menorot* are mentioned in I Kings 7:49: "the lampstands – five on the right side and five on the left – in front of the Shrine, of solid gold; and the petals (*perah*), lamps, and tongs, of gold." There is no reason to suppose on the basis of this verse that these *menorot* were seven-branched; they appear, rather, to have been the lampstands with a floral element, probably at the top, serving as the base for a single lamp. Nor do they appear to have been connected with the cult; in all likelihood, they served to illuminate the large hall. The Tabernacle menorah used for cultic purposes was presumably among the sacred vessels that the priests and Levites transferred to the Temple together with the Tent of Meeting (I Kings 8:4); it was not included among the other ten.

The description suggests that the ten *menorot* in Solomon's Temple and the Tabernacle menorah, which also featured floral elements, were likewise lampstands of the type described above, current among the archaeological finds from the First Temple period and earlier. This type consists of cultic lampstands and incense burners with flaring bases and floral capitals.

** The term *menorot*, the Hebrew plural of menorah, is used here at the authors' request.

The Menorah in the Vision of Zechariah

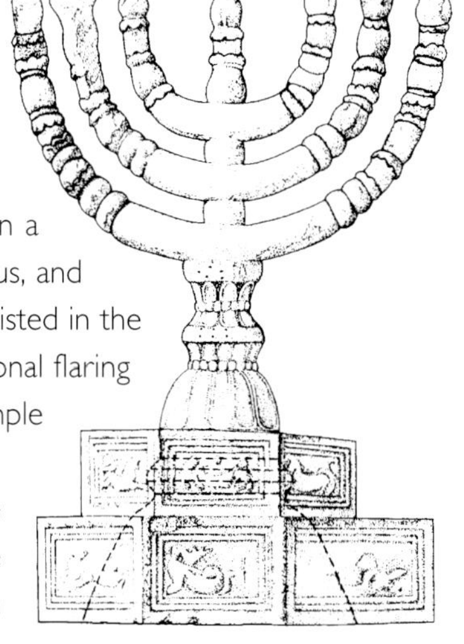

4
The Temple menorah carved in relief on the Arch of Titus, Rome

An additional menorah is mentioned in the Book of Zechariah, ascribed to the 6th century BCE, the period following the Return to Zion. It is described as: "a lampstand all of gold, with a bowl (*gullah*) above it. The lamps on it are seven in number, and the lamps above it [i.e., on the bowl] have seven pipes (*mutzakot*)" (Zechariah 4:2–3). Here, for the first time, a menorah with seven lamps is cited.

The prophet Zechariah describes the menorah as if it had been revealed to him in a dream, but it is reasonable to assume that his description was not fundamentally fictitious, and that its details had a basis in reality; in other words, that a menorah with seven lamps existed in the period concerned. While the base is not described, we believe that it was of the traditional flaring type – standard for the early *menorot* as for the later version from the Second Temple period. But what, however, is the *gullah* at the top of the stand?

The term *gullah* also appears in I Kings 7:41 and in II Chronicles 4:12 with reference to the columns of Jachin and Boaz: "the two globes (*gullot*) of the capitals upon the columns." It should be noted that *gullah* is translated here differently from its translation above as "bowl", an example of the inconsistency in the translation of terms. We understand *gullah* as apparently referring to the torus (a ring-like, convex molding) beneath the capitals. We may thus postulate that the *gullah* of Zechariah's menorah could be interpreted as a torus-like element on top of the base, upon which seven lamps with pinched lips were placed or attached.

Among the archaeological material from the Ancient Near East are several pottery vessels whose shape facilitates our understanding of Zechariah's menorah. These objects belong to a group of cultic utensils, referred to as *kernoi*, that are characterized by a hollow ring to which containers, floral elements, and animal heads are attached. It appears that in the 6th–5th century BCE, vessels combining some of the features associated with Zechariah's menorah – a stand with several containers – were known. Among them are even examples with seven receptacles, which scholars have claimed were used for illumination (fig. 3).[4] Since Zechariah's menorah comprised seven lamps – not one, as we have inferred for the Tabernacle menorah and for those of the First Temple period – we believe that it represents a transitional stage between the early lampstand with a single lamp and the seven-branched menorah of the Second Temple period.

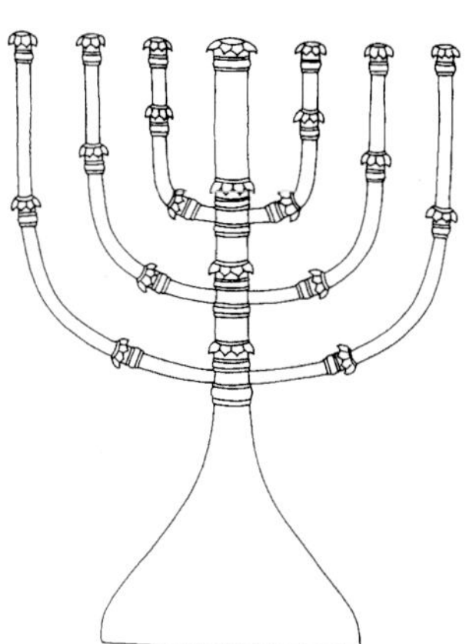

5
Suggested reconstruction of the form of the seven-branched menorah as described in the Book of Exodus

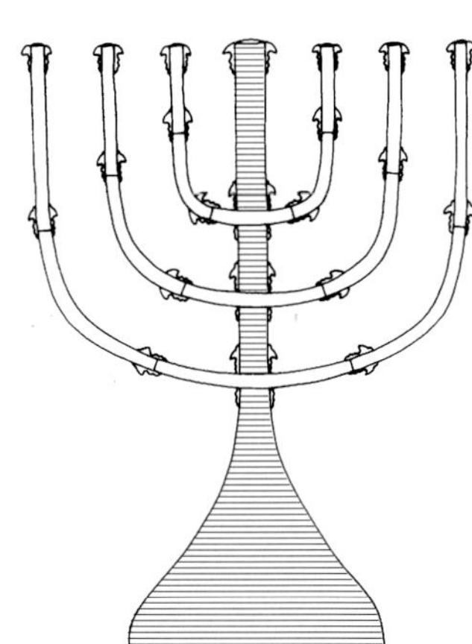

6
Cross section of the reconstuction in fig. 5

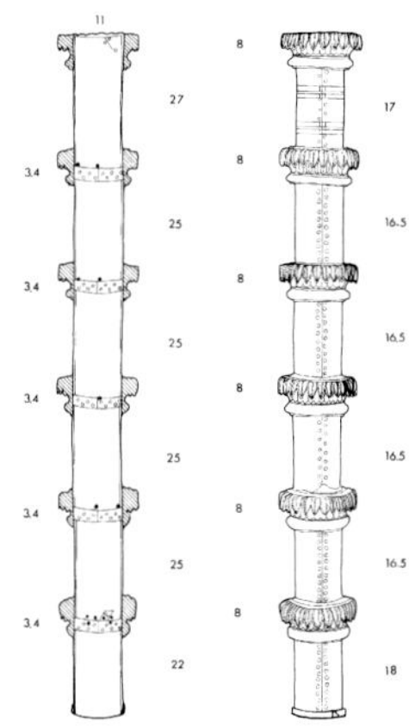

7
Cross section and exterior view of the candelabrum from Urartu (p. 32)

The Menorah of the Second Temple Period

With the return of the Babylonian exiles to Zion, the Temple was rebuilt (Ezra 3:10–11). Cyrus, King of Persia, consigned the sacred vessels to Sheshbazzar, and they were transported to Jerusalem (Ezra 1:7–11). From the text it is unclear whether a menorah was among them.

Evidence for the use of the menorah in the new Temple is provided by several sources: In the Book of Ben Sira (26:17), ascribed to the beginning of the 2nd century BCE, it is written: "as bright as the light on the sacred lampstand." In I Maccabees 1:21 it is recounted that Antiochus (in 168 BCE) removed from the Temple in Jerusalem: "the golden altar, the lampstand with all its equipment." Further on in this book (I Maccabees 4:49) we read that during Judas Maccabaeus' purification of the Temple (in 165 CE): "They renewed the sacred vessels and the lampstand, and brought the altar of incense and the table into the temple."

Concrete finds testifying to the existence of the seven-branched menorah in the Temple do not predate the end of the Hasmonean period, that is to say, the second half of the 1st century BCE. From this point on, however, their number increases steadily. Examples from the 1st century BCE until the 1st century CE, when the Second Temple was destroyed, include the following: the menorah on the coins of Mattathias Antigonus (40–37 BCE), the earliest possessing an absolute date (see p. 156, top); a menorah graffito in plaster on the wall of a Herodian-period house, discovered during the excavations of Jerusalem's Jewish Quarter (p. 27); a menorah engraved on a sundial from the Temple Mount excavations, ascribed to the Herodian period; and menorah graffiti on the wall of Jason's Tomb in Jerusalem (p. 65),[5] dated to the end of the 1st century BCE. The most notable menorah is depicted in relief on the Arch of Titus in Rome (fig. 4 and pp. 190–191): the relief shows the menorah along with the shewbread table and trumpets being borne in a victory parade celebrating the Temple's destruction and the fall of Jerusalem (Josephus, *Jewish War*, VII, v, 5,7). This depiction of the menorah is presumably faithful to the original except for the base, which is hexagonal in shape and engraved with images of animals and monsters, in contrast to the Jewish artistic conventions of the Second Temple period. In our opinion, the most convincing explanation of this phenomenon is that what appears to be the base is actually an addition that was not a part of the menorah,[6] but rather a hexagonal or octagonal *ferculum* into which the flaring base was inserted, to make the menorah easier to carry. Indeed, the relief clearly shows the poles that passed through the crate's bottom in order to transport the menorah (see D. Sperber's article in this volume).

The Second Temple period *menorot* enumerated above have several common features: a flaring base, curving branches reaching a uniform height, and a thickening at the end of the branches, which betokens an oil container – apparently a small bowl. Scholars agree that these represent the type of menorah that stood in the Temple.

Reconstruction of the Seven-Branched Menorah

The reconstruction of the menorah[7] submitted here is based upon our understanding of the text in Exodus and on comparative archaeological material from Israel and neighboring lands (figs. 5, 6, 7, and p. 32).

The base and the shaft: Our reconstruction includes a flaring base (*yarekh*), from which the shaft *(kaneh)* rises. Its shape is derived from the bases of early incense burners and lampstands. This type of base was common in ancient times; it also served as the base for *tymiateria* and basins, as seen in Assyrian reliefs, for stands discovered in Etruscan tombs, and so forth. The presence of bases of this type in Jewish art is attested by the Second Temple period menorahs.

The arrangement of the branches: The shaft *(kaneh)* that rises from the base of the lampstand constitutes the central branch of the seven branches *(kanim)* of the menorah: "six branches (*kanim*) issued from its side: three branches from one side of the lampstand and three branches from the other side of the lampstand" (Exodus 25:32). The six branches are equidistantly spaced, curve upward parallel to one another, and terminate at the same level. There is no direct evidence for this arrangement from the biblical text. The reconstruction is based on finds from the end of the Hasmonean period until the destruction of the Second Temple. An additional source for the shape is provided by Josephus' description of the Temple menorah (*Antiquities*, III, vi, 7), which presumably reflects the Temple menorah of his day.

In Jewish art of the 2nd–3rd century CE, there is a marked increase in the types of different branch arrangements for the menorah (figs. 8, 9). In all likelihood, these variations represent a later development.

The decorative elements: The ornamentation of the menorah – both the branches and the central unit – consists of floral segments integrated into its construction, contributing greatly to its ornate appearance. The branches are described in Exodus 25:33: "On one branch there shall be three cups *(gevi'im)* shaped like almond-blossoms, each with calyx *(kaftor)* and petals *(perah)*, and on the next branch there shall be three cups *(gevi'im)* shaped like almond-blossoms, each with calyx *(kaftor)* and petals *(perah)*; so for all six branches issuing from the lampstand."[8] In our opinion, the text does not refer to three separate decorative elements, but rather describes almond-shaped cups *(gevi'im)* which combine two elements – a torus-like lower section *(kaftor)* crowned with a flower *(perah)* – together forming a kind of floral capital. The account in Exodus specifies that each branch had three such floral capitals, without, however, indicating their position. In our proposed reconstruction, the three floral capitals have been evenly spaced, with the third placed at the top of the branch.

After describing the branches, the text refers to the floral decoration of the central section of the menorah: "And on the lampstand itself there shall be four cups *(gevi'im)* shaped like almond-blossoms, each with calyx *(kaftor)* and petals *(perah)*; and a calyx *(kaftor)*, of one piece with it, under a pair of branches . . . so for all six branches issuing from the lampstand" (Exodus 25:34–35; 37:20–21). Accordingly, in our reconstruction we placed a torus-like ring *(kaftor)* underneath each respective pair of branches. The text, however, does not specify the place of the four floral capitals (*gevi'im* – each comprising *kaftor* and *perah*). In our proposal we placed three out of the four above the point at which each pair of branches meets the central shaft (the most plausible location), and the fourth at the shaft's top (figs. 5, 6).

The oil lamps: At the close of the menorah's description, it is written: "Make its seven lamps" (Exodus. 25:37); lamps are also mentioned further on (35:14; 37:23; 39:37). The lamps were made separately, but were included in the talent of pure gold allotted for the menorah and its accessories. It appears that the floral capitals (*gevi'im*) that surmounted each branch served as the base upon which a lamp or small bowl was placed. The text does not specify the shape of these lamps – whether the typical oil lamps or simply small bowls. The lamps on the menorah graffito from the Jewish Quarter and on the Arch of Titus resemble small bowls, whereas the later menorah shown in the paintings above the Torah niche in the synagogue at Dura Europos (3rd century CE) features the typical oil lamps used during that period (fig. 8).

The Bible does not relate the method of manufacture of the menorah. However, it is possible to infer the working methods from the nature of the description and its accompanying terms. The menorah comprises three elements: 1) the basic unit – the base and shaft (*yarekh* and *kaneh*); 2) six branches (*kanim*); 3) floral decoration – floral capitals (*gevi'im*), each consisting of *kaftor* and *perah*.

The basic unit (base and central shaft) had to sustain the weight of the branches and the elaborate floral decorations; the flaring base was meant to stabilize the structure. These two components, together with the six branches, were to form a single unit (Exodus 25:31). The weight indicated for the menorah and its accessories – "a talent of pure gold" (i.e., 30 kilograms) – supports the assumption that the central unit possessed thick walls or was even made solid at its base.

In order to affix the branches to the shaft, three pairs of holes were necessary, which the branches passed through: "Six branches (*kanim*) issued (*yotzim*) from its sides: three branches from one side of the lampstand, and three branches from the other side of the lampstand" (Exodus 25:32) is meant to convey that the six branches were not attached to the surface of the main unit, but issued from within, that is to say, from six points along the central shaft; the term *kanim*, in our view, indicates that the branches were shaped as hollow tubes. Technically, this would fit a menorah of such a large size. One would also assume that the curving branches were not made of a single piece, but rather composed of units of standard size that were fitted together. This supposition is supported by early bronze lampstands. One such lampstand, of monumental size, is in the shape of a long hollow tube, which is actually composed of several hollow cylindrical units joined together, the joins of which are covered by floral ring-like capitals which are separate elements (fig. 7 and p. 32).[9] A similar construction could well fit the menorah. Thus, apart from their purely decorative function, the floral elements may have acted to protect and conceal the structural seams of the hollow tubes which composed the branches (figs. 5, 6).

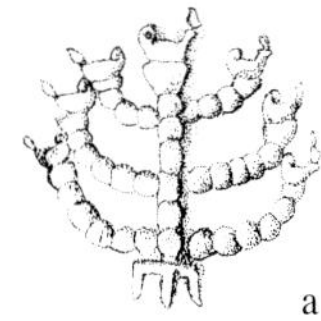

a

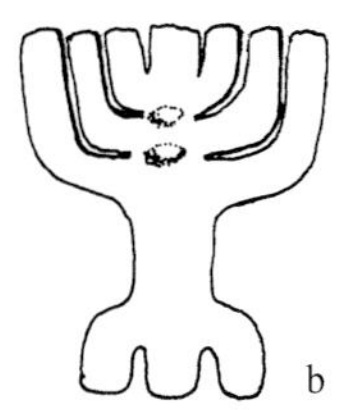

b

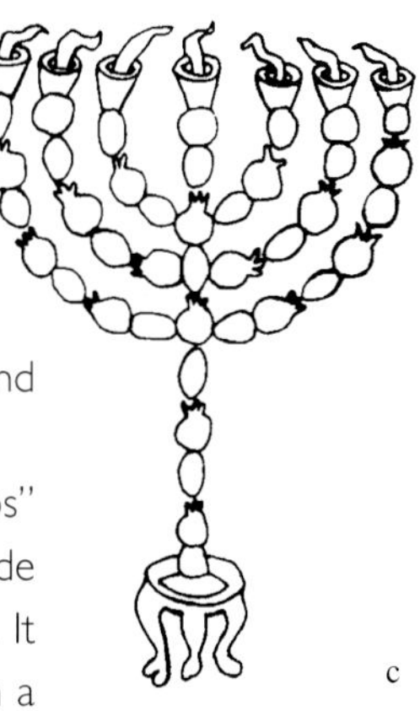

c

8

Branched *menorot* from the period of the Mishnah and Talmud

a Menorah carved on a sarcophagus from Rome

b Menorah on a pottery oil lamp

c Menorah on the mosaic floor of the synagogue at Hammath Tiberias

In this proposed structure, each pair of branches possessed one common unit – the middle one – which traversed the central shaft. It thus follows that each pair consisted of five units of equal length.

As stated, each of the menorah's branches was decorated with three floral capitals consisting of *kaftor* and *perah.* Accordingly, our reconstruction places a similar floral element at each of the two weak points, the joins, along the branch and the third at the end, to reinforce and thicken the apex and to serve as a base for the lamp. The three additional torus-like *kaftorim* of the central shaft mentioned in the description also served to bolster the points where the branches issued from either side.

Concerning the total sum of the parts from which the menorah was composed, note should be taken of Josephus' description of the Tabernacle menorah: "It was made up of globules and lilies, along with pomegranates and little bowls, numbering seventy in all" (*Antiquities,* III, vi, 7). On the basis of our reconstruction, the menorah indeed consists of seventy pieces: the central section (base and shaft = 1; five units for each of the three pairs of branches = 15; the *gevi'im* decorating the branches combining: *kaftorim* = 18 and *perahim* = 18; the *gevi'im* decorating the central shaft: *kaftorim* = 4 and *perahim* = 4; additional *kaftorim* decorating the central shaft = 3; lamps = 7, altogether 70 elements.

Summary and Conclusions

In this article, we have aimed to show that the early cultic menorah – according to tradition, the menorah of the Tabernacle – was not seven-branched, despite the conventional view inspired by the text of Exodus. We believe that the description there contains both earlier and later layers, and, as we have sought to prove, the earlier component, called the "menorah," was a lampstand with a flaring base decorated on its upper section with a floral capital and topped with a lamp, as was common during the early periods.

Haran and Sperber, scholars who have dealt with this subject, contend that the Tabernacle menorah possessed seven branches, as did the ten *menorot* in Solomon's Temple.[10] Concerning the latter, it can be averred that the shape attributed to them is not attested in the Bible. In Meyers' opinion,[11] the Tabernacle menorah had seven branches and a flaring base, while the ten *menorot* of Solomon's Temple were lampstands. She further maintains that no seven-branched menorah stood in Solomon's Temple, but that this type returned to currency in the Second Temple period. It is our view that since the Bible states that the equipment of the Tent of Meeting was transferred to Solomon's Temple at its inauguration (I Kings 8:4), it follows that a cultic menorah stood there in addition to the other ten. However, there is no mention of seven branches. The shape of the ten *menorot* that stood in the Temple, described as having floral capitals at the top with no mention of seven branches, corresponds explicitly to the early lampstand type.

The menorah in Zechariah's vision provides the first indication of a more elaborate menorah with seven lamps, though it is not described as having branches. It is only toward the end of the Second Temple period that we have clear evidence on the coins of Mattathias Antigonus of the form of the menorah that stood in the Temple: it possessed seven curving branches terminating at the same level and a central shaft with a flaring base (p. 156). From then until the time of the Temple's destruction, the number of illustrations of this type of menorah continued to grow.

9
Menorah painted above the Torah niche from the 3rd-century CE synagogue at Dura Europos

It follows that the seven-branched menorah originated in the time span between the Return to Zion and the Hasmonean period, and that the description in Exodus of the Tabernacle menorah is a projection backwards of the Second Temple type, which retains elements dating to the Tabernacle menorah as well as the version that evolved following the Return to Zion.

The number seven was sacred, and there is apparently an affinity between the seven branches of the menorah and the seven days of the week. It is possible that the seven-branched menorah served as a kind of calendar of the daily and weekly cult conducted in the Temple (Exodus 27:21; 30:7–8; Leviticus 24:2–4).

The menorah illustrated in the mid-3rd century CE synagogue wall painting at Dura Europos (fig. 9) represents a further development. Its branches do not terminate on the same level, and three knobbed legs are attached to its flaring base. From this point on, the base of the menorah changes from flaring to tripodal, and the branches are variously fashioned, as the archaeological finds – sculptures, mosaics, oil lamps, and so forth – attest (fig. 8 and pp. 69, 95, 97, 108).[12]

The Second Temple menorah, featured on the coins of Antigonus, on the wall of the house unearthed in Jerusalem's Jewish Quarter, and on Titus' Triumphal Arch, is accompanied by the shewbread table – the Temple's second sacred article. It follows that in this period, the menorah and shewbread table were believed to be the more important cultic objects in the Temple in Jerusalem, chosen as motifs to represent it, and that no symbolic meaning should be ascribed to them beyond this. It was only after the Temple's destruction that the menorah became the symbol of Judaism, and only since has its representation become common on various articles associated with burial and synagogue art, both in the land of Israel and the Diaspora.[13]

---

1 The word "branches" is commonly used to describe the seven arms of the menorah. However, the word in the Hebrew text is *kaneh* (pl. *kanim*), which means "reed." This meaning is confirmed in the Septuagint by the Greek term **καλαμισκοι**, which also describes the arms of the menorah as hollow pipes. Thus, the word "branches" is used here only in the literary sense, born by the pictorial association. We reject, however, the interpretation suggested by some scholars that the menorah represents a symbolic tree or the Tree of Life.

2 One talent equals approximately 3,000 shekels: a shekel equals 10 grams. Thus one talent equals 30 kilograms, the amount allotted for the menorah and its utensils.

3 We will relate to the terms of the floral decoration further on when discussing the decorative elements.

4 For an additional example in metal see our article in *Eretz-Israel* (above, *), 258, pl. 51:4.

5 B. Mazar, "Excavations near the Temple Mount," *Qadmoniot* 5 (1972): 82 (Hebrew); L. Y. Rahmani, "The Tomb of Jason," *Israel Exploration Journal* 17 (1967): 73–74, fig. 7, pl. 22A.

6 W. Wirgin, "Two Notes: On the Shape of the Foot of the Menorah," *Israel Exploration Journal* 11 (1961): 152, figs. 1, 2; M. Pfanner, *Der Titusbogen* (Mainz am Rhein, 1983), 54, 74, fig. 39.

7 The only one to have attempted a reconstruction of the seven-branched menorah was M. Haran, *Encyclopedia Biblica*, s.v. "Menorah" (Hebrew).

8 The English translation offered here for the floral elements constitutes one version among others that appears in English translations of the Bible. *Gavi'a* (pl. *gevi'im*) has been translated as "cup", "bowl"; *kaftor* (pl. *kaftorim*) as calyx, ornamented knob; *perah* (pl. *perahim*) as petal, flower.

9 R. Merhav, Urartu, *A Metalworking Center in the First Millennium BCE*, exh. cat. (The Israel Museum, Jerusalem, 1991), 264, 270, pl. 11 a, b, fig. 11 on p. 352; R. Merhav and A. Ruder, "The Construction and Production of a Monumental Bronze Candelabrum of King Menua of Urartu," in *Anatolian Iron Ages*, eds. A. Cilingiroglu and D. H. French (Oxford, 1991), 75–96, figs. 06.1.1–1.2.

10 See M. Haran (above, n. 5); D. Sperber, "The History of the Menorah," *Journal of Jewish Studies* 16 (1965): 135–159.

11 C. L Meyers, *The Tabernacle Menorah: A Synthetic Study of a Symbol from the Biblical Cult*, AASOR Dissertation Series 2 (1976); idem, "Was There a Seven-Branched Lampstand in Solomon's Temple," *Biblical Archaeology Review* 5 (1979): 51–55.

12 R. Hachlili, *Ancient Jewish Art and Archaeology in the Land of Israel* (Leiden, 1988), 236–253; idem, *Ancient Jewish Art and Archaeology in the Diaspora* (Leiden, 1998), 212–344.

13 Hachlili (above, n. 12, *Land of Israel*), 254–255.

Daniel Sperber

Between Jerusalem and Rome

The History of the Base of the Menorah as Depicted on the Arch of Titus*

1
Examples of menorahs from the cemetery at Beth She'arim

The Shape of the Temple Menorah in the Hasmonean Period

The earliest known representation of the menorah is on a coin minted by the last Hasmonean king, Mattathias Antigonus (reigned 40–37 BCE; p. 156). The die-cutter was probably acquainted with the menorah fashioned in the early days of Hasmonean rule (or, at least, with a candelabrum of that type), and on that basis he designed the depiction of the menorah on the coin. As it would be unreasonable to expect to find on such a small coin, made using a fairly simple technique, a precise, fully detailed representation of the menorah, there is no sign in the coin of the cups, knobs (*kaftorim*), and flowers referred to in Exodus 25:35–36. Nevertheless, the general shape of the menorah may be compared with the following account in the Talmud:

> Said Samuel in the name of an old sage: The height of the menorah is eighteen handbreadths: The legs and the flower – three handbreadths, two handbreadths – smooth; then a handbreadth in which are a cup and a knob and flower, and two handbreadths smooth; then a handbreadth with a knob, and two branches issue from it, one on this side and one on that, reaching up to the height of the menorah; then a handbreadth smooth, and a handbreadth with a knob, and two branches issue from it, one on this side and one on that, reaching up to the height of the menorah; then a handbreadth smooth, and a handbreadth with a knob, and two branches issue from it, one on this side and one on that, reaching up to the height of the menorah; and two handbreadths smooth. There remain three handbreadths, in which are three cups and a knob and flower . . . (Babylonian Talmud, Menahot 28b).

In this description, all the branches of the menorah end at the same height, as is the case on Antigonus' coin. Moreover, the base of the menorah on the coin is indeed supported by (three?) small legs, in agreement with the above passage, which also refers to legs, though without specifying the number. The representation on the coin agrees with the proportions specified in the Talmud: the legs (i.e., the base, that is "The legs and the flower – three handbreadths – make up one sixth of the whole menorah, which is eighteen handbreadths high – more or less the proportion seen on the coin. No further details of the shape of the menorah can be inferred, however, from this small illustration.

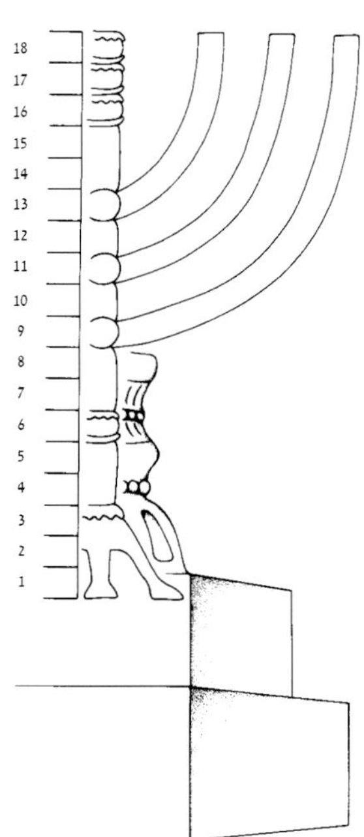

2
Dimensions of the menorah according to rabbinic sources in comparison with the menorah on the Arch of Titus

Base or Legs

We know of several representations of the menorah from slightly later than the Herodian period: a graffito of the menorah incised on plaster, found in the Jewish Quarter excavations (p. 27); a menorah carved on a stone sundial discovered in the excavations south of the Temple Mount; and menorah graffiti on the wall of Jason's Tomb in the Rehavia neighborhood of Jerusalem. However, none of these provides a distinct picture of the base of the menorah, as they are all crudely executed and lacking in detail. One conclusion, though, may be drawn: all show the base with legs of some kind, in accordance with the above-mentioned rabbinic tradition. The issue of the number of legs is addressed in medieval sources.

* This account is based on my article "The History of the Menorah," *Journal of Jewish Studies* 16 (1965): 171– 204, which may be consulted for further sources and comments. Both articles covered a much longer span of time, while here I have concentrated on the history of the menorah from the Hasmoneans to the Herodian period and treated a few topics in some detail.

Maimonides, in *Hilkhot Bet Habehirah* 3:2, writes: "It [= the menorah] had three legs," while Rashi, in his commentary to Exodus 25:31, remarks: "That is the lower leg, fashioned like a kind of box, and three legs issue from it downward . . ." We may assume that these great scholars, who made no statements without sufficient support, based themselves on a reliable source.

In addition, there is an abundance of drawn or engraved representations of the menorah, dating from the 1st–6th century CE, all with a base of three legs (fig. 1 and pp. 97, 108, 135, 198). We may reasonably assume, therefore, that this shape reflects a reliable tradition of a menorah with three legs. In Rome itself, where one could see the relief of the menorah on the Arch of Titus, with its heavy, stepped hexagonal base, menorahs with legs were depicted on gold-glass bases (p. 62). It thus appears that the tradition that the menorah had a three-legged base antedates the Arch of Titus and stands on its own.

3
Base of a column from the Temple of Apollo at Didyma

The Problematic Shape of the Menorah on the Arch of Titus

At first glance, the menorah depicted on the Arch of Titus (p. 191) looks rather strange, as its two parts – the base and the upper half – show a lack of stylistic cohesion and balance: The base is massive and heavy, and the branches seem to "grow" out of the trunk above the base in an inorganic and inelegant way. In fact, the proportions violate the conventions of Hellenistic-Roman art. This, coupled with the fact that the upper part of the menorah is in general accordance with rabbinic tradition and in a style quite foreign to Roman art, makes it quite probable that this depiction faithfully represents the original shape of the menorah.

The lower part of the menorah on the Arch of Titus, however, is inconsistent with all the descriptions in the rabbinic tradition and with the archeological evidence: instead of legs it has a solid base, much larger than that shown on Antigonus' coin. According to the Talmudic description cited above, the lower part of the menorah was smaller than the upper part (eight out of eighteen handbreadths); in the depiction on the Arch of Titus, the lower part is larger than the upper (fig. 2). If one were to reconstruct the menorah on the basis of halakhic sources, it would be very similar to the depiction of the menorah in the ancient synagogue of Dura Europos, which dates to the mid-3rd century CE. Taking into account all of the above, we may conclude that the lower part of the menorah was altered at some point, the alteration occurring after the rule of Mattathias Antigonus, that is, after 37 BCE; for judging from the coin, at that time, the base of the menorah was still similar to that described in rabbinic sources.

The Base of the Menorah on the Arch of Titus

Examination of the base of the menorah of the Arch of Titus immediately reveals that it consists of two hexagonal bases or podia, the upper one smaller in diameter than the lower. Various reliefs are carved on the paneled faces of the two podia. On the upper base, in the center panel, are two eagles holding an arc-shaped wreath of leaves; in the right and left panels are sea monsters with fishtails pointing to the center panel. The center panel in the lower base depicts a single dragon, while the right and left panels each contain two winged, bird-headed dragons. If, as suggested above, these decorations were not additions made by the artists who built Titus' triumphal arch, but were faithfully copied from the plundered Temple menorah, they are entirely inconsistent with Jewish tradition. The Mishnah, for example, rules; "If a man found objects on which is a figure of the sun, a figure of the moon, or a figure of a dragon, he shall throw them into the Dead Sea" (Avodah Zarah 3:3), that is, it is forbidden to derive any benefit from such figures because of their association with idolatry. But here we have dragons in the Temple itself!

A prototype of this hexagonal base may be seen in the great Temple of Apollo at Didyma (southwest Turkey), where the earliest example of a polygonal podium, with dragons carved on its paneled faces, was found. The creatures shown in the menorah's side panels, with fishtails and bird's heads, also have counterparts at Didyma. As for the foliate profile above the base – a familiar motif in Roman architectural sculpture beginning in the 1st century CE – this too can be traced to Didyma (figs. 3, 4).

A more detailed comparison of the Didyma prototype with the base of the menorah on the Arch of Titus reveals further points of similarity. The twisting dragons on the lower base of the menorah are almost exact "copies" of those at Didyma, even in terms of their pose and direction. As for the fishtailed monsters, such creatures have parallels in ancient art, but they are generally depicted with frills or ruffs around their necks, as usual in representations of dragons; those on the menorah have smooth necks – a rather rare design. Moreover, the dragons at Didyma have nymphs riding on their backs; this common motif is also missing on the menorah. Most probably, the absence of the nymphs riding the dragons and of frills on the monsters' necks is not accidental, but rather a concession to the requirements of Jewish law, done out of a consideration for popular feeling. Indeed, we read in the Tosefta: "What kind of dragon is forbidden? Rabbi Simeon ben Eleazar says: any dragon with frills coming out of its neck. But if it was smooth, it is permitted" (Avodah Zarah 5:2). And the Talmud elaborates: "Our Rabbis taught: What is the shape of a dragon? Rabbi Simeon ben Eleazar explained: Anything that has frills between its joints. Rabbi Assi added: between the joints of its neck. Said Rabbi Hama ben Rabbi Hanina: The law agrees with the view of Rabbi Simeon ben Eleazar" (Babylonian Talmud, Avodah Zarah 43a). It follows that the nude nymph were removed from the dragons' backs and the frills from their necks out of consideration for the feelings of the people, who would have surely been incensed by the introduction of idolatrous images to the Temple. As for the double-stepped structure of the base, which is exceedingly rare in Roman sculpture, it may allude to the following description in the Mishnah: "There was a stone before the menorah in which there were three steps; on this the priest stood to trim the lamps. He left the *kuz* [a kind of pitcher] on the second step and came away" (Tamid 3:9). It is possible that the stepped podium was the stepped stone on which the priest used to stand to trim the lamps.

4
Carved panel from the base of a column, Temple of Apollo at Didyma, Turkey

When was the Shape of the Menorah Altered?

It would appear, therefore, that the alteration in the shape of the menorah – particularly in that of its base – was done by a person familiar with Roman culture or very eager to emphasize Roman sovereignty in the region, as shown by the eagles on the base. These Roman symbols, introduced into the Temple, essentially proclaimed that the Temple was under the dominion of the Roman eagle. This could have occurred only after the death of Mattathias Antigonus in 37 BCE. We can reduce the possible time span even further, suggesting that the change was introduced before the time of Philo (c. 20 BCE – c. 40 CE). In his work *Quis rerum divinarum heres,* Philo discusses the numerical symbolism of the shape of the menorah in the Temple (218–220N, Loeb ed., vol. IV, pp. 391–393). Though the discussion hinges on combinations of the numbers three and seven, Philo makes no mention of the menorah having three legs. Had the menorah still had three legs, Philo would surely have cited this in his calculations.

It may thus be concluded that the shape of the menorah was altered during Herod's reign. Indeed, we need not be surprised that he introduced Roman eagles into the Temple, as we know that, defying public opinion, he affixed a large golden eagle above the Temple gate (Josephus, *Jewish War,* I, xxxiii, 2; *Antiquities*, XVII, 151). Herod, having ascended the throne with Roman support, made every effort to prove his loyalty to the Roman imperial government, as witness the eagle on his coins which, like the eagle on the base of the menorah and that surmounting the Temple gate, was a visible emblem of

Roman rule. All his coins, with their pagan symbols, clearly express this policy; special emphasis is placed, moreover, on the symbols of the god Apollo (e.g., the tripod, incense bowl, palm branches, and the Macedonian shield with the sun motif). Herod's choice of these symbols may have been based on the fact that his patron, the Emperor Augustus, attributed his own victory at Actium to Apollo, the god whose main cultic center was at Didyma.

One may in fact venture to suggest the reason for the replacement of the menorah base at this particular time: Herod became king after the death of Mattathias Antigonus, during whose reign the Parthians had conquered and sacked Jerusalem (40 BCE). We may assume that they also damaged the Temple and its appurtenances (Antiquities XIV, 363–364). The weak point in the structure of the menorah was, of course, the point where the upper, branched part was attached to the base. Perhaps the menorah had indeed been broken at that point, the upper part being separated from the lower part. When Herod rebuilt the Temple and repaired its implements, he took the opportunity of creating a new base for the menorah, in the style of the temple at Didyma, featuring symbols from the cult of Apollo so revered by his patron.

From that point on, the light of the menorah was, so to speak, dimmed for the Jews, for it no longer symbolized the kingdom and sovereignty of the true God, representing instead Roman domination of their homeland. Thus, the very menorah that had, under the Hasmoneans, symbolized the spiritual and political independence of the people of Israel became a symbol of its submission to the might of Rome and to pagan culture. Little wonder, then, that in later generations, after the destruction, groaning under the yoke of the Roman Empire, the Jews "restored" the three-legged menorah of the Hasmoneans, preferring it over the menorah whose shape appeared on the Arch of Titus – Herod's menorah (see articles by L. Levine and D. Barag in this volume).

פרופ. ב. שץ
ירושלם הבנויה
חלום בהקיץ
אמר ר' הושעיא: עתידה
ירושלם לעשות פנס
לאמות העולם והם
מהלכין לאורה (פסיקתא)

Hope for Redemption

The prophet Zechariah lived during the time of the Return to Zion and the building of the Second Temple in Jerusalem. In his vision, he beheld a golden menorah flanked by two olive trees – an allegory of the Temple. This was the first time the menorah was referred to not as a cultic object, but as a symbol of the Temple itself.

With the destruction of the Second Temple in 70 CE, the menorah ceased to serve as a cultic vessel, and its evolution as a symbol proceeded with increasing intensity. Depictions of the menorah along with the other Temple appurtenances – the shewbread table, the golden altar, the four species, the *shofar* (ram's horn), and the incense shovel, in a variety of different combinations – began to represent not only the Temple that had been destroyed but also the hope for its restoration at the End of Days. Such depictions are found in tombs and on tombstones, on the mosaic floors of ancient synagogues, and later on various objects used in synagogues throughout the Jewish Diaspora. In illuminated manuscripts of the Bible, as well, this concept is expressed through illustrations of the same array of objects: the oldest example is found in a Pentateuch that was written in the land of Israel or Egypt in the year 929 CE. Among the Sephardi Jews, a Bible was called a *miqdashiya* (Temple), and many Sephardi Bibles bear depictions of the sanctuary appurtenances on their opening pages. Such scenes, which bore eschatological significance, also made their way into Christianity and are frequently seen in Christian manuscripts and church wall paintings.

When the Zionist movement was founded in the late 19th century, it quite naturally adopted the menorah, with its messianic connotations, as its symbol. On the roof of the Bezalel School of Art and Crafts in Jerusalem, a menorah was erected – expressing hope for the renewal of the arts in the land of Israel and the Zionist ideology of the institution. The establishment of the State of Israel marked the realization of the dream guiding the nation's return to its homeland: the choice of the menorah as the State emblem added yet another layer of meaning to the menorah's messianic significance.

Previous page:
Drawing for the title page of the book *Jerusalem Rebuilt*, ca. 1924
Ze'ev Raban, 1890–1970
Pen and india ink on paper
36 x 27 cm
Israel Museum Collection

Opposite:
Zechariah's vision of the menorah from an illuminated Pentateuch
Scribe: Samuel ben Abraham
Illuminator: Joseph Hatzarfati
Cervera, Spain, 1300
Handwritten in ink on parchment, gold leaf and tempera
28.2 x 21.7 cm
Biblioteca Nacional, Lisbon

Depictions of the appurtenances of the sanctuary are extremely rare in Ashkenazi manuscripts of the Middle Ages. This manuscript was clearly influenced by similar illustrations appearing in Sephardi Bibles, but the style of the drawings and the colors are typical of southern Germany. The appearance of Aaron in priestly vestments, extending his arm to light the menorah, is a particularly unique feature.

Aaron the High Priest lighting the Tabernacle menorah
From a manuscript containing the Pentateuch, the Scrolls, and the *Haftorot*
Regensburg, Bavaria, Germany, ca. 1300
Handwritten in ink on parchment, tempera, and gold leaf
18.5 x 24.5 cm
Israel Museum Collection

Postcard for the founding congress of the New Zionist Organization
"All Who Believe in Complete Redemption"
Vienna, September 7th, 1935
Collection of Alain Roth, Herzliya

Opposite:
Page from the album *Seven Etchings for the Book of Zechariah,* 1996–97
Igael Tumarkin, b. 1933
Etching, aquatint, dry-point, cut and folded paper
81.5 x 44.5 cm
Courtesy of Har'el Printers and Publishers, Jaffa

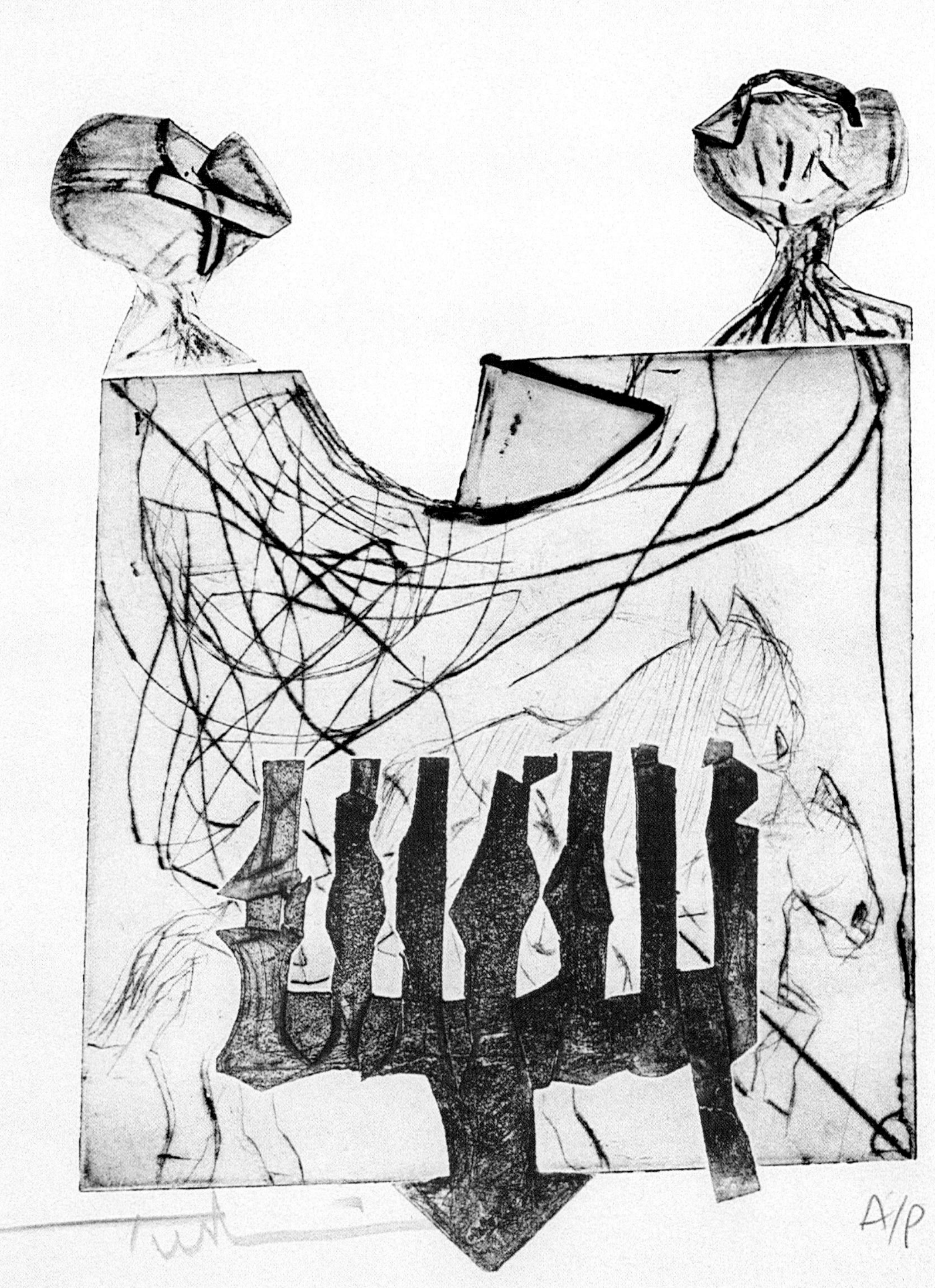

Gold-glass base from
a Jewish catacomb
Rome?, 4th century CE
Glass and gold-leaf
D 10.0 cm
Israel Museum
Collection, gift of
Yacob Michael,
in memory of his wife,
Erna Sondheimer-
Michael

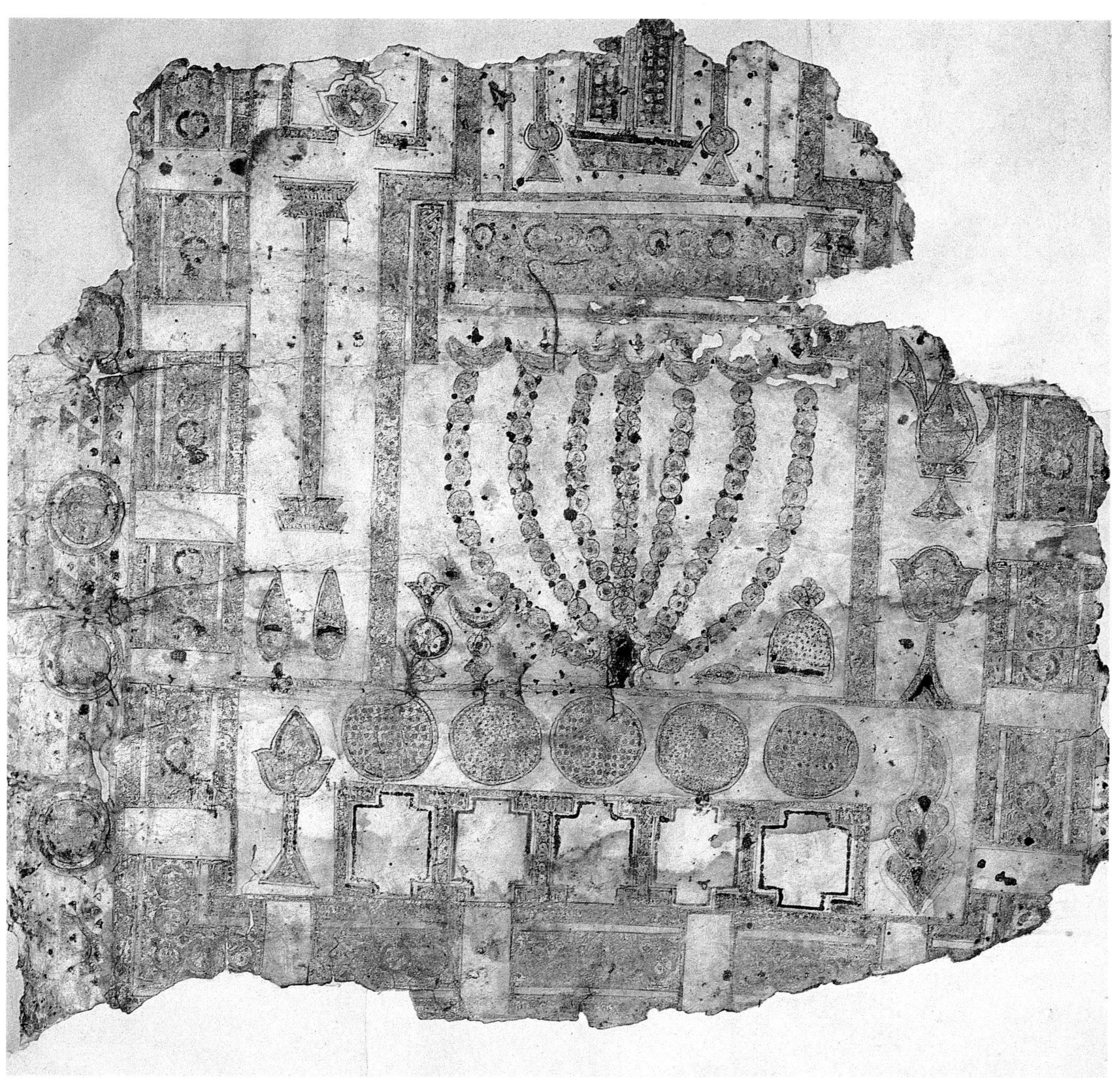

Page from the
First Leningrad Pentateuch
Scribe: Solomon Halevi son of Bouya'ya
Egypt, 929
Handwritten in ink on parchment and gold leaf
40 x 47 cm
The National Library of Russia, St. Petersburg

This page, one of only two that have survived, is one of the earliest illustrations from a Bible known to us today. It depicts the Tabernacle and its appurtenances, with the menorah in the center.

The ark, built to resemble the facade of a shrine with two columns supporting a gable, is almost five meters high and is entirely covered with a rich repertoire of carved vegetal motifs. The central motif of the upper section is a depiction of the menorah based on Zechariah's vision. An inscription in Hebrew verse, appearing on either side of the ark, refers to the artist: "Eliahu," and an acrostic also alludes to a man called Moses, who donated the wood for the ark. According to the inscription, the work was completed on the 17th of the month of Ab, 1891. Another date according to the Seleucid era is also mentioned: 2202.

Decoration for the top of a Torah ark
Parur, India,
dated: 1891
Carved teak
480 x 287 cm
Israel Museum Collection, gift of Della and Fred Worms, London and Jerusalem

Opposite:

Torah ark doors from the synagogue of Rabbi Moses Isserles (the Rema)
Artists: "Zalman and Hayim and Anya(?) Schnitzer and Welwel KS"
Cracow, Poland, beginning of the 17th century
Lead and tin alloy, painted wood
154 x 33 cm
Israel Museum Collection, gift in memory of Mattityahu Jacubowicz, Wadowice, Poland, who perished in the Holocaust, and his wife, Haya Rivka (Helena)

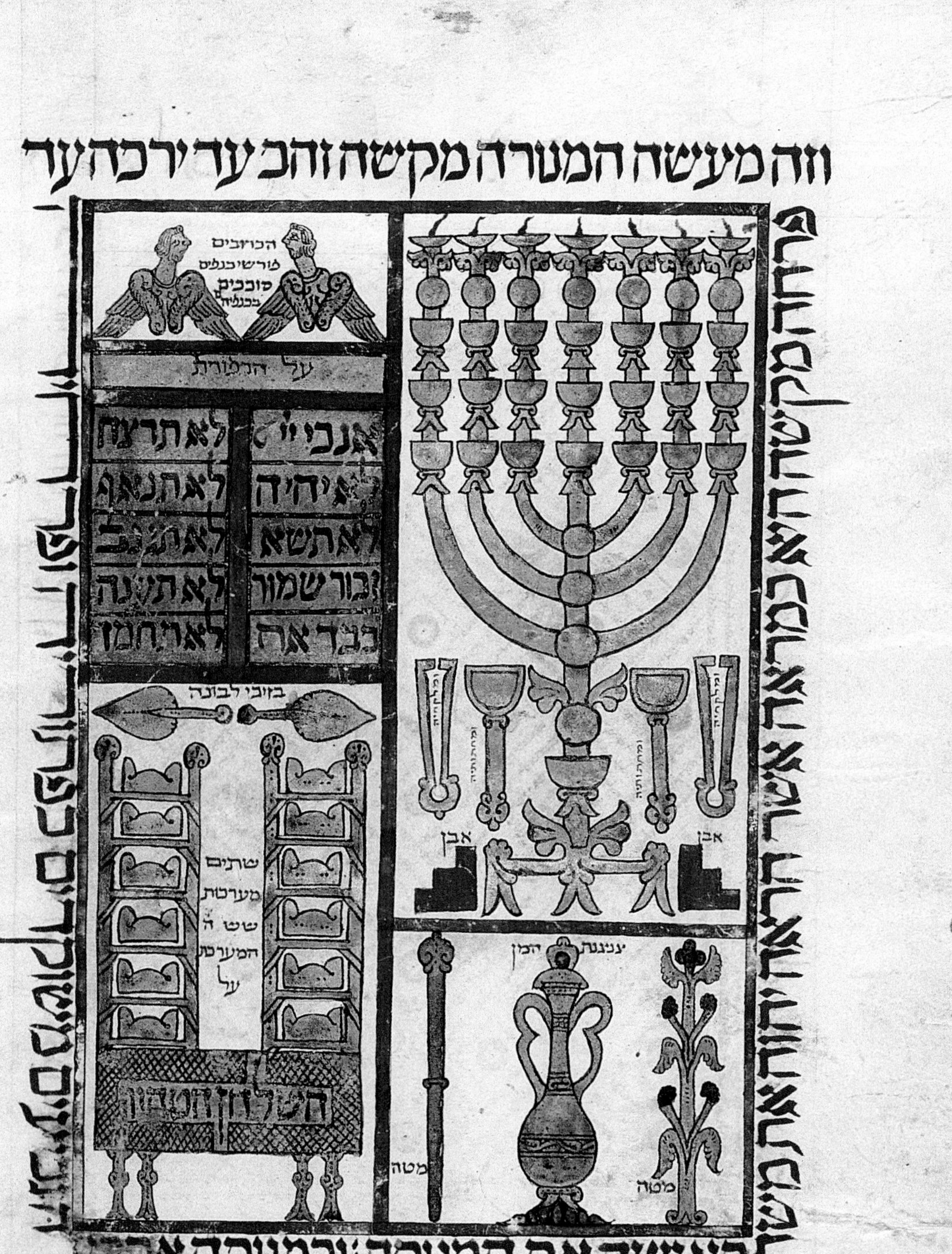
וזה מעשה המנרה מקשה זהב עד ירכה עד
כן עשה את המנורה
אבן
אבן
מטה
מטה

The synagogue at el-Khirbeh, like most Samaritan synagogues, faces Mt. Gerizim, which is sacred to the Samaritans. In the center of its floor, the sanctuary appurtenances are depicted – the menorah with tongs and a pair of trumpets and the shewbread table bearing various implements and loaves of bread – along with a structure consisting of four columns supporting a gable, in front of which a curtain hangs, its edge wrapped around one of the columns. This is the earliest known depiction of the sanctuary appurtenances on a synagogue floor. Similar representations of the menorah together with an architectural structure became common decorative motifs in the 4th–6th century CE. The shewbread table, however, is very rare – the only other place it has been found is on the mosaic from the synagogue at Sepphoris; the tongs are known only from the el-Khirbeh mosaic.

Section of a mosaic floor from the Samaritan synagogue at el-Khirbeh, Samaria
Byzantine period, 4th century CE
Stone, 266 x 136 cm
Courtesy of the Staff Officer for Archaeology, Judea and Samaria

Opposite:
The sanctuary appurtenances on the opening page of a Bible, Perpignan, Kingdom of Majorca, 1299
Handwritten in ink on parchment, tempera and gold leaf
32.5 x 23.5 cm
Bibliothèque Nationale de France, Paris

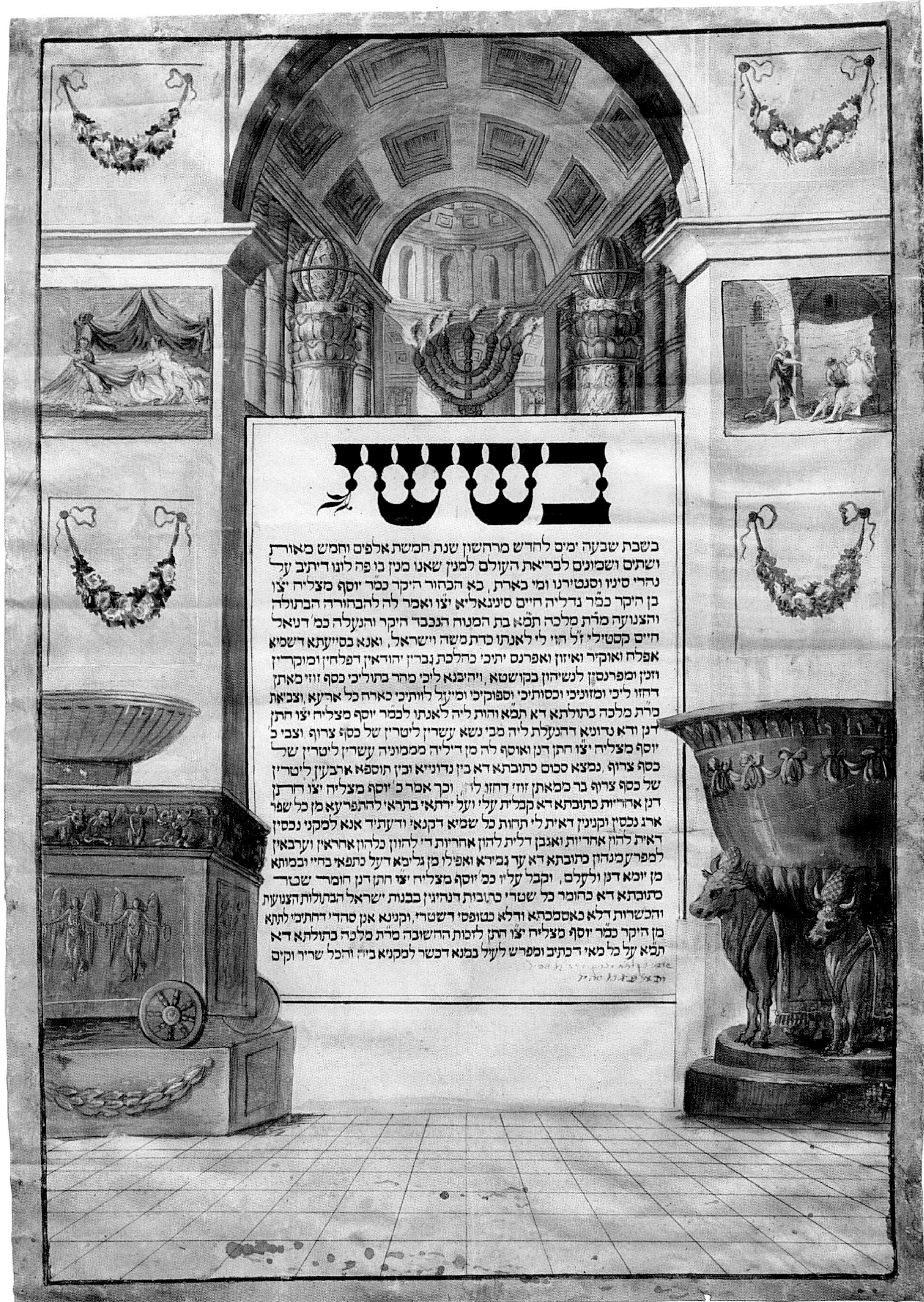

בששי

בשבת שבעה ימים לחדש מרחשון שנת חמשת אלפים וחמש מאות
ושתים ושמונים לבריאת העולם למנין שאנו מנין בו פה לונו דיתיב על
נהרי סיניו וסנטירנו ומי בארת, בא הבחור היקר כמ״ר יוסף מצליח יצ״ו
בן היקר כמ״ר גדליה חיים סינגאליא יצ״ו ואמר לה להבחורה הבתולה
והצנועה מ״רת מלכה תמ״א בת המנוח הנכבד היקר והנעלה כמ׳ דניאל
חיים קסטילי ז״ל הוי לי לאנתו כדת משה וישראל, ואנא בסייעתא דשמיא
אפלח ואוקיר ואיזון ואפרנס יתיכי כהלכת גברין יהודאין דפלחין ומוקרין
וזנין ומפרנסין לנשיהון בקושטא, ויהיבנא ליכי מהר בתוליכי כסף זוזי מאתן
דחזו ליכי ומזוניכי וכסותיכי וספוקיכי ומיעל לוותיכי כארח כל ארעא, וצביאת
מ״רת מלכה בתולתא דא תמ״א והות ליה לאנתו לכמ״ר יוסף מצליח יצ״ו חתן
דנן ודא נדוניא דהנעלת ליה מבי נשא עשרין ליטרין של כסף צרוף, וצבי כ׳
יוסף מצליח יצ״ו חתן דנן ואוסף לה מן דיליה ממוניה עשרין ליטרין של
כסף צרוף, נמצא סכום כתובתא דא בין נדונייא ובין תוספא ארבעין ליטרין
של כסף צרוף בר ממאתן זוזי דחזו לה, וכך אמר כ׳ יוסף מצליח יצ״ו חתן
דנן אחריות כתובתא דא קבלית עלי ועל ירתאי בתראי להתפרעא מן כל שפר
ארג נכסין וקנינין דאית לי תחות כל שמיא דקנאי ודעתיד אנא למקני נכסין
דאית להון אחריות ואגבן דלית להון אחריות די להוון כלהון אחראין וערבאין
למפרע מנהון כתובתא דא עד גמירא ואפילו מן גלימא דעל כתפאי בחיי ובמותא
מן יומא דנן ולעלם, וקבל עליו כמ׳ יוסף מצליח יצ״ו חתן דנן חומר שטר
כתובתא דא כחומר כל שטרי כתובות דנהיגין בבנות ישראל הבתולות הצנועות
והכשרות דלא כאסמכתא ודלא כטופסי דשטרי, וקנינא אנן סהדי דחתימי לתתא
מן היקר כמ״ר יוסף מצליח יצ״ו חתן לזכות החשובה מ״רת מלכה בתולתא דא
תמ״א על כל מאי דכתיב ומפרש לעיל במנא דכשר למקניא ביה והכל שריר וקים

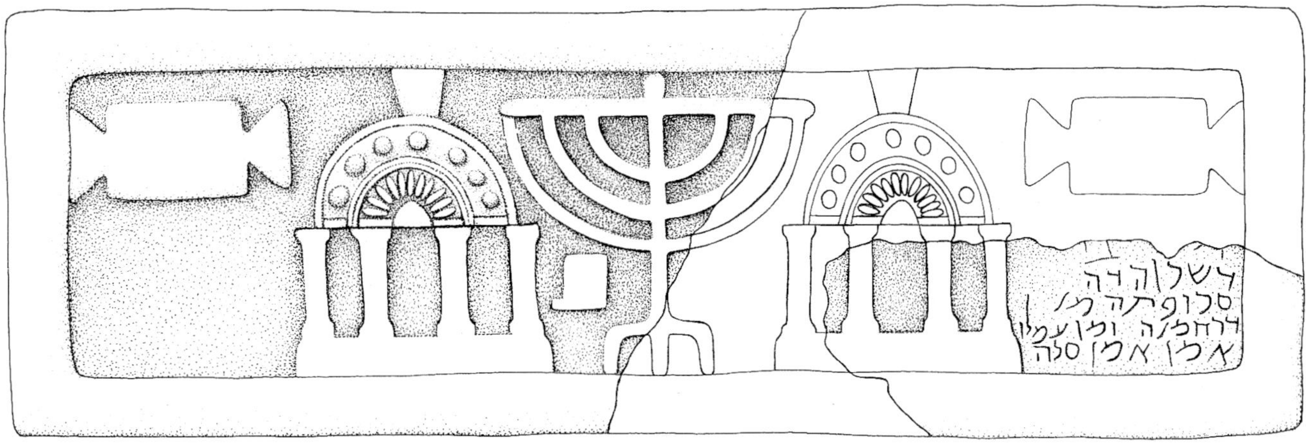

Lintel decorated in relief from a synagogue? at Kokhav Hayarden
Byzantine period, 4th–5th century CE
Basalt, L 112 cm
Israel Antiquities Authority Collection

Proposed reconstuction of the missing section of the lintel

Opposite:
Solomon's Temple and its appurtenances as decoration for a *ketubbah*
Lugo, Italy, 1821
Handwritten in ink on parchment, watercolor
65 x 47 cm
Israel Museum Collection

Plan of the Tabernacle from the *Christian Topography* by Constantine of Antioch (Cosmas Indicopleustes) 11th century CE Library of St. Catherine's Monastery, Sinai

Dan Barag

The Menorah as a Messianic Symbol in Antiquity

The earliest depictions of the seven-branched menorah are from the Hasmonean period. These, however, are very rare, and it appears that the menorah only became a common motif in Jewish art in the 3rd century CE. Archaeological and numismatic discoveries from the second half of the 19th century until today have shed light on developments in the menorah's styles of representation and in its significance. The research until now has been largely confined to clarifying the morphological issues (that is to say, the menorahs have been classified typologically into groups) and the significance attributable to the menorah's appearance in this period of antiquity.[1] Various interpretations of the menorah's symbolic meaning have been advanced; E. R. Goodenough has divided them into four categories:

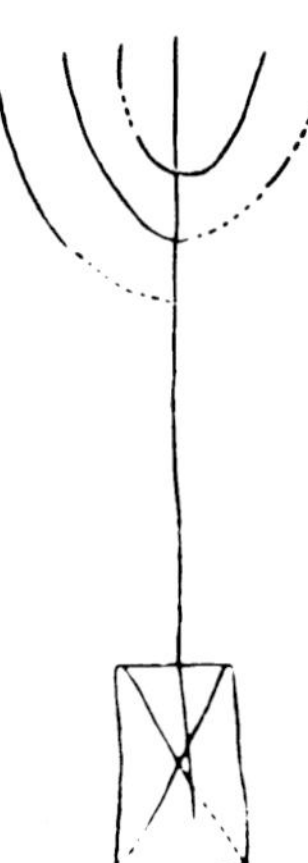

1
Graffito from Jason's Tomb, Jerusalem

A. The menorah as a emblem intended to identify a synagogue, a tomb, or an object belonging to Jews
B. Symbolic interpretations concerning the celestial sphere, i.e., astral explanations
C. The menorah as an expression of the "Light of the Torah"
D. The menorah as an apotropaic symbol

In his study, Goodenough cited a wide range of interpretations that Jews have given to the menorah: it has been viewed as a symbol of God, the source of light, a symbol of the Torah, the Tree of Life, the path to God, a symbol of motherhood, and so forth.[2] Cecil Roth saw in the menorah a messianic emblem, one of a wide, and certainly exaggerated, aggregate of symbols to which he ascribed similar meaning.[3] Arnold Goldberg has shown that the depictions of the menorah together with the Holy Ark represented the Temple and expressed the hope and expectation for redemption.[4]

It appears that the menorah's various artistic representations and their meaning should be divided into two periods: 1) the period preceding the destruction of the Second Temple, when the menorah was still in use in the Temple; 2) the period following the Temple's destruction and the Bar Kokhba Revolt, during which the menorah became Judaism's central symbol.

Mattathias Antigonus, the last of the Hasmonean kings (reigned 40–37 BCE), introduced an important innovation in the annals of Jewish art. He minted a bronze coin which bears the shewbread table encircled by the Hebrew inscription "Mattathias the High Priest" on the obverse and a seven-branched menorah encircled by the Greek inscription "[belonging to] King Antigonus" on the reverse (p. 156). This coin suggests that the shewbread table was regarded as more important than the menorah and was thus struck on the side with a Hebrew inscription. The very minting of such a coin demonstrates that it was not, in fact, forbidden to depict the Temple appurtenances.

In the sumptuous Jason's Tomb in western Jerusalem, various menorah graffiti were discovered (fig. 1). This tomb apparently served an eminent priestly family during the Hasmonean and early Herodian periods. The excavations of ancient Jerusalem's Upper City revealed fragments of wall plaster from the 1st century BCE, in which a seven-branched menorah was incised (fig. 2): discernible to its right are the remains of depictions of the shewbread table and the incense altar, and to its left a fragment of the stone on which the priest stood in order to trim the lamps (Mishnah Tamid 3:9).[5] The excavators surmised that the depiction may have been incised on the wall of a priestly house for the purpose of instructing novices. These discoveries indicate that from the days of the Hasmoneans until the destruction of the Temple, while the shewbread table and the menorah were still in use, there

2
Graffito incised on the wall of a house excavated in the Jewish Quarter of Jerusalem
Israel Antiquities Authority Collection

was no prohibition against artistic representations of the Temple appurtenances, though this was indeed not a common practice.[6]

In the 1st century CE, the menorah's symbolic meaning engaged the attention of the Jewish philosopher Philo of Alexandria, as well as the historian Flavius Josephus. Philo interpreted the menorah as an emblem of the stars, the zodiac, and the seasons, whereas Josephus asserted that its seven branches represent the seven stars (i.e., planets; *Jewish War,* V, v, 5; *Jewish Antiquities*, III, 144–145, 182). Both Philo and Josephus discuss the menorah after their discussion of the shewbread table (corresponding to the order in Exodus 25:31–40; 37:17–24). Moreover, in Josephus' account of the victory procession in Rome in 71 CE (*Jewish War,* VII, v, 5) and on the relief on Titus' triumphal arch (pp. 190–191), the menorah follows the shewbread table, which is carried first because of its greater importance. Neither Philo nor Josephus mentions any ban on the artistic depiction of either the shewbread table or the menorah.

3
Facade of the Temple depicted in a wall painting from the synagogue at Dura Europos

The large silver tetradrachms minted after the Temple's destruction at the time of the Bar Kokhba Revolt bear on the obverse a facade of the Temple with four pillars, one pair to the right, another to the left, and between them the shewbread table; the reverse shows a *lulav* (palm branch) and an *etrog* (citron). The ideological message of these coins is clear: redemption will bring about the rebuilding of the Temple and the renewal of the cult and of pilgrimage to Jerusalem on Sukkot (the Feast of Tabernacles) and the other festivals. From this coin, it seems that Bar Kokhba and his followers also preferred the shewbread table to the menorah.[7] (The assumption that the menorah appears, with various alterations, on Jewish ceramic oil lamps characteristic of Judea in the period between the Temple's destruction and Bar Kokhba's Revolt is doubtful.)

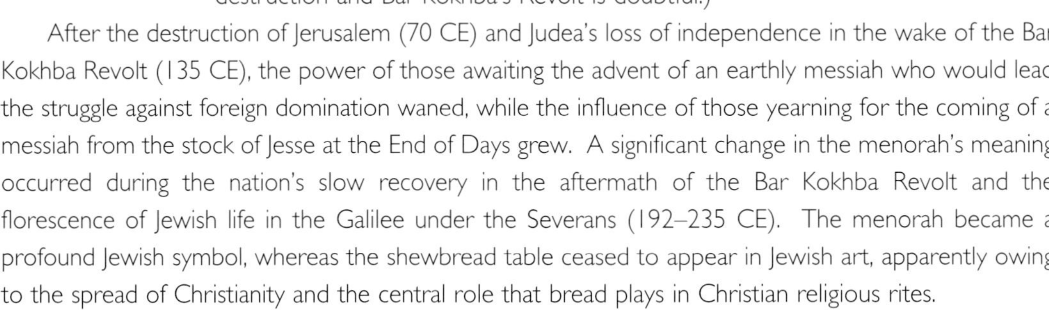

After the destruction of Jerusalem (70 CE) and Judea's loss of independence in the wake of the Bar Kokhba Revolt (135 CE), the power of those awaiting the advent of an earthly messiah who would lead the struggle against foreign domination waned, while the influence of those yearning for the coming of a messiah from the stock of Jesse at the End of Days grew. A significant change in the menorah's meaning occurred during the nation's slow recovery in the aftermath of the Bar Kokhba Revolt and the florescence of Jewish life in the Galilee under the Severans (192–235 CE). The menorah became a profound Jewish symbol, whereas the shewbread table ceased to appear in Jewish art, apparently owing to the spread of Christianity and the central role that bread plays in Christian religious rites.

The profound change in the importance of the menorah and its significance, which occurred between the end of the 2nd and the middle of the 3rd century CE, led to a shift in the manner in which the menorah was depicted. Henceforth, the menorah was represented as standing on a tripodal base accompanied by all or some of the following symbols: the *lulav* (palm branch), the *etrog* (citron), the *shofar* (ram's horn), and the incense shovel.

In the wall paintings of the synagogue at Dura Europos on the banks of the Euphrates river, the facade of the Temple was portrayed in the middle of the wall facing Jerusalem; it closely resembles the facade depicted on the silver tetradrachms of Bar Kokhba (fig. 3). To the right, the binding of Isaac is portrayed – the symbol of salvation on Mount Moriah, identified here with the Temple Mount; to the left of the facade, the menorah appears. It is doubtful that this scheme, executed ca. 245 CE, originated in the border city of Dura Europos, even though it is the earliest example of the type known to us. Situated in the most important place in the synagogue, the scheme expresses the hope for redemption and the rebuilding of the Temple.

The mosaic floor of the synagogue at Hammath Tiberias, from the 4th century CE, depicts a menorah with a tripodal base, together with a *lulav*, *etrog*, *shofar*, and incense shovel, on either side of the Holy Ark. Its message is similar to that of the wall painting from Dura Europos, despite the many differences (the Holy Ark, for instance, occupies the place of the Temple facade, and the menorah and other sacred objects are depicted on both sides of it). This artistic scheme, appearing for the first time at Hammath Tiberias, became the standard scheme for mosaic floors of synagogues in land of Israel during the Byzantine period.

In the cemetery of Beth She'arim (3rd – mid-4th century CE),[8] the menorah appears quite frequently, generally without the *lulav, etrog, shofar*, and incense shovel (figs. 4, 5). In the catacombs of the Jews of Rome, it is sometimes depicted on either side of the Holy Ark, usually in conjunction with the typical accessories (see article by L. Habas in this volume). The Temple menorah taken as booty from Jerusalem was at that time kept in a pagan sanctuary (*Templum Pacis*) in Rome, after it had been depicted in relief on the Arch of Titus. Nevertheless, the Jews of Rome still preferred to depict on their graves the tripodal menorah, as was customary in Jewish art of that time. As such, they expressed their identification with the menorah of profound symbolic value, as opposed to the "captive menorah" seen on the Arch of Titus (see article by D. Sperber in this volume). Depictions of the menorah also became fairly common on daily objects, including, starting in the 3rd century CE, ceramic oil lamps (p. 155), generally in combination with some or all of the sacred implements. In the 3rd–4th century CE, the menorah appears on gold-glass bases from Rome (p. 62), and in the 3rd–7th century on jewelry and other objects. In the last quarter of the 6th through the beginning of the 7th century, it adorns glass vessels produced for Jewish pilgrims to Jerusalem (fig. 6).

The rabbinic proscription that one may not make "a menorah in the form of a menorah, but rather with five or six branches or eight; but not with seven, even of other types of metals" (Babylonian Talmud, Rosh Hashanah 24a, b; Menahot 28b; Avodah Zarah 43a) was preserved solely in a *baraita* (a teaching not included in the official Mishnaic corpus), not in the Mishnah compiled by Rabbi Judah Hanasi. Rabbi Jose ben Rabbi Judah, quoted in connection with the aforementioned ruling, belonged to the last generation of Tannaim (the end of the 2nd to the beginning of the 3rd century CE). It seems that the ruling does not reflect the earlier state of affairs, but rather the reality of the sages living during the period directly following the Bar Kokhba Revolt, during which the menorah had taken on special meaning; moreover, they apparently did not prohibit its artistic representation altogether, but rather decreed that menorahs imitating the Temple exemplar should not be produced. The proscription against producing menorahs for synagogue use was apparently scrupulously enforced. The synagogue at Ein Gedi yielded a cast-bronze menorah from the 5th century CE (p. 103); this menorah, however, appears to have been symbolic, not an object of actual use; it probably served to decorate the Holy Ark. In the stone menorah discovered by Nahum Slouschz in the synagogue at Hammath Tiberias (p. 95), only the upper section is rendered, not the shaft and base, and it has depressions at the top for holding ceramic oil lamps. Though this was indeed an object intended for actual synagogue use, measures were clearly taken to ensure that it would not be "a menorah in the form of a menorah," even in terms of the material from which it was made – limestone. In the synagogue at Horvat Ma'on fragments of a menorah carved in marble (p. 102; estimated height over 1.6 m) were discovered, but here too, it can be assumed that the object was symbolic and not intended for actual use. It is noteworthy that until today there is no known inscription from the Holy land mentioning the donation of a synagogue menorah. The finds discovered to date prove that in the synagogues and private houses of antiquity, menorahs in the fashion of the Temple exemplar were not used – certainly not ones of metal. The artistic representations, by contrast, are not of contemporary objects, as E. R. Goodenough believes, but rather of the Temple menorah (see article by L. Levine in this volume).

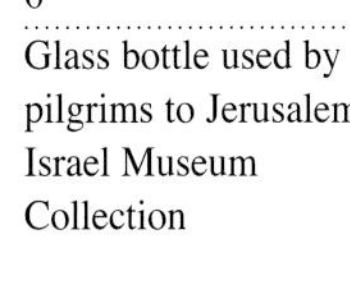

6
Glass bottle used by pilgrims to Jerusalem
Israel Museum Collection

The development in the representations of the menorah and in the menorah's meaning can thus be traced quiet clearly. There can be no doubt that until the Bar Kokhba Revolt, the shewbread table was perceived as more important than the menorah. Artistic depictions of the menorah are rare at this time, not because illustrating it was forbidden, but simply because it had not yet received the primacy it would later acquire. The change occurred in the days of Rabbi Judah Hanasi – in the late 2nd – early 3rd century CE, or slightly later. From this point on, the menorah occupies a prominent position in synagogue decoration, usually accompanied by a *lulav, etrog, shofar,* and incense shovel. At this time, it seems to symbolize – whether portrayed together with the Temple facade, as at Dura Europos, or with the Holy Ark, as in later depictions – the hope for rebuilding the Temple, for renewing the daily cult and the pilgrimage festivals in Jerusalem, and the coming of the messiah (Bamidbar Rabbah 15:10).

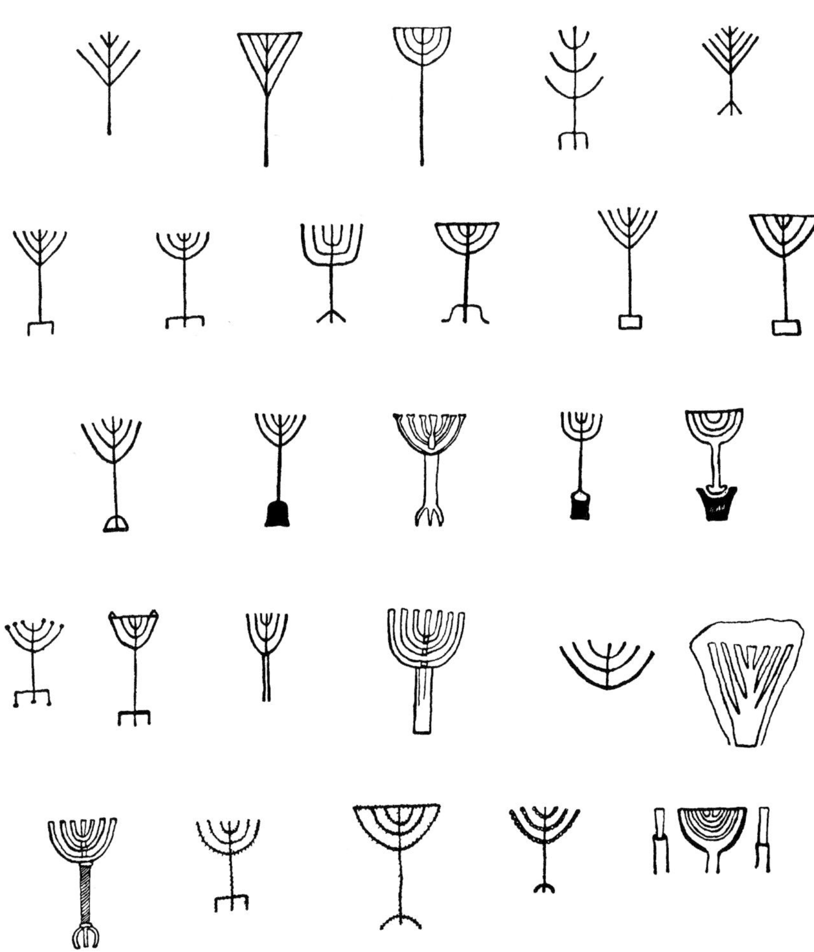

4
Menorah motifs from the cemetery at Beth She'arim

In cemeteries, the menorah expresses the hope that the general redemption contingent upon the coming of the messiah will entail personal redemption – that is to say, the resurrection of the dead. As a symbol of the belief in resurrection, the menorah frequently appears in cemeteries in the land of Israel without the accompanying motifs. Its representation in cemeteries and in synagogues expresses the same concept from two parallel perspectives: the belief in redemption and the coming of the messiah, which will bring about the rebuilding of the Temple and the resurrection of the dead. This development occurred sometime during the end of the 2nd to the mid-3rd century CE. With remarkable speed, the menorah achieved tremendous popularity throughout the Jewish world and was regarded as a major symbol in both East and West. This phenomenon suggests that the menorah and the accompanying objects conveyed a clear and intelligible message with which all Jews could identify, wherever they lived. The use of the menorah as a symbol was further intensified, apparently in the first half of the 4th century. When Christians began using a combination of the first two letters of the word "Christ" (meaning messiah in Greek) as an expression of their belief that the messiah had already arrived, the Jews used the menorah as symbol of the messiah's future coming. Over time, after this interpretation of the menorah had been accepted throughout the Jewish world, additional, on the whole simplistic, meanings were attached to the menorah motif, and it became, for example, a sign of Jewish identity, a protective amulet, and so forth.

The depictions of the menorah in synagogues and cemeteries of the 3rd to the 7th century CE should not be perceived as indicative of impatience for the messianic era or a call for direct confrontation with Roman rule, but rather an expression of hope – which was later formulated in Maimonides' Thirteen Principles of Faith – for the coming of the messiah and resurrection the of the dead at the End of Days.

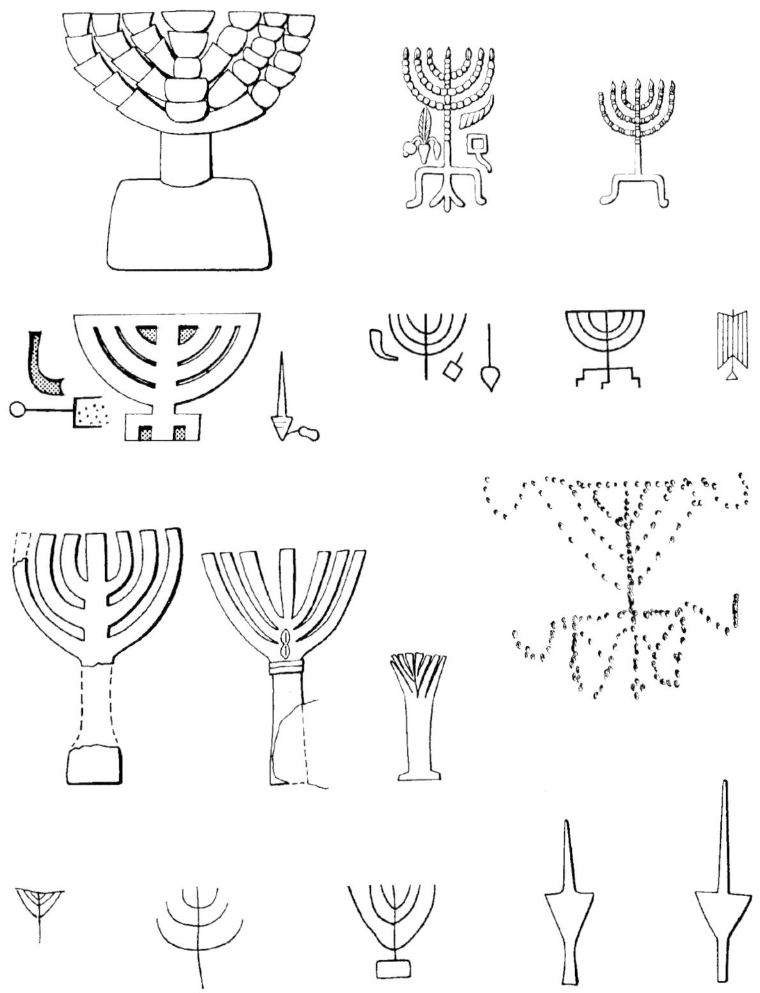

5
Menorah motifs from the cemetery at Beth She'arim

1 Among the rich literature on this subject, the following works are particularly important for our purposes: A. Negev, "The Chronology of the Seven-Branched Menorah," *Eretz-Israel* 8 (1967): 193–210 (Hebrew); N. Avigad, *Beth She'arim*, vol. 3 (Jerusalem, 1976), 268–274 (Hebrew); R. Hachlili, *Ancient Jewish Art and Archaeology in the Land of Israel* (Leiden, 1988), passim; C. L. Meyers, *The Tabernacle Menorah: A Synthetic Study of a Symbol from the Biblical Cult*, AASOR Dissertation Series, no. 2 (1976); L. Yarden, *The Tree of Light* (London, 1971).

2 E. R. Goodenough, *Jewish Symbols in the Greco-Roman Period*, IV (New York, 1954), 71–98; XII (1965), 79–83.

3 C. Roth, "Messianic Symbols in Palestinian Archaeology," *Palestine Exploration Quarterly* 87 (1955): 152f.

4 A. M. Goldberg, "Der siebenarmige Leuchter, zur Enstehung eines jüdischen Bekenntnissymbols," *Zeitschrift der Deutschen Morgenländischen Gesellschaft* 117 (1967): 232–246.

5 Fig. 2 presents a proposed reconstruction with the stone on which the priest stood to the left of the menorah. See D. Barag, "The Temple Cult Vessels Graffito from the Jewish Quarter Excavations at Jerusalem," in H. Geva (ed.), *Ancient Jerusalem Revealed* (Jerusalem, 1994), 274, 277–8, which contains the reconstruction proposed by N. Avigad, who excavated the graffito.

6 The coins dating from the Jewish War (66–70 CE) depict various objects used in Temple, but for reasons that are still unclear, they do not represent the shewbread table and the menorah.

7 D. Barag, "The Shewbread Table on the Facade of the Temple on Coins of the Bar Kokhba Revolt," in Geva (above, n. 5), 272–276.

8 For a different view, see article by L. Levine's in this volume.

Lihi Habas

Identity and Hope
The Menorah in the Jewish Catacombs of Rome

1
The "Good Shepherd" on the ceiling of a burial chamber in the Christian catacomb of Priscilla

The absence of the menorah among the archaeological finds of the First Temple period and its rarity among those of the Second Temple period stand in striking contrast to the menorah's importance in the biblical text and its central position in the Tabernacle and the Temple.

It seems that the menorah first appeared as a symbol of Jewish identity among the Diaspora communities, where is was used in the context of death and interment.[1] In the Jewish catacombs of Rome, it was painted on tomb walls, engraved beside the epitaphs on the slabs that sealed the burial niches, and carved on the facades of the sarcophagi. Owing to their physical distance from the land of Israel, the Jews of the Diaspora were forced to deviate from the burial customs practiced by their ancestors in their homeland. Jewish interment in the land of Israel during the First and Second Temple periods was in family burial caves, in which a number of generations were buried, the dead attended by their kin. The Jews of the Diaspora, having lost their property and lands, had no choice by to adopt the burial practices of their new environs, and thus, the Jewish community in Rome took on the custom of public burial in subterranean systems (catacombs), as practiced by the pagans and Christians among whom they lived.

In order to understand the choice of the menorah as a symbol of Jewish identity in funerary art, it is necessary to understand the funerary art of the pagans and, especially, the Christians, from the end of the 2nd to the 4th century CE.

Before the crucifix became the symbol *par excellence* of Christianity, the walls of the early Christian catacombs in Rome were mainly decorated with the peacock, the anchor, and the fish, as well as depictions of the "Good Shepherd." In addition to these symbols, the walls of the burial chambers (*cubicula*) bear detailed representations of biblical episodes that express God's deliverance of the individual or the collective: the Sacrifice of Isaac; the Exodus from Egypt and the crossing of the Red Sea; the miracles in the desert; the story of Jonah; the rescue of Daniel from the lions' den and the three Hebrews from the fiery furnace; and so forth. These biblical themes were supplemented by stories from the New Testament, especially those connected with miracles performed by Jesus, such as the raising of Lazarus and the healing of the blind man, the paralytic, and the woman with an issue of blood, as well as stories from the lives of mythological heroes, such as Hercules and Orpheus – mortals who entered the realm of Hades, God of the Underworld, but managed to return to the world of the living. Identical depictions occur in the reliefs on marble sarcophagi, also used for burial at this time. In both cases, the images seek to express a message of redemption for the believer.

2
Ceiling of a burial chamber decorated with mythological figures in the Jewish Vigna Randanini catacomb

The distribution of biblical motifs in Christian funerary art should be understood in the context of the Church Fathers' use of biblical stories – both literally, as part of the prayers and supplications for salvation, and allegorically, whereby they were construed as prefigurations of the precepts of Christian faith.[2] In funerary art, events and personalities associated with redemption were selected, and they were presented to the viewer as heralds of rebirth in the new, Christian era. It is on this ideological basis that the use of the menorah in the funerary art of the Jews should be examined, beginning with the paintings on the catacomb walls.

3
Ceiling of a burial chamber decorated with the menorah in the Torlonia catacomb

Christian Catacomb Paintings

The ceilings of the Chrisitian catacombs were painted according to a scheme originating in the pagan world, but which was also accepted in antiquity by Christians and Jews. In this scheme, the central area of the domed or vaulted ceiling consists of a central circle with concentric bands around it, while the sides and corners contain secondary, usually semicircular, units. The different·units are filled with figures, objects, and floral motifs. The figure or symbol in the innermost circle is always one associated with the heavenly sphere, expressing the hopes of the faithful for redemption.[3] The variety in the symbols and figures is produced mainly in the secondary units.

A common motif appearing in the central circle on the ceilings of burial chambers in Christian catacombs is that of the "Good Shepherd." One of the most notable surviving examples of this type is found in the burial chambers of Bottai and Velatio in the catacomb of Priscilla, from the second half of the 3rd century (fig. 1). In Early Christian art, the "Good Shepherd" is analogous to Jesus, while the sheep represent the believers and the souls of the deceased. In this visual metaphor, Jesus protects his believers just like the shepherd, who guards his flock from beasts of prey and the forces of nature; and like the shepherd carrying a ewe upon his shoulders, he bears the souls of the deceased to an eternal life of bliss.[4]

Jewish Catacomb Paintings

The "celestial ceiling" (Dome of Heaven) also decorates the Jewish catacombs of Vigna Randanini and Torlonia. One of the chambers in the Vigna Randanini catacomb features the usual scheme, but the geometric units are empty, devoid of symbols, figures, or objects; in two others, however, the central circle is occupied by mythological figures: in the first, Victoria, the winged goddess of Victory, holds a palm branch in one hand, while with the other she crowns a nude youth with a wreath (fig. 2); in the second room, the goddess Fortuna or Tyche holds a cornucopia in her left hand, while she pours a libation from a flask with her right.[5]

4
Back wall of an *arcosolium* decorated with menorahs and a Torah shrine in the Torlonia catacomb

The owners of the Torlonia catacomb preferred to place Jewish symbols in the center of the "celestial ceiling." Here, the seven-branched menorah replaces the "Good Shepherd" and the Goddess of Victory (fig. 3).[6] It is surrounded by circles decorated with geometric and floral patterns creating a stylized wreath. The semicircles around the central circle each contain a dolphin with a trident. The corners are decorated with vine scrolls and a *shofar* (ram's horn) and *etrog* (citron) within concentric circles.

Along the walls, *arcosolia* (vaulted niches containing coffin-shaped graves; sing: *arcrosolium*) were installed. The menorah also appears on the vaulted ceilings of these niches, within a scheme similar to the "celestial ceiling," but in partial representation, as dictated by the contour of the arch. In the middle, in concentric circles/wreaths, is a lit menorah; to either side are semicircles, one of which contains a pomegranate, the other a *shofar*, in one grave, the semicircles feature a pomegranate and a Torah scroll.[7]

According to pagan belief, dolphins led the souls of the dead to the realm of Hades, God of the Underworld, and the pomegranate was the symbol of Persephone, his wife. The wreath, a symbol of victory, originated in the Dionysian world and the aspect of rebirth associated with it. All of these symbols were therefore common in pagan funerary art, as they were related to the concept of rebirth and victory over death. In the Jewish catacombs, these pagan motifs were combined with the *shofar*, *etrog*, *pomegranate*, and Torah scroll, and in the place reserved for the symbol of the hope for life after death, the menorah was depicted. Thus, the common pagan "celestial ceiling" was in use in Jewish art – an inseparable mixture of pagan and Jewish motifs.

These changes in Jewish art at the end of the 2nd century and the free use of pagan symbols should be understood against the background of the decline of pagan culture, which no longer constituted a significant religious threat. During this period, mythological motifs were copied in Jewish contexts merely as decorative patterns, or as generally accepted symbols, and were not perceived as having any real religious meaning.[8]

5

Relief of the menorah on the facade of a Jewish sarcophagus from the Vigna Randanini catacomb Soprintendenza Archeologica di Roma, Museo Nazionale Romano, Rome

6

Relief of the menorah on the facade of a Jewish sarcophagus from the Torlonia catacomb Soprintendenza Archeologica di Roma, Museo Nazionale Romano, Rome

The menorah appears in a complex composition on the back wall of an *arcosolium* in one of the burial chambers of the Torlonia catacomb. In the center of the composition, the Torah shrine is depicted with its doors wide open (fig. 4). Inside the Torah shrine, resting on the shelves, are scrolls. The shrine's gabled roof is decorated on top with a circle surmounted by a large star, with the sun, the moon, and clouds to either side. The shrine is flanked by two menorahs whose seven branches are decorated with "knobs and flowers" supporting burning oil lamps. The composition is completed by an *etrog*, a knife, a *shofar*, a vase, a pomegranate, and a *lulav* (palm branch). Above is a curtain drawn aside.[9] The symbols are all presented against a celestial background in an eschatological context, which implies that the objects belong to the realm that the deceased is about to enter.

In the pagan and Christian sarcophagus reliefs of this period, it was customary to place a portrait of the deceased (or of the deceased couple) in the center of the coffin facade. In some cases, this portrait, or an epitaph, appears within a seashell, a medallion, or a shield held by the goddesses of victory – a motif betokening the triumph over death. In Jewish sarcophagi, however, the seven-branched menorah replaces the portrait. Thus the basic composition was retained, but by means of the menorah, the deceased or his family proclaimed their Jewish identity. On the facade of a sarcophagus from the Vigna Randanini catacomb, there is a relief of two winged Victories holding a shield in their hands; but here, instead of the expected portrait bust, a seven-branched menorah with oil lamps at the top is carved (fig. 5). Though only the central portion of the original sarcophagus has survived, on the basis of comparison with similar sarcophagi, it is possible to reconstruct that the sides of the facade featured personifications of the four seasons in the form of winged Erotes. The sole extant example represents Autumn, who holds a basket of fruit in one hand and a pair of geese in the other. Of the figure of Winter next to it, only a trace of a wing, one leg, and an uplifted hand holding a wild boar caught in a hunt remains. Underneath the menorah's medallion are putti treading grapes in a vat with lion-headed spouts. An additional cupid, to the right, is shown riding a hare, while his companion rides a dog.

Fragments of another sarcophagus facade from the same catacomb depict a menorah, with branches terminating in oil lamps, which is flanked by palm trees. Between these trees, rosettes, *lulavim*, an *etrog*, and two disks are carved. A simpler menorah representation is found in the center of a sarcophagus facade discovered in the Torlonia catacomb; it is accompanied by an *etrog* and a *lulav* (fig. 6).[10]

The Jewish catacombs have yielded hundreds of gravestones that were used to seal the graves (*loculi*), and in which epitaphs were carved; most are in Greek, while some have additions in Aramaic and

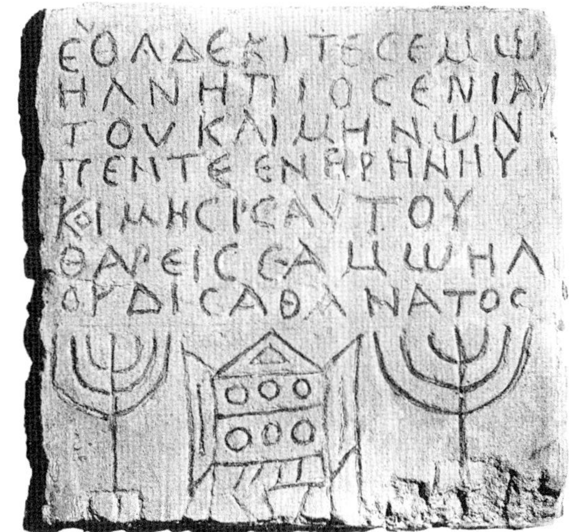

a

b

7
The menorah motif on Jewish gravestones from the Monteverde catacomb

Hebrew. The latest of these epitaphs were written in Latin. About half of these gravestones were also adorned with Jewish symbols. The Monteverde catacomb produced over two hundred such slabs, of which forty-seven were adorned with the menorah, sometimes as the only symbol, sometimes alongside the Torah shrine, as, for instance in a gravestone containing a touching inscription in Greek: "Here lies Samuel, an infant of one year and five months. May he rest in peace! Be brave, Samuel! No one is immortal" (fig. 7a). The menorah also appears in a complex composition, which includes additional objects and symbols, such as an amphora, *lulav*, *etrog*, *shofar*, and ivy leaves in various arrangements and versions, as on the gravestone of Salo, on which the following epitaph is inscribed: "Here lies Salo, the daughter of Gadias, Father of the Synagogue of the Hebrews. She lived forty-one years. In peace she sleeps" (fig. 7b).[11] Like the wall paintings in the catacombs and the reliefs on the sarcophagi, the Jewish gravestones were also influenced by their Christian counterparts, on which the main symbols are the anchor and the fish, originally pagan symbols of salvation.[12]

After the destruction of Jerusalem and the razing of the Second Temple, the Jewish communities of Rome adopted the seven-branched menorah as a symbol of Jewish identity, in order to distinguish themselves from the Christians and pagans. It was chosen in spite of its being a symbol of defeat, of lost nationhood, and of the Temple's destruction. For the Jews of Rome, the relief of the menorah on Titus' Triumphal Arch situated in the heart of the city must have been a constant, painful reminder of their loss. It is perhaps for this reason that they deliberately distanced themselves from the model of the menorah featured on the Arch, designing instead simple, stylized menorahs, linear or floral in mode. They also avoided compositions which combined the menorah with trumpets and the shewbread table – the absence of which is striking in the funerary art of the Jewish catacombs.

Thus, the symbol of national defeat ultimately became a mark of Jewish identity. In funerary art, however, under the influence of the pagan and Christian art of the same time and place, the menorah acquired an additional layer of meaning: it became an eschatological symbol, comparable to the other symbols concerned with both individual and collective redemption and the triumph over death (see article by D. Barag in this volume). Its location in the catacombs and sarcophagi is also parallel to that of the depictions of the stories of deliverance from the Bible, the New Testament, and mythology.

In the 3rd century, the menorah, enriched with new meaning, returned to the land of Israel by way of the cemeteries in which local and Diaspora Jews were buried together. It appears, both individually and as part of complex compositions, on tomb walls, gravestones, and sarcophagi in the cemeteries of Jaffa, Caesarea, and Beth She'arim. From there it spread to the realm of synagogue decoration, beginning with architectonic sculpture and afterwards extending to mosaic floors (see article by L. Levine in this volume).

1 M. Avi-Yonah, "The Symbol of the State Emblem from an Historical Perspective," *Moladeti* 13–15 (1950): 96–97 (Hebrew).

2 The early Church Fathers, from the end of the 2nd and the 3rd–4th centuries (Origen of Alexandria, Tertullian, Clement of Alexandria, Ambrose Bishop of Milan, and others) dealt in their writings with the symbolism of Old Testament occurrences and their parallelism to the New Testament. They created a kind of concordance whereby they classified typologically events, figures, and objects which prefigure Jesus and his doctrine.

3 E. R. Goodenough, *Jewish Symbols in the Greco-Roman Period,* vol. II (New York, 1953), 17; K. Lehmann, "The Dome of Heaven," *Art Bulletin* 27 (1945): 1–27.

4 M. Gough, *The Origins of Christian Art* (London, 1973), 18–48.

5 Goodenough (above, no. 3), vol. 2, 16–21; vol. 3, figs. 737–743, 748–749, 759–760.

6 Goodenough (above, no. 3), vol. 2, 36–37; vol. 3, fig. 806; H. W. Beyer and H. Lietzmann, *Jüdische Katakombe der Villa Torlonia in Rom* (Berlin, 1930), 9–10, pl. 7a.

7 Beyer and Lietzmann (above, no. 6), 10–21, pls. 4, 6.

8 E. A. Urbach, "The Laws of Idolatry in the Light of Historical and Archaelogical Facts in the Third Century," *Eretz-Israel* 5 (1958): 189–205 (Hebrew); L. Habas, "The Image of Man and Animals in Ancient Jewish Art," *Mahanaim* 10 (1995): 14–29 (Hebrew).

9 Beyer and Lietzmann (above, no. 6),16, 24–26, pl. 12.

10 Goodenough (above, no. 3), vol. 2, 26–29, 41, figs. 788–789, 818; Beyer and Lietzmann (above, no. 6), 44, pls. 26a–28.

11 Goodenough (above, no. 3), vol. 2, 4–14, figs. 706, 721; J. B. Frey, *Corpus inscriptionum Judaicanum,* vol. 1 (Rome, 1936), 310, 318 (nos. 706, 416).

12 The fish was a cryptogram – the letters of the word "fish" in Greek, ΙΧΘΥΣ, are the initials of a profession of faith: "Jesus Christ, Son of God and Savior."

Bezalel Narkiss

The Menorah in Illuminated Hebrew Manuscripts of the Middle Ages*

Introduction

The shape of the seven-branched menorah in the Middle Ages differs little from its shape in antiquity, and this image continued to serve as a symbol of the Temple in Jerusalem that would be rebuilt in days to come. The most common representations of the menorah during the late Middle Ages is within an array of sacred implements from five different sanctuaries: the Tabernacle in the desert; Solomon's Temple; the Second Temple; Herod's Temple; and the ideal temple of Ezekiel's vision. The objects are arranged haphazardly and do not represent an accurate ground plan of any of the above sanctuaries; such depictions should be regarded, therefore, as symbolic descriptions of the Temple to be rebuilt in the End of Days.

1
Opening page of the *Cambridge Alphabet Book for Children*
Egypt, 11th century
University Library, Cambridge
T-S K5.13

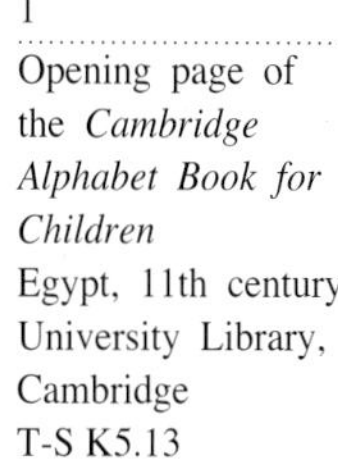

The tradition of depicting a haphazard array of sanctuary implements dates back to antiquity; it is found on objects of clay, metal, and glass, on the mosaic floors of synagogues, in wall paintings, and on funerary plaques – from both the land of Israel and the diaspora and dating from the 2nd–6th century CE. This type of scheme continued to appear in the Middle Ages, mainly on the carpet pages of Hebrew biblical illuminated manuscripts from Islamic countries dating from the 9th century on. The idea of placing illuminated carpet pages at the beginning and end of sacred books may have been influenced by illuminated manuscripts of the Koran. The array of sanctuary implements was produced in all the main medieval Jewish regional cultures: in the Near East and Spain, in the Ashkenazi communities of France, Germany, and Northern Italy, and, later, in Eastern Europe. The fact that these communities shared a similar tradition may imply the existence of a common model, which was apparently based on a comprehensive array or a ground plan of the Temple created either in antiquity or the early Middle Ages. Such a plan can be seen, perhaps, in a graffito of the menorah, shewbread table, and incense altar found in Jerusalem in a Herodian-period house (p. 27).[1] This kind of model was at the disposal of the different communities, each of which developed its own version of the menorah and other implements, but also enabled one culture to influence the scheme of another.

2
Enrico Nahum Pentateuch
Spain, ca. 1300
Jewish National and University Library, Jerusalem

Near Eastern Manuscripts

The earliest known representation of the menorah among sanctuary implements in a Hebrew illuminated manuscript appears in the *First St. Petersburg Pentateuch,* which was written in 929 in either the land of Israel or Egypt.[2] In the manuscript, two menorahs are depicted along with other sanctuary implements on two opposing pages. Despite the general impression of symmetry, based on the central position of each of the menorahs and the stylized arks above them, most of the implements appear to have been strewn randomly across the pages. Moreover, a different menorah is depicted on each page. On one page (fol. 4v; p. 63), the menorah has the usual curved branches; on the other, the menorah's branches are angular.[3] The branches of both menorahs are decorated with a continuous line of flowers, rather than

* I would like to thank Yaffa Levy and Ariella Amar for assisting me with the research of this topic and for their insightful comments on this article.

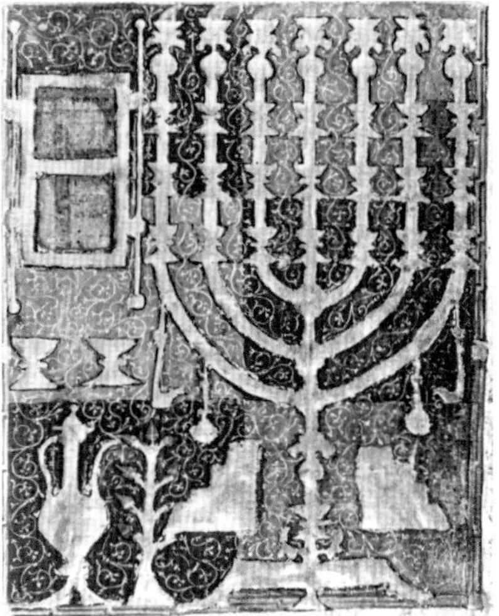

3
Harley Catalan Bible
Catalonia, 14th century
The British Library, London

the prescribed cups or goblets (*gevi'im*), knobs (*kaftorim*), and flowers (*perahim*) (Exodus 25:31–35). This is also the case on many menorahs from ancient times, which are ornamented with stylized flowers, though the menorah depicted in the graffito from Jerusalem is decorated with straight lines and circles. Both of the menorahs in the Pentateuch lack a base, perhaps because the base is not described in the biblical text. This may indicate that the Pentateuch was commissioned by a Karaite patron, for the Karaites based their laws on the Bible alone (see article by R. Hachlili and R. Merhav in this volume).[4]

Menorahs with a central shaft and base are commonly found in manuscripts from the 11th century onward. One example can be seen on a carpet page of the *Cambridge Alphabet Book for Children,* which was found in the Cairo Genizah (fig. 1).[5] These depictions of the menorah are part of a long tradition, extending from antiquity to the late Middle Ages, the finest examples of which can be found in the Sephardi illuminated Bibles.

Sephardi Manuscripts

The menorah's shape and ornamentation began to be depicted in detail in Sephardi manuscripts of the 13th century. These depictions are based mainly on the commentaries of Rashi (1040–1105) on the Bible and Maimonides (1138–1204) on the Mishnah and Talmud, as well as on Maimonides' *Mishneh Torah.*[6] Though none of the menorahs appearing in the Sephardi Bibles is completely in keeping with Rashi's and Maimonides' interpretations, they do reflect them in certain details. For example, the three-legged base of the Sephardi menorah, which is commonly found in depictions of the menorah from antiquity, was formulated for the first time in Rashi's explanation of the base of the menorah in his commentary on Exodus 25:31: "fashioned like a kind of box, and three legs issue from it downward . . ." In terms of the number of decorative elements and their placement, the Sephardi menorah corresponds to Maimonides' commentary to the Mishnah (Menahot 3.7). Here he explains that each of the branches and the upper part of the central shaft, called the menorah, were decorated with three goblets (*gevi'im*) that narrowed toward the bottom and that above each of the goblets was an ovoid, as opposed to spherical, knob (*kaftor*), which was in turn surmounted by a flower (*perah*) shaped like a lily (*shoshan*), or, in the words of the Talmud, "like the blossoms on the capitals of columns" (Babylonian Talmud, Menahot, 28b). In most of the Sephardi menorahs, the flower resembles a fleur-de-lis or two serrated wing-like leaves. The seven lamps, one atop each of the six branches and another above the central shaft, were, in Maimonides' view, an integral part of the menorah, "a kind of small bowl into which the oil and wicks were put" (*Mishneh Torah, Hilkhot Bet Habehirah* 3: 7–8). According to both Rashi and Maimonides, the flames were turned toward the central lamp, called in the Talmud the "western lamp." The lower part of the shaft was decorated with an additional goblet surmounted by a knob and flower. A flower was placed at the junction of the shaft and its base.

4
Duke of Sussex Catalan Bible
Catalonia, 14th century
The British Library, London

Certain additional objects usually appear together with the menorah in these Sephardi Bibles: Two pairs of tongs and two incense shovels, which are mentioned in the Bible,[7] are depicted flanking the menorah, or hanging from its lower branches. At some point in the 14th century, the incense shovels were replaced by censers, resembling the kind used in churches; they are shown suspended from the lower branches of the menorah by chains, as in the *Enrico Nahum Pentateuch* from Spain (fig. 2).[8] Also appearing in the Sephardi Bibles is a third object, mentioned only in the Mishnah: "There was a stone before the menorah in which were three steps; the priest stood on this to trim the lamps" (Tamid 3:9). One such stepping stone was drawn on either side of the menorah, probably for the sake of symmetry. A small pitcher is sometimes depicted next to the menorah, or on the second step of the stone. It might represent the *kuz,* a kind of pitcher which the priest used to add oil to the lamps.

In Hebrew illuminated manuscripts from medieval Spain, the menorah appears in three different contexts: A. as part of a ground plan of the Temple; B. as part of an array of sanctuary implements; C. on its own. The menorahs are similar in shape and ornamentation in each of these contexts, and they all have messianic significance.

An example of a ground plan of the Temple has survived in a fragment by the renowned scribe-artist, Joshua son of Abraham ibn Gaon (the fragment is from a manuscript he made in Soria, Spain in 1306). It was bound together with the *Second Kennicott Bible*[9] and depicts, in great detail, the right wing of the Second Temple, with a view of the right side of the menorah, which is portrayed as having angular branches. Joshua Ibn Gaon also used an angular menorah in the margin of the *First Ibn Gaon Bible,* which he copied and illuminated in 1301.[10]

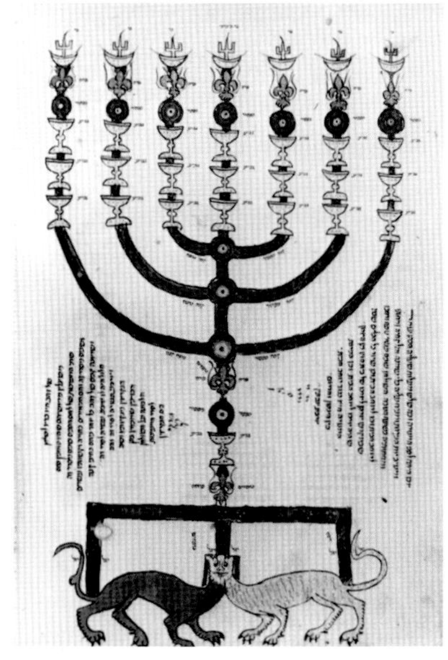

5
Maimonides' *Mishneh Torah,* southern Germany, late 13th century
The Jewish Theological Seminary of America, New York

There are about thirty extant Sephardi illuminated Bibles with depictions of sanctuary implements; in each case, the menorah occupies a prominent position.[11] Occasionally, the objects are surrounded by biblical verses describing the form of the menorah and concluding with the hope for the rebuilding of the Temple in the near future. The earliest of these Bibles was produced in Toledo and dates from 1277; the latest is from the last decade of the 15th century, just before the expulsion of the Jews from Spain in 1492. In most of them, the sanctuary appurtenances are depicted on two or more pages. The arrangement of the objects varies according to school, place, and time. Over the years, several distinct types emerged.

The Toledan Type includes the *Toledo Bible of Parma,*[12] the *Perpignian Bible* of 1299 (the best-preserved of the group, see p. 66),[13] as well as other biblical manuscripts with a similar compositional arrangement, in which each object is depicted within its own frame, with the menorah usually on the upper right.[14] In the Intermediate Type, the objects are laid out somewhat differently, and the menorah occupies the full height of the framed page. The ark of the covenant and the tablets of the law are left of the menorah, above Aaron's flowering rod. An example of this type is the *Harley Catalan Bible* (fig. 3).[15] Two additional manuscripts of this type were discovered in Karaite synagogues in Cairo and Istanbul. The Intermediate Type also includes manuscripts in which the objects are drawn with micrographic letters. One of these is the *Micrographic Bible from Barcelona,* owned by the Jewish community of Rome.[16] The second is the *Catalan Micrographic Mahzor* of the late 14th century, in the collection of the Jewish National and University Library, Jerusalem.[17] In the Catalan Type, the menorah fills the entire page and is sometimes flanked by objects besides the traditional tongs, shovels, and steps. About twelve Bibles belonging to this type have come down to us; most are of the 14th century. The earliest is the *Foa Bible,*[18] and the best-preserved example is the *Duke of Sussex Catalan Bible* (fig. 4).[19]

6
Kaufmann Mishneh Torah, northeastern France, 1296
Library of the Hungarian Academy of Sciences, Budapest

In several Hebrew illuminated manuscripts from Spain, the menorah appears on its own, without the other sanctuary appurtenances, as in the *Cervera Bible* of 1300.[20] There, another type of menorah appears – the menorah described in Zechariah's vision (Zechariah 4:4), which is flanked by two olive trees (p. 57; see article by R. Sarfaty in this volume). A stylized menorah can be seen on a single page from the late 15th century, in the collection of The Israel Museum, Jerusalem (MS 180/159). Single menorahs also occasionally appear in law codes, next to the section dealing with the laws of the Temple, as in the first book of Maimonides Mishneh Torah. A late example of a single menorah is from the *Catalan Mishneh Torah of Jerusalem* of 1460 (p. 30).[21] These menorahs are quite different from one another, perhaps because each artist interpreted the text differently. One of the most fascinating single menorahs is a kabbalistic example from the manuscript of *Sha'arei Orah* (Portals of Light) by Joseph Gikatilla, copied in Toledo in 1485–90 (p. 142).[22]

Ashkenazi Manuscripts

The menorahs in Ashkenazi illuminated manuscripts vary, depending on the manuscripts in which they appear, but they are mainly based on the writings of Rashi and Maimonides. The manuscripts of the Bible usually depict the menorah on its own, or as part of a scene with Aaron the High Priest. In the manuscripts of the *Mishneh Torah*, the menorah appears as part of a ground plan of the Temple, though in one case, it is part of an array of sanctuary appurtenances similar to the Catalan Type.

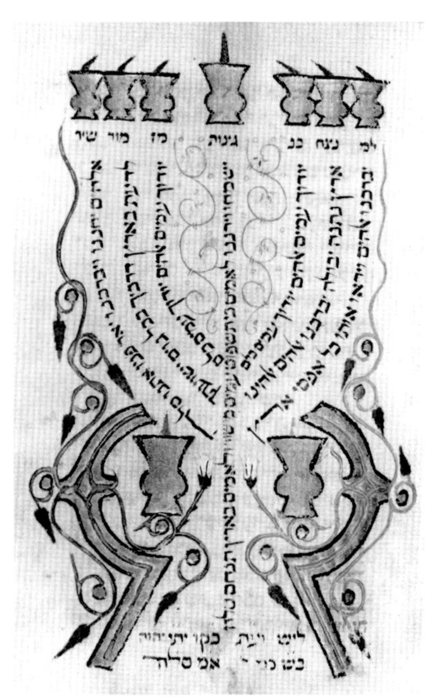

7
Yehiel ben Matitiah Mahzor
Pisa, 1397
Private collection

A single menorah appears in one of the earliest Hebrew illuminated manuscripts from Europe, the *Rashi Biblical Commentary* (Würzburg 1233).[23] The branches of the menorah are thin and emerge from the shaft diagonally, turning upward at the middle. Each branch bears three small goblets with a fleur-de-lis on top. Round knobs decorate the joins. The central shaft, which is supported by a stepped, three-legged base, bears a knob, a fleur-de-lis, and a goblet. The menorah is surrounded by a frame that conforms to its shape, and the background appearing between its branches is multicolored. In the sketches of the ground plan of the Temple appearing in 14th- and 15th-century copies of the *Mishneh Torah* from Germany, the menorahs are positioned in accordance with Maimonides' view.[24]

Manuscripts of the *Mishneh Torah* from southern Germany usually depict single menorahs as an illustration to Maimonides' detailed descriptions. One example shows a colorful menorah with curved branches, decorated with large yellow goblets, green knobs, and reddish-brown fleurs-de-lis, and a rectangular three-legged base. Under the base are two lions sharing a single head (fig. 5).[25] Another single menorah appears in the *Kaufmann Mishneh Torah*, made in northeastern France in 1296 (fig. 6).[26] The goblets, knobs, and flowers decorating its curved branches and short shaft differ from earlier depictions. In addition, the menorah is flanked by trees, a possible allusion to Zechariah's vision.

Scenes of Aaron pouring oil into the menorah or lighting it are found in illuminated manuscripts from northern France and southern Germany. In the *London Miscellany* of ca. 1280, possibly from Amiens or Troyes in northeastern France, these scenes are illustrated together on a full page, on which the menorah is portrayed with angular branches.[27] A representation of Aaron lighting the menorah, outlined in micrography, appears in the *Franconian Giant Bible* in the Bibliothèque Nationale de France, Paris, which dates from 1294.[28]

The most interesting Ashkenazi illustration of the menorah is found in the Regensburg Pentateuch of ca. 1300, which shows a clear Sephardi influence and was made by an artist who copied from a source without actually understanding the significance of its details and the differences between the various objects (pp. 58–59): On the left-hand page, Aaron the High Priest is depicted among the sanctuary implements wearing a long robe, a miter, and a breastplate inscribed with the names of the twelve tribes; in his right hand he holds the pitcher (*kuz*), while his left hand, which holds a torch, is outstretched to light the menorah depicted on the right-hand page. The menorah is gold and has curved branches, which rise vertically toward their ends. Each branch has three sets of stylized, ring-shaped knobs, fleurs-de-lis, and goblets. The short central shaft is decorated with three rings, and the three-legged base terminates in animal paws. The base is flanked by two rampant lions, perhaps symbols of the Lion of Judah, the precursors of the Messiah.

Italian Manuscripts

The few depictions of menorahs in Italian Hebrew manuscripts are based, for the most part, on the Sephardi model. For example, at the end of the Pentateuch in the *Bolognese Harleian Hebrew Bible*, from the end of the 13th century, is a colorful menorah with curved branches, each of which is decorated with three goblets, a round knob, and a fleur-de-lis.[29] Knobs also cover the points where the branches meet the shaft, while the shaft itself is ornamented with a goblet, a knob, and two flowers. The rectangular, three-legged base supports two trees, which may relate to Zechariah's vision. Flanking the shaft are two monkey-headed lions blowing *shofarot* (ram's horns). Each part of the menorah is inscribed with the relevant section from the *Mishneh Torah.*

Beginning in the 14th century, the Italian communities began producing depictions of the menorah formed from the words of Psalm 67. According to its kabbalistic interpretation, this psalm was believed to possess protective powers. Such depictions of the menorah also contain a detailed explanation of the menorah's mystical elements, placed next to the image. The belief was that "whoever recites Psalms 67 from a text whose words are set out in the form of a menorah, no evil shall befall him" (see articles by M. Idel and E. Yuhasz in this volume). The base of the menorah is made of verses and acronyms related to the various names of God. One of the earliest known illustrations of Psalm 67 in the shape of a menorah is in the *Yehiel ben Matitiah Mahzor* copied in Pisa in 1397 by the renowned scribe Meir ben Samuel Deslois from Arles in Provence (fig. 7).[30] The menorah resembles the Sephardi type, particular in terms of the lamps and the parts illuminated in gold. It may indicate that the Sephardi influence on the Italian menorah was via Provence.

Conclusion

The shape of the menorah in medieval Hebrew illuminated manuscripts takes different forms. It evolved from the seven-branched candelabrum decorated with flowers, which symbolized the Temple, found in Near-Eastern examples of the 10th century, to the distinctive Sephardi menorah, produced from the 13th century onward, whose details clearly reflect the various interpretations of the biblical text. The symbolic meaning of the menorah, as an expression of the hope for redemption, was preserved in the Sephardi depictions of the sanctuary implements. This random array of implements was presumably devised in antiquity, a ground plan of the Temple that was perfected in Spain. The Ashkenazi tradition tended more toward narrative depictions, such as scenes of Aaron pouring oil into the menorah or lighting it. Yet the array of sanctuary implements in the Ashkenazi *Regensberg Penateuch* reflects both Sephardi and Ashkenazi models. The Italian menorahs were also influenced by the Sephardi tradition, but the Italian scribe-artists devised a way of drawing the menorah with the text of Psalm 67, thereby stressing the magical nature of the menorah and placing it within the sphere of Kabbalah.

1 B. Narkiss, "A Scheme of the Sanctuary from the Time of Herod the Great," *Journal of Jewish Art* 1 (1974): 6–14.

2 St. Petersburg, Russian National Library, MS Firk. Hebr. II. B.17, fols. 4v–5. Y. Levy, "Ezekiel's Plan in an Early Karaite Bible," *Jewish Art* 19–20 (1993/4): figs. 18–19; B. Narkiss, *Hebrew Illuminated Manuscripts* (Jerusalem, 1969), pl. 1a (fol. 5), pp. 42–43.

3 For examples of lamps with angular branches from ancient times, particularly ceramic oil lamps from Cyrenaica in North Africa, see A. Reifenberg, *Ancient Hebrew Arts* (New York, 1950), pl. 145:4.

4 All the sanctuary appurtenances depicted in this Pentateuch are from the Tabernacle and Solomon's Temple; none are from the Second Temple or Herod's Temple. See Levy (above, n. 2), 68–85.

5 Cambridge University Library, MS T–S.K5. 13; B. Narkiss, "Illuminated Hebrew Children's Books from Egypt," *Scripta Hierosolymitana* XXIV (Studies in Art) (1972): fig. 6; B. Narkiss, *Hebrew Illuminated Manuscripts* (Jerusalem, 1984), ill. 15, pp. 25, 28 (Hebrew).

6 A detailed description of the menorah and the other sanctuary implements, as well as a discussion of the textual and visual interpretations, is found in B. Narkiss, A. Cohen, A. Tcherikover, *Hebrew Illuminated Manuscripts in the British Isles, Catalogue Raisonné. Vol. I: Spanish and Portuguese Manuscripts* (Jerusalem and London, 1982), 101–104.

7 Exodus 25:38; 37:23; Numbers 4:9. The role of the tongs, according to Rashi, was "to take the wicks out of the oil, to straighten them, and to pull them out of the mouths of the lamps"; the shovels were "like small vessels used to remove the ash from the lamps each morning." The tongs may have appeared as early as the 4th century in the mosaic floor of the Samaritan synagogue of el-Khirbeh, between the inner branches of the menorah (p. 61).

8 Jerusalem, Jewish National and University Library, MS 40 5147, fol. 6v. The replacement of the shovels with similar censers is also known from the Roman-Byzantine period, the 5th–6th century CE, as in the mosaic floors from the synagogue at Na'aran and the House of Leontis at Beth Shean (today in the Hecht Museum, Haifa).

9 Oxford, Bodleian Library, MS Ken. 2, fols. 1v–2; Narkiss et al. (above, n. 6), no. 3, pp. 24–29, figs. 9, 10.

10 Paris, Bibliothèque Nationale de France, MS hébr. 20, fol. 54; B. Narkiss, G. Sed-Rajna, "La première Bible de Josué ben Abraham Ibn Gaon," *Revue de études juives* CXXX (1974), 1, 1, 4.

11 Narkiss (above, n. 2), 21–25.

12 Parma, Biblioteca Palatina, parms 2668, fols. 7v–8; C. O. Nordström, "Some Miniatures in Hebrew Bibles," *Synthronon* II (1968), figs. 49–50.

13 J. Gutmann, *Hebrew Manuscript Painting* (London, 1979), pls. 6–7.

14 *Copenhagen Bible*, 1301, Copenhagen, Royal Library, MS Heb. 2, fols. 11v–12; *Catalan Bible from Modena*, Modena, Biblioteca Estense, MS T.3.8, fols. 25v–26; *Sephardi Bible from Frankfurt*, private collection, formerly in the Stadtsbibliothek, Frankfurt, Ausst. 4, fols. 25v–26. See G. Swarzenski, R. Schilling, "Die Illuminierten Handschriften und Einzeliminaturen des Mittelalters und der Renaissance," in *Frankfurter Besitz* (Frankfurt A.M., 1929), no. 48, pp. 50–51, pl. XXIX. The details of the objects in the Sephardi Bible from Frankfurt resemble those appearing on a double page depicting the sanctuary appurtenances in a Latin commentary on the Bible, Peter Comestor, *Historia Scholastica*, copied in Aragon in the 14th century, Madrid, Biblioteca Nacional, Cod. Res. 199, fols. 6v–7; Nordström (above, n. 12), pls. 2, 3.

15 London, British Library, MS Harley 1528, fols. 7v–8; Narkiss et al. (above, n. 6), no. 20, pp. 107–109, figs. 324–327.

16 Rome, Jewish community, MS 19a, fol. 213v.

17 Jerusalem, Jewish National and University Library, MS 8° 6527, p. 12; see *Books from Spain*, exh. cat., Israel Museum (Jerusalem, 1992), no. 31, pp. 60–65 and photograph on p. 65.

18 Paris, Bibliothèque de la Compagnie des Prêtres de Saint-Sulpice, MS 1933, fols. 5v–6; M. Garel, "The Foa Bible," *Journal of Jewish Art* 6 (1979): 78–85.

19 London, British Library, Add. 15250, fols. 3v–4; Narkiss et al. (above, n. 6), no. 19, pp. 105–107, figs. 310–323.

20 Lisbon, Biblioteca Nacional, MS IL. 72, fol. 60; B. Narkiss, A. Cohen-Mushlin, *The Kennicott Bible*, Facsimile Editions, text vol. (London, 1985), 47–48, fig. 20.

21 Jerusalem, Jewish National and University Library, MS heb. 4o 1447, fol. 182. An earlier version is a colorful menorah appearing in the *Catalan Mishneh Torah*, dated to 1306, Vatican Library, MS Vat. Ebr. 173, fol. 7.

22 Paris, Bibliothèque Nationale de France, MS hébr. 819, fol. O recto; G. Sed-Rajna, *Les manuscrits enluminés des bibliothèques de France* (Leuven-Paris, 1994), no. 40, pp. 108–109; M. Garel, *D'une Main Forte*, exh. cat. (Paris, 1991), no. 53.

23 Bayerische Staatsbibliothek, Munich, Cod. hebr. 5/1, fol. 65; *Jüdische Lebenswelten*, exh. cat. (Berlin, 1991), no. 6/44. In the *Rashi Commentary on the Pentateuch* from Berlin, 14th century, there is a pen drawing of a menorah with curved branches and a lion to its left: Staatsbibliothek, Berlin, MS or. fol. 1210, fol 135; *Jüdische Lebenswelten*, no. 6/47.

24 R. Wischnitzer, "Maimonides' Drawings of the Temple," *Journal of Jewish Art* 1 (1974): 16–27. This type of pen drawing of the menorah was widespread in the depictions of the Temple plan in Latin encyclopaedic manuscripts of the 12th century from southern Germany, such as the menorah appearing in the plan in Herrad of Landsberg (1167–1195), *Hortus Deliciarum*, fols. 45v–46; R. Green and M. Evans, *Hortus Deliciarum* (London, 1979), pls. 63–64, pp. 80–81, cf. 11, fig. 70.

25 New York, Jewish Theological Seminary, MS Rab. 350, fol. 274v.

26 Budapest, Library of the Hungarian Academy of Sciences, Kaufmann Collection, MS A 77/111, fol. 3v; Sed-Rajna, "The Budapest Mishneh Torah," *Journal of Jewish Art* 6 (1979): 64–77.

27 London, British Library, MS Add. 11639, fols. 114 and 552v; Narkiss (above, n. 2), pl. 23, pp. 86–87; J. Leveen, *The Hebrew Bible in Art* (New York, 1939), pl. XXV, pp. 72–84. An additional French manuscript depicting Aaron lighting a menorah with angular branches is found in the Polini Pentateuch from 1300: Paris, Bibliothèque Nationale de France, MS hébr. 36, fol. 283v; Garel (above, n. 22), no. 72; Narkiss (above, n. 2), pl. 24, pp. 88–89.

28 Paris, Bibliothèque Nationale de France, MS hébr. 5, fol. 118–119; Garel (above, n. 22), 87–88. This drawing is preceded by earlier micrographic drawings, one of which depicts olive-picking from a seven-branched tree and two men producing oil from the olives (p. 31).

29 London, British Library, MS Harley 5710, fol. 136; Narkiss (above, n. 5), 58, ill. 55.

30 Private collection, formerly in the collection of S. D. Sasson, *Ohel David* (Oxford and London, 1932), MS 1028, fol. 31; Narkiss (above, n. 5), 59; B. Narkiss, "Three Jewish Art Patrons in Medieval Italy," in the *Reuben Hecht Jubilee Volume* (Jerusalem, 1979), 317–327, ill. 12 (Hebrew).

Rachel Sarfaty

Promise of Redemption
Zechariah's Vision of the Golden Menorah

I see a lampstand all of gold, with a bowl (gullah) *above it. The lamps on it are seven in number, and the lamps above it have seven pipes* (mutzakot)*; and by it are two olive trees, one on the right side of the bowl* (gullah) *and one on its left." I, in turn, asked the angel who talked with me, "What do those things mean, my lord?" . . . Then he explained to me as follows: "This is the word of the Lord to Zerubbabel: Not by might, nor by power, but by my spirit – said the Lord of Hosts. . . ." And what," I asked him," are those two olive trees, one on the right and one on the left of the lampstand?" And I further asked him, "What are the two tops of the olive trees that feed their gold through those two golden tubes* (tzanterot)*?" . . . Then he explained, "They are the two anointed dignitaries who attend the Lord of all the earth.* (Zechariah 4: 2–14)

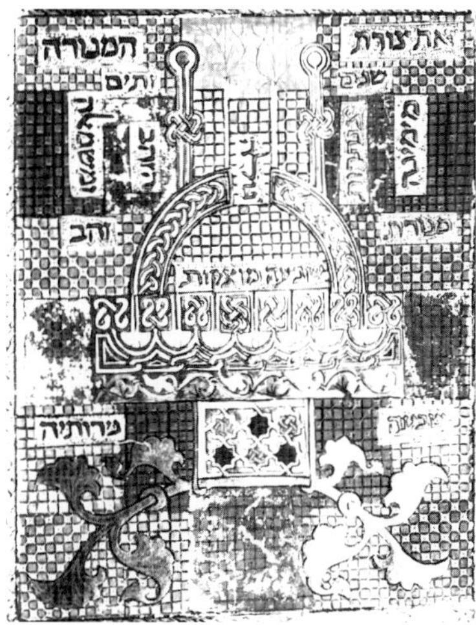

1
Farhi Bible
Provence, 1366–1382
Sassoon Collection

Thus reads the biblical account of the vision seen by the prophet Zechariah in 520 BCE, the second year of the reign of Darius. What was it that Zechariah actually saw? And how are we to understand such enigmatic terms as *mutzakot* and *tzanterot* mentioned in the description? Many commentators and biblical scholars have wrestled with this passage, which continues to defy attempts to derive a clear picture of the object it describes. Rashi, Ibn Ezra, and other traditional commentators – whose interpretations guided the work of different artists – believed that the text describes the menorah, the seven-branched candelabrum of the Temple, surmounted by a large, round bowl (the *gullah*), which held oil. The oil entered the bowl from the *tzanterot* (receptacles of some sort) in which olives from the trees flanking the menorah were crushed. It then passed out of the bowl through short pipes (*mutzakot*) and filled the lamps.

The meaning of the vision is provided by the angel, who tells Zechariah: "This is the word of the Lord to Zerubbabel: Not by might, nor by power, but by my spirit – said the Lord of Hosts. . . ." This message must be understood in the light of its historical context – the period of the Return to Zion, when the Babylonian exiles returned to Jerusalem to rebuild the Temple. This was a time of political and economic weakness, and construction of the Second Temple was delayed by both the Persian authorities and by tensions with neighboring peoples. The prophets of this period, Haggai, Zechariah, and Malachi, sought to encourage the builders and bring their enterprise to a speedy conclusion. In this vision, God therefore says to Zechariah, although you have little might and are ruled by powerful foreign nations, the Temple will be rebuilt, for its existence depends not on physical strength, but on my spirit.

2
Title page of *Sefer Menorat Hama'or*
Metz, France, 1829
The Jewish National and University Library, Jerusalem

Generations of commentators attempted to understand the vision by interpreting its various components, adding to the explanation already given by the angel. Some (Rashi, Ibn Ezra, and David Kimhi) write that just as the olives were pressed into oil for the bowl without human intervention, so too will the Temple be rebuilt by the spirit of God. Rashi, in his explanation of the repetition of the word "seven" in verse 2, emphasizes the eschatological meaning of the vision. He writes that Zechariah's menorah had forty-nine lamps in allusion to messianic times, when the light of the sun will be "seven times more powerful than the light of seven days," that is, forty-nine times more powerful than daylight. Like Rashi, Abarbanel also stresses the eschatological significance of Zechariah's menorah: according to him, the golden menorah is a metaphor for the future redemption of the Jewish people, which will be like a shining lamp for the nation that presently stumbles in darkness; the phrase "all of gold" refers to that fact that in the days of the Messiah, all twelve tribes will be reunited in the land of Israel; and the word *gullah* in the phrase "with a *gullah* above it" is interpreted as the crown that the Jewish people is destined to wear when, no longer subjugated by others, it will take its place at the head of the nations. Song of Songs Rabbah (4:7) plays on the words *gullah, golah* (exile), and *ge'ulah* (redemption); according to this interpretation, when the Jews were exiled from their land, God went into exile with them, thereby ensuring their redemption. Thus all of these commentaries regard Zechariah's vision of the golden menorah as a messianic prophesy, expressed against the background of the hope for imminent salvation from foreign oppression inspired by the building of the Second Temple.[1]

The Vision of the Menorah in Jewish Art

The earliest known depictions of Zechariah's vision of the menorah are found in illuminated Bible manuscripts from Spain, such as the Cervera Bible, illustrated by Joseph Hatzarfati in 1300 (p. 57). The illustration at the end of the book of Zechariah shows the golden candelabrum against a geometric background, flanked by two fairly realistic olive trees. The *gullah* and *tzanterot* are situated above, between the treetops, and depicted as three golden bowls. The olives fall into the two upper bowls, and the oil from them flows into the lower bowl.

The second biblical manuscript is the Farhi Bible (Sassoon Collection, MS 368), which was written and illustrated in the years 1366–82 by Elisha ben Abraham ben Benveniste. The manuscript opens with texts on various topics and some illuminated pages, including a depiction of Zechariah's vision. Unlike the Cervera Bible, this depiction is extremely stylized; the various elements are geometrical in form and feature interlace ornamentation (fig. 1). The menorah, set against a colorful checkered background, has a rectangular base and is surmounted by a bar supporting a row of seven lamps. The *mutzakot* are depicted as seven rectangles, and the *gullah* takes the form of an inverted dome above the menorah, topped by two slender olive trees. The *tzanterot* alongside the trees are depicted as two columns with round capitals. Each component is accompanied by an identifying inscription. It is clear that the illustrator based his work on a different interpretation than that which informed the illustrations of the Cervera Bible, but the fact that both devoted an entire page to Zechariah's vision indicates the importance it had for them. Undoubtedly eschatological, its subject matter is typical of the opening pages of Spanish Bibles of the time, which include depictions of the Tabernacle and Temple appurtenances (see article by B. Narkiss in this volume). Such depictions also reflect the belief that the Bible – known in this period as *mikdashiya* (derived from *mikdash* meaning, "sanctuary," or the Temple) – was in a sense a substitute for the Temple in Jerusalem that had been destroyed.[2]

3
Paper-cut
Turkey, 19th–20th century
Israel Museum Collection

The artistic tradition of Spanish manuscripts is echoed in a number of 16th-century scrolls containing lists of holy sites in the land of Israel. Such lists are based on the anonymous text *Yihus Ha'avot*, written in the Holy Land in the 15th century.[3] Three scrolls belonging to this group that were transcribed and illustrated in the land of Israel begin with a quotation from Zechariah's vision (vv. 2–4), below which appears an inverted dome labeled *gullah*.[4] This simple allusion to the vision, which is reminiscent of the *gullah* in the Farhi Bible as well as other representations from this manuscript, among them the depictions of the Temple appurtenances and the city of Jericho in a labyrinth beneath the same verses from

Zechariah, suggests a link between these scrolls and the illuminated manuscripts of the Bible from Spain.[5]

Manuscripts detailing the holy sites in the land of Israel were distributed by emissaries to Diaspora communities as a method of fund-raising. These were not geographical tracts; rather, they had a mystical and messianic message, to which Zechariah's vision was well suited. Because of their wide distribution, these manuscripts inspired Jewish artists all over the Diaspora, and imitations of their illustrations may be found in later centuries in countries such as Italy, Turkey, and Persia.

We also have a number of visual depictions of Zechariah's vision from the modern period, which indicates that this subject was a common one in recent times as well. The title page of *Sefer Menorat Hama'or,* a collection of legends and homilies written by Isaac Abohab in the 14th century and printed by Ephraim Hadamar in Metz, France in 1829, features a detailed depiction of the vision with each component identified by a quotation from the biblical text (fig. 2). The artist's desire to reconcile the vision with the laws of physics is clear: the *gullah* appears as a stylized dome suspended from chains over the candelabrum; the *tzanterot* are capitals atop columns; and the oil comes out through a pipe at the base of each capital. The visual interpretation here is similar to that found in the Farhi Bible. Below the *gullah,* slender pipes are arranged in groups of seven over the seven branches of the menorah, as in Rashi's interpretation of the text.

4
Hanukkah lamp
Italy, 1864
Israel Museum
Collection

Further examples are provided by two beautiful paper-cuts from the late 19th or early 20th century, which were created for synagogues in Turkey. One of them, made by David Algranati, is similar in form and in its use of gold and light blue to the illustration in the Cervera Bible; its floral border contains painted medallions with quotations from Zechariah (Israel Museum Collection 168/58; fig. 3).[6]

Zechariah's vision is also represented on an unusual Italian Hanukkah lamp from 1864 (Israel Museum Collection 118/345; fig. 4): on a silver panel set behind the candelabrum, there appears – between two olive trees – a depiction of the *gullah,* this time in the form of a fountain spouting oil. However, in this case, the lamp has eight, rather than seven, branches. The craftsman may have combined the eight-branched Hanukkah lamp with the prophetic description of the seven-branched menorah because Zechariah's vision is read in the synagogue on the Sabbath during Hanukkah; alternatively, it may have been the overall connection between the menorah as a symbol of the Temple and the story of Hanukkah that inspired his design.

These few examples from the 19th to early 20th century may provide some indication of the way in which visual depictions of Zechariah's vision found their way to the Jews of Cochin. The Israel Museum recently acquired a carved wooden Torah ark dating from 1891 from the synagogue in Parur, a town near Cochin in the southwestern Indian state of Kerala (p. 65). The carvings on the upper part of the ark depict the vision. The seven-branched menorah stands in the center flanked by its accessories, the tongs and the incense shovels, and by the steps the high priest climbed to light the lamps (according to the Mishnaic description in Tamid 3:9). On either side is a vase out of which a fruit-bearing tree or vine grows. This plant looks very much like a stylized date palm; there are no olive trees in India, and presumably the craftsman was not sure what the tree mentioned in Zechariah actually looked like. The *tzanterot* are depicted as small bowls, topped by an oval *gullah* from which the oil flows into the seven lamps. The entire scene is framed by an arch inscribed with a quotation from Zechariah (4:3–4).

5
Decoration above the entrance to the synagogue in Chennamangalam
Early 20th century
Center for Jewish Art, The Hebrew University of Jerusalem

We also know of two other depictions of Zechariah's vision found in the synagogues of the Cochin community: a Torah ark curtain (*parokhet*) for the Day of Atonement, dating from 1927, which was dedicated to the Kadavumbagam synagogue in Ernakulam,[7] and the decoration above the entrance to the synagogue in Chennamangalam, dating from the early 20th century (fig. 5). These two stylized depictions contain fewer elements than the panel from the Parur Torah ark. The menorah stands in the center, surmounted by the *gullah* in the shape of a wide bowl; like the Parur Torah ark, the olive trees at the sides take the form of a stylized vegetal motif that fills the background.

6
Torah breastplate
Frankfurt, 1904
Gross Family Collection

Why did the Jews of Cochin attribute such importance to Zechariah's vision? Did the prominence of this motif as synagogue decoration reflect the community's choice, expressing both local beliefs and artistic traditions as well as their own messianic longings, or was it determined by non-Indian influences? It is clear that the Cochin Jews were exposed to the artistic tradition of Hebrew books printed in Europe. From the 16th century until the time when a Hebrew press was established in India in the 19th century, the religious books required by the community were imported from Livorno or Amsterdam.[8] The community's familiarity with European traditions is evident in, for example, the form of the menorah and its accessories on the Parur Torah ark, which is undoubtedly based on a depiction of the menorah that was widespread from the 14th century on (pp. 66, 82). It is also possible that they became acquainted with the significance of Zechariah's vision through written texts and adopted it as a central motif in the decoration of their synagogues.

All of these visual depictions testify to a very old messianic tradition which found expression mainly in the 14th century in Spanish Bible manuscripts, in the 16th century in scrolls depicting holy sites in the land of Israel, and in the modern age, in the synagogues of Cochin, India.

Yet another link in this chain of tradition comes to us in the form of a Torah breastplate created by Leo Horovitz in Frankfurt in 1904 (fig. 6). What is unusual about its representation of Zechariah's vision is the design of the menorah, which is based on the menorah depicted on the Arch of Titus in Rome. This particular design was characteristic of Jewish art inspired by the Zionist movement of the time. One generation later, with the creation of the State of Israel, this form of the menorah – flanked by olive branches – would be adopted as the new country's national emblem (see article by A. Meshori in this volume).[9] It thus seems that the long tradition of depicting Zechariah's vision had reached the end of its journey, having evolved from an expression of the longing for redemption by the Jews of the Diaspora to a symbol of the Jewish people's return to its homeland.[10]

1 Y. Kaufmann, *History of Israelite Religion* (Jerusalem–Tel Aviv, 1960), 249 (Hebrew).

2 B. Narkiss, *Hebrew Illuminated Manuscripts* (Jerusalem, 1984), 25 (Hebrew).

3 E. Reiner, "Oral Versus Written Traditions of Holy Places in Medieval Palestine," in *Offerings from Jerusalem: Portrayals of Holy Sites by Jewish Artists*, ed. Rachel Sarfaty, exh. cat. (The Israel Museum, Jerusalem, forthcoming).

4 S. Zucker, "*Yihus Avot* or *Eleh Mas'ei* — Scrolls of Holy Sites," *Of Books and People: Bulletin of the Jewish National and University Library* 10 (Jerusalem, 1996): 4 (Hebrew).

5 See R. Sarfaty, "Illustrations of *Yihus Avot* as a Link in an Artistic Tradition," in *Offerings from Jerusalem* (above, n. 3).

6 E. Juhasz, ed., *Sephardi Jews in the Ottoman Empire: Aspects of Material Culture*, exh. cat. (The Israel Museum, Jerusalem, 1990), pl. 59.

7 O. Slapak, ed., *The Jews of India: A Story of Three Communities*, exh. cat. (The Israel Museum, Jerusalem, 1995), pp. 57–67 and ill. p. 64, right.

8 W. J. Fischel, "Literature of the Jews on the Malabar Coast," *Eretz-Israel* 10 (Jerusalem, 1971): 221–25 (Hebrew).

9 In the original, fuller article published in *Cathedra* in 1987, Meshori first made the connection between the olive branches in the national emblem and Zechariah's vision.

10 I am grateful to Orpa Slapak, Daisy Raccah-Djivre, Osnat Sirkin, and Chaya Benjamin for their help in assembling the material for this article.

זה השער לה'
צדיקים יבואו בו

A Lesser Sanctuary

Following the destruction of the Temple, the synagogue came to be regarded as a kind of "substitute Temple," in which prayers were offered in place of sacrifices. The menorah was and remains a popular decorative motif in synagogues of all periods, appearing in reliefs, mosaics, and wall paintings, on Torah ark curtains and on ritual objects. The earliest depiction of a menorah in a synagogue is from the synagogue at Dura Europos in Syria (3rd century CE), the oldest synagogue to have survived with its decorations intact. Despite the rabbinic prohibition against making menorahs resembling the one that stood in the Temple – "[It is permitted] to make [a menorah] with five branches or six branches or eight branches, but no one shall make one with seven branches, even of other types of metal" (Babylonian Talmud, Menahot 28b) – three-dimensional menorahs have been discovered in several ancient synagogues. We have no way of knowing, however, whether they were used for illumination, for ceremonial or commemorative purposes, or for decoration.

Of particular interest is the custom of decorating Hanukkah lamps with depictions of the seven-branched candelabrum. The combination of the two lamps alludes to the miracle of the cruse of oil in the time of the Maccabees, which kept the menorah in the Temple burning for eight days.

Previous page:
Sketch for a Torah ark curtain (detail), after 1923
Meir Gur-Arieh, 1891–1951, and Ze'ev Raban, 1890–1970
Industrial Art Studio craft shop, Bezalel School, Jerusalem
Watercolor and pencil on paper
32.5 x 41 cm
Collection of Itzhak Einhorn, Tel Aviv

Medal and stamp sheet produced in honor of the dedication of the Israel Museum, 1965
Design: Miriam and Mordechai Gumpel
Brass, D 4.5 cm; paper
Israel Museum Collection
The motif is based on the menorah from the synagogue at Hammath Tiberias (opposite).

Carved menorah from the synagogue at Hammath Tiberias
Byzantine period, 4th–6th century CE
Limestone, W 60 cm
Israel Museum Collection
The depressions at the tops of the branches were meant for holding oil lamps.

Section of the mosaic floor from the synagogue at Sepphoris
Byzantine period, 5th century CE
Stone, H 163
Courtesy of the Sepphoris Expedition, The Institute of Archaeology, The Hebrew University of Jerusalem

Opposite:
Synagogue menorah
Italy, late 18th century
Gilt carved wood and metal, glass
H 85 cm
Collection of Georges Weil, Israel

Plaque for a synagogue memorial lamp
Rissani, Morocco, 19th–20th century
Carved and painted wood, metal, and iron
H 67 cm
Israel Museum Collection

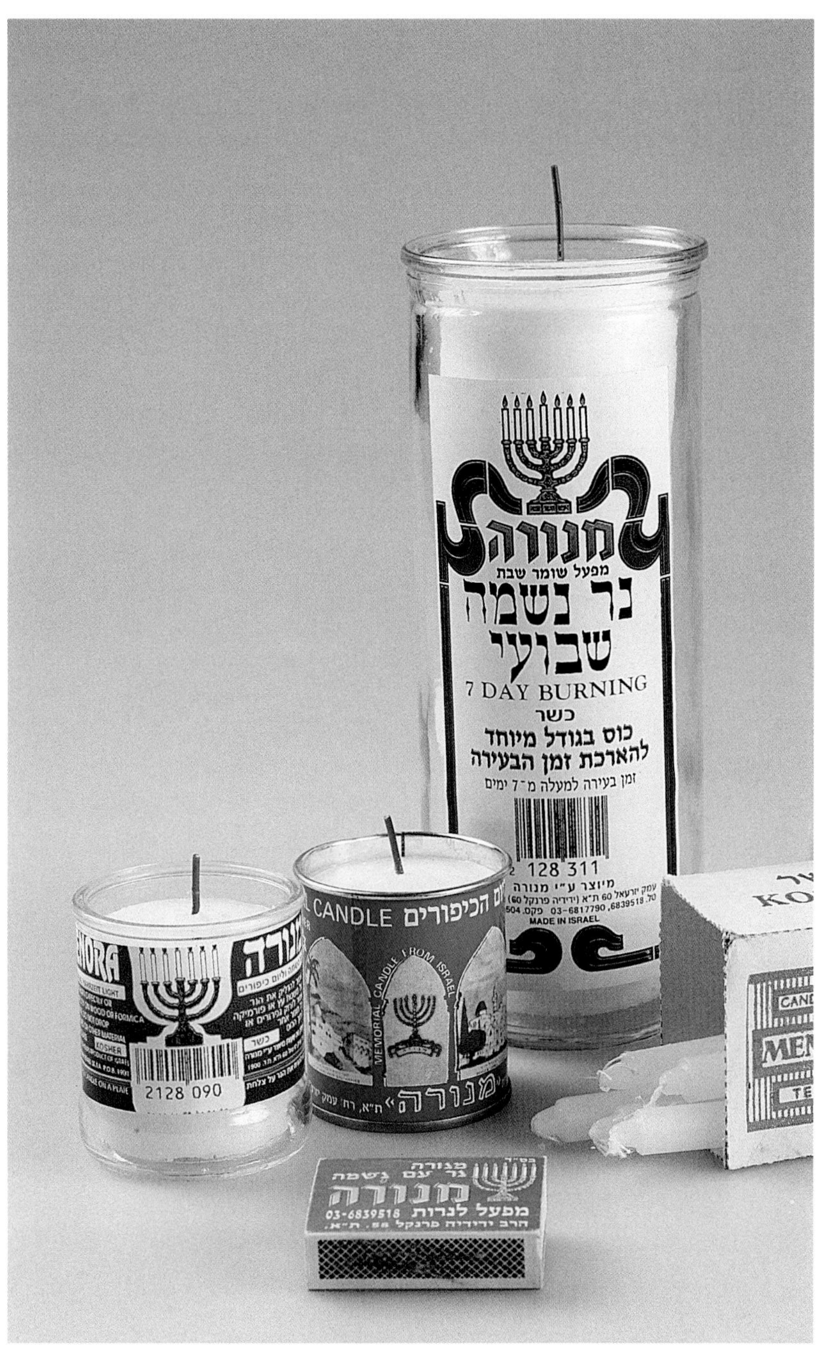

Candles and matches manufactured by the Menorah Candle Factory, currently sold in supermarkets and stores all over Israel

Decoration from the *sukkah* of Rabbi Immanuel Loew (1854–1944)
Szeged, Hungary, late 19th – early 20th century
Oil on canvas mounted on wood
176 x 100.3 cm
Israel Museum Collection

Plaque with a menorah carved in low relief
Horvat Qoshet, near Qiryat Tivon
Late Byzantine – early Umayyad period, 6th–8th century CE
Marble, H 64 cm
Israel Antiquities Authority Collection
Restored in the Israel Museum Laboratories through a donation by Janis and Harold Cooper, Florida

Three-dimensional menorah with oil lamps atop its branches from the synagogue at Ma'on, southern Hebron hill region
Late Byzantine period, 6th–7th century CE
Marble, H 88 cm
Courtesy of the Staff Officer for Archaeology, Judea and Samaria
Reconstructed from several fragments in the Israel Museum Laboratories through a donation by Janis and Harold Cooper, Florida

Most of the ancient stone and marble menorahs that have come to light are carved in relief; very few are sculpted in the round. In the excavations of the synagogue at Ma'on, twelve fragments of a marble menorah were discovered. Upon its reconstruction, it became apparent that this was not only the largest three-dimensional menorah ever discovered, but that it also had oil lamps at the tops of its branches which had actually been lit. This find seems to run counter to the sages' objection to fashioning seven-branched candelabra resembling the one used in the Temple. Moreover, it supports the theory that menorahs stood and were even lit in synagogues for symbolic, ornamental, or ceremonial purposes.

Cast menorah and wine goblet from the synagogue at Ein Gedi
Byzantine period, 6th century CE
Bronze, H of menorah: 14.5 cm
H of goblet: 11 cm
Israel Antiquities Authority Collection

Torah ornaments from Venice, Italy inlaid with depictions of the sanctuary appurtenances

Finials: 19th century
Silver, repoussé and cast, partly gilt
H 65 cm
Israel Museum Collection, gift of the Jewish community of Venice

Crown: 1712–1749
Silver, repoussé, pierced, and cast, partly gilt
H 22.5 cm, D 26 cm
Israel Museum Collection, Steiglitz Collection, made possible through a donation by Erica and Ludwig Jesselson, New York, to American Friends of the Israel Museum

Opposite:
Torah ark curtain and valance embroidered with silver and gold
Embroiderer: Jacob Koppel Gans
Bavaria, 1772/73
Velvet, silk and metal threads, 213.4 x 163.8 cm
Collection of The Jewish Museum, New York

Relief depicting the menorah flanked by Moses and Aaron on a Hanukkah lamp from Germany, 1769
Silver, repoussé, engraved, and cast, partly gilt
H 27.5 cm
Israel Museum Collection, gift of Ignazio Bauer, Madrid

Opposite:
Torah ark curtain decorated with a menorah in the appliqué technique
Turkey, 19th–20th century
Felted wool, appliqué of silver and gilt-silver, studs and plaques
200 x 126 cm
Israel Museum Collection, purchased by courtesy of Jerome L. Stern, New York

שדי
זה השער לה״

Left:
Capital decorated with a menorah from the synagogue at Caesarea
Byzantine period, 5th century CE
Marble, H 40 cm
Israel Antiquities Authority Collection

Below, left:
Pedestal decorated with a menorah from a synagogue? at Ashkelon
Byzantine period, 4th century CE
Marble, H 70 cm
Israel Antiquities Authority Collection

Below, right:
Pedestal decorated with a menorah from the synagogue at Ein Neshut, Golan Heights
Byzantine period, 5th–6th century CE
Basalt, H 150 cm
Israel Antiquities Authority Collection

Lee I. Levine

The Menorah in the Ancient Synagogue

Of the numerous examples of ancient synagogue art from Roman-Byzantine times, the menorah is the most common and displays the richest variety of forms. The menorah served as a decorative motif and symbol – often the main symbol – in synagogues throughout the land of Israel and the Diaspora, from Dura Europos in the east to Italy and North Africa in the west. It is usually portrayed with other Jewish motifs, such as the *lulav* (palm branch), *etrog* (citron), incense shovel, and *shofar* (ram's horn), but is no less often found on its own.

The menorah symbol appears on various architectural elements of the synagogue building: on capitals (Beth Guvrin; Caesarea, p. 108; and Capernaum, fig. 1); columns (Gaza); pedestals (Ashkelon, p. 108); chancel screens (Ashdod; Ashkelon, p. 198; Hammath Gader; Naveh; Susiya, p. 37); friezes (Nabratein); architraves (Ostia); pediments (Pergamum); lintels (Kokhav Hayarden, p. 69; Nabratein; Yafia; Eshtemoa, fig. 2); stone slabs (Priene); unidentifiable architectural fragments (Capernaum; Chorazin; Eshtemoa); wall paintings (Dura Europos); and, above all, mosaic floors.

1
Capital from the synagogue at Capernaum

The most common scheme depicted on mosaic floors consists of a pair of menorahs flanking a Torah ark, as found at Hammath Tiberias, Beth Alpha (fig. 3), and Na'aran; two menorahs without an ark appear at Husifa, and menorahs flanking the facade of a building (the Temple?) are found at Susiya. The menorah is portrayed in a highly schematic form at some sites (as at Jericho), while at others it is represented in a detailed, naturalistic fashion. In spite of the great diversity in the scope of the decoration, there is a high level of uniformity in the general shape of the menorah: its six branches – three on either side of the central stem – are partly curved; it almost always stands on three legs (appearing in different styles); and only occasionally is its base shown as solid and stepped; its branches are relatively simple or are decorated with "cups shaped like almond-blossoms, each with calyx and petals (*kaftor vaferah*)" (Exodus 25:33). They almost always end at the same level, though a few menorahs have branches of differing heights, lending them a "stepped" look. In many cases, a horizontal bar lies across the tops of the branches and probably served to support the lamps or the bowls containing oil and wicks.

Three-Dimensional Menorahs

Three-dimensional menorahs have been found in synagogues in Israel and the Diaspora. For example, the remains of a stone menorah were found in the 1921 excavations of Hammath Tiberias; it had seven depressions on top, which probably held the oil lamps (p. 95), and its branches were decorated with buds and pomegranates. Three-dimensional menorahs have also been found at four other sites, all in Judea: Eshtemoa, Susiya, Ma'on, and Ein Gedi (fig. 4 and pp. 102–103). The bronze menorah from Ein Gedi is relatively small, while that from Ma'on is much larger, almost as tall as a person and, as suggested by the reconstruction of the remaining fragments, was decorated with pairs of lions standing on their hind legs and grasping the central stem.

2
Lintel from the synagogue at Eshtemoa
Israel Antiquities Authority Collection

It is difficult to determine whether it is significant that most of the menorahs known to us from Israel (80%) were found in Judea. This distribution might be completely random, but it is also possible that it points to a regional tradition, which preserved a closer link to Temple-related activities than was the case in other areas. This explanation, if true, is in keeping with another practice encountered in the synagogues of the Judean region (Susiya, Eshtemoa, Ma'on, and Anim), namely, the custom of placing synagogue entrances on the eastern sides of the building, like the entrances to the Tabernacle and the Temple (see Tosefta, Megillah 3: 22). Evidence of three-dimensional menorahs in synagogues is also known from the Diaspora. In Sardis, for example, the remains of three free-standing menorahs have been found, and an inscription from Asia Minor mentions the donation of two menorahs to a synagogue in Sida.

Was the Menorah a Regular Feature in the Synagogue?

The discovery of menorah fragments in Israel and abroad lends support to the hypothesis that the menorah was indeed displayed on a permanent basis in the synagogue. This hypothesis is further corroborated by the frequency of the menorah's appearance, together with the Torah ark and other symbols, on the building's focal wall. It is possible that the mosaic panel closest to the *bima* (elevated platform) reflects, even if not exactly, the items that stood on the *bima* of the synagogue. Moreover, the fact that in a number of synagogues niches have been found (as at Eshtemoa), as well as *bimot* (as at Sardis, Merot, and Nabratein), flanking the main entrance suggests that menorahs may have been placed there. Further confirmation of this phenomenon has been preserved in several rabbinic traditions about the menorah in the synagogue. The most famous refers to the Emperor Antoninus, the friend of Rabbi Judah Hanasi: "Antoninus made a menorah for the synagogue. Rabbi heard and said: 'Blessed be God, Who inspired him to make a menorah for the synagogue'" (Jerusalem Talmud, Megillah 3:2, 74b).

If we assume that a menorah was indeed displayed in many synagogues, this raises the question as to whether it was purely ornamental or whether it served some liturgical-religious function. There is no certain information in this regard, and the only evidence for the use of the menorah in the synagogue comes from a Genizah fragment of Midrash Hagadol to Leviticus 6:2 (ed. Steinsaltz, p. 141), which describes the menorah as a permanent fixture in the synagogue that was perceived as an imitation and continuation of the Temple menorah:

> "Command Aaron." It is taught: Why was this not said or told, but commanded, since a command [implies] diligence in performance immediately and in the generations [to come]? Three things were commanded which were established immediately and for the generations to come. The lamps, the sending away of unclean persons, and the daily offerings. The lamps – "And thou shalt command the children of Israel that they bring thee pure olive oil . . ." (Exodus 27:20) – was established immediately and for generations to come. Even though the Temple has been destroyed and the lamps have been abandoned, the synagogues and academies in which lamps are lighted are called "a miniature temple," as it is said: "I will be to them a minature temple in the countries to which they have come" (Ezekiel 11:16).

3
Part of the mosaic floor from the synagogue at Beth Alpha, 6th century CE

The Menorah as a Symbol

The extensive distribution of the menorah in Late Antiquity raises the question of the menorah's significance in synagogues in particular and in Jewish art in general. Many theories have been suggested to date. The menorah is a general symbol of Judaism; it represents the stars and the signs of the zodiac; it is a symbol of light and the Torah; it bears messianic and salvational implications; it represents the Temple and hopes for its speedy rebuilding; it stands for God as the source of light, for *halakha* (Jewish law), or for the Tree of Life; and it functioned as a symbol around which the Jews, as a minority, could rally in the face of the pagan-Christian presence. Some have pointed to the success of Christianity in the 4th century as a factor in the widespread use of the menorah; it served as a clear Jewish counterpart to the Christian cross.

In attempting to explain the meaning of the menorah, we shall address some of the basic assumptions that underlie the above suggestions. One such assumption, based on finds from the catacombs of Rome, which until recently were dated from the 1st to the 3rd century CE (see article by L. Habas in this volume), is that the menorah first appeared in the Diaspora and only later reached the land of Israel. Since these finds were believed to predate the use of the menorah as a symbol in Israel, it was often assumed that the symbol in fact originated outside the country. However, studies over the last decade have demonstrated that the Roman catacombs should be dated to the 3rd–5th century, thereby providing evidence that is later than – or at least contemporary with – what we know from Israel. The artistic evidence from Israel – as at Beth She'arim, where the menorah symbol was widely used – likewise dates to the early 3rd–5th century (for a different view see article by D. Barag in this volume). Moreover, examples of menorahs have been found in Israel from the late Second Temple period as well as from the period between the First and Second Revolts (70–132 CE); even though they are few in number, their very presence indicates that the representation of the menorah was familiar at least to Jews within certain circles in Israel.

Another assumption, namely, that the sages had a decisive say in the way in which the symbol of the menorah was used and interpreted, is related to a broader issue which has recently come under debate, i.e., that the sages had a marked influence on the design of synagogues. Since the menorah symbol does not only appear at Tiberias and Sepphoris, where sages resided, but also in many other places throughout Israel where few (if any) of them lived, as well as in places in the Diaspora where their influence was not felt at all, it would appear difficult to claim that the sages had any influence on the extensive use of this symbol.

4
Three-dimensional marble menorah from the synagogue at Susiya (proposed reconstruction)

The reliance upon rabbinic literature to understand the meaning of the menorah in the synagogue is problematic. Not only did the sages hardly ever discuss the menorah or its contemporary symbolic significance – except in their commentaries on the Tabernacle and the Temple menorah – but there is an explicit *baraita* appearing three times in the Babylonian Talmud that records the sages' rooted opposition to replicating the Temple menorah. "As it was taught, no one shall make a house after the pattern of the [Temple] sanctuary, or an exedra after the pattern of the [Temple] porch, or a courtyard like the [Temple] court, or a table like the [Temple] table, or a menorah like the [Temple] menorah. But [it is permitted] to make [a menorah] with five branches or six branches or eight branches, but no one shall make one with seven branches, even of other types of metal" (Rosh Hashanah 24a–b; Avodah Zarah 43a; Menahot 28b). Furthermore, the wide appearance of the menorah not only in synagogues but also in cemeteries and on small objects, such as gold glass and ceramic oil lamps, clearly indicates that this symbol was used over many generations and by Jews of all socioeconomic levels.

Any single explanation would be insufficient to account for the phenomenon of the menorah in antiquity. Presumably, this symbol was originally associated with the Temple and the priests, which would thus explain its appearance on a coin of Mattathias Antigonus, king and high priest; in Jason's Tomb in Jerusalem, which probably belonged to a priestly family; in the Upper City of Jerusalem, in a house that probably belonged to priests; and on a sundial found in the excavations near the western wall of the Temple Mount, which may also have been linked in some way or another to the Temple area. And, of course, the menorah depicted on the Arch of Titus in Rome represents the Temple spoils as displayed in Titus' triumphal procession in Rome.

At a later stage, from the 3rd–4th century on, the popularity of menorah increased geometrically. A plethora of reasons have been suggested, some of which have been noted above. Many, perhaps all, of those mentioned are undoubtedly correct. Yet, like every successful symbol, the menorah could be interpreted and understood in innumberable ways. There is no doubt that some Jews saw it as a profound symbol of immense significance, while others regarded it simply as a general representation of Judaism and Jewishness. Equally interesting is why such an object had become so popular at this time. To explain this phenomenon, two contextual factors should be considered. In the first place, ancient art generally was moving from a more representational mode to one featuring symbols with multiple meanings, a trend particularly characteristic of and in tandem with Christian art. The use of symbols had thus become more ubiquitous than ever before; while Christianity spearheaded this development with all the imperial and ecclesiastical means at its disposal, Jews could hardly remain unaffected.

The second contextual factor to be taken into consideration when explaining the popularity of the menorah in the Byzantine period is the widespread emergence of the cross. By the 4th and 5th centuries, this symbol appeared everywhere – in Christian buildings, at burial sites, and in homes – and was worn by individuals as well. The use of the menorah, in part as a Jewish response to the cross, is not simply a theoretical possibility. In a number of archaeological finds, we find the menorah appearing precisely where a cross would have been depicted in a Christian context. For example, a menorah was engraved on a chancel screen at Hammath Gader, as was a cross on a chancel screen at Massuot Yitzhaq (p. 159). Crosses decorate late Byzantine oil lamps (p. 155) as well as glass jugs and jars from Byzantine Jerusalem and elsewhere in precisely the place where menorahs appear.

Whatever the reasons for its popularity, the menorah is an outstanding example of a symbol that was accepted not because of the dictates of leaders or some supreme authority, but because it sprang from the people themselves in many different places and at roughly the same time. It provided a symbol with which Jewish communities throughout the world could readily identify and which helped them to cope with the challenges of their times and their surroundings.

Selected Bibliography

D. Amit, "A Seven-Branched Menorah Carved in Marble from the Excavations of the Synagogue at Ma'on," in *Proceedings of the Tenth World Congress of Jewish Studies*, B/I (Jerusalem, 1990) 53–59 (Hebrew).

D. Barag, "The Menorah in the Roman and Byzantine Periods: A Messianic Symbol," *Bulletin of the Anglo-Israel Archaeological Society* (1985/86): 44–47.

Y. Brand, *Ceramics in Talmudic Literature* (Jerusalem, 1953), 296–314 (Hebrew).

A. Eitan, "The Menora as Symbol," *Israel Museum News* 3/1–2 (1968): 45–49.

S. Fine and B. Zuckerman, "The Menorah as Symbol of Jewish Minority Status," in *Fusion in the Hellenistic East*, ed. S. Fine, B. Zuckerman (Los Angeles, 1985) 24–31.

E. R. Goodenough, *Jewish Symbols in the Greco-Roman Period*, vol. 4 (Princeton, 1954), 71–98.

V. A. Klagsbald, "The Menorah as Symbol: Its Meaning and Origin in Early Jewish Art," *Jewish Art* 12 (1987): 126–134.

L. Levine, "The History and Significance of the Menorah in Antiquity," *From Dura to Sepphoris: Studies in Jewish Art and Society in Late Antiquity*, ed. L. Levine and Z. Weiss (Ann Arbor, forthcoming).

M. Muncaczi, "The Menora: The True Symbol of Judaism," in *Semitic Studies in Memory of Immanuel Löw*, ed. A. Scheiber (Budapest, 1947) 125–146 (Hebrew).

A. Negev, "The Chronology of the Seven-Branched Menorah," *Eretz-Israel* 8 (1967): 193–210 (Hebrew).

W. Wirgin, "The Menorah as Symbol of Judaism," *Israel Exploration Journal* 12 (1962): 140–142.

Elisheva Revel-Neher

A Shadow of the Past or an Image of Theological Truth?

The Menorah in Byzantine Illuminated Manuscripts

The Epistle to Hebrews (10:1) states: "For the Law contains but a shadow, no true image of the realities yet to come." This verse was interpreted by Cyril of Alexandria using examples taken from the world of art: "We say that the law was a shadow and a type, and like unto a picture set as a thing to be viewed before those watching reality. The underdrawings of artist's skill are the first elements of the lines in pictures, and if the brightness of the colors is added to these, the beauty of the picture flashes forth."[1] To Cyril, the Old Testament played the role of a preliminary artist's sketch, an outline that emphasizes and brings to light the more precise and absolutely perfect overpainting, which is the true image, while also serving as a frame for the figuration. From this point on, the Byzantine Church Fathers began using the artistic metaphor as a form of allegoric exegesis, clarifying biblical descriptions by means of Byzantine art.

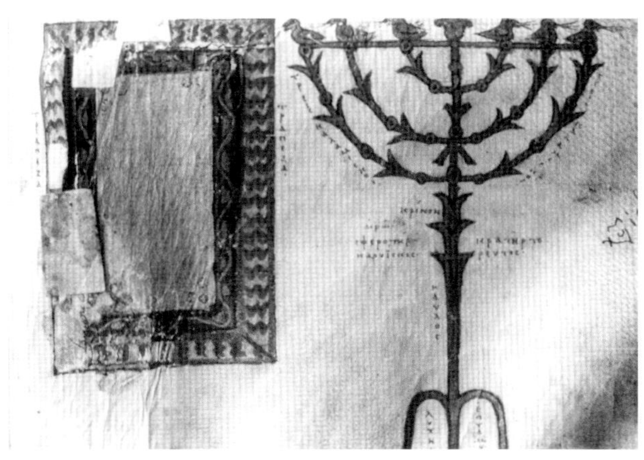

1
The menorah and shewbread table
From a miniature in the *Christian Topography*, 11th century
Library of St. Catherine's Monastery, Sinai

The menorah, as one of the Tabernacle appurtenances, is mentioned only once in the New Testament: "The first Covenant also had cultural institutions and a sanctuary, belonging to this world. A tent had been built – the anterior tent – where stood the candlestick [menorah], the table and the shewbread; it was called the Holy" (Epistle to Hebrews 9:1–2). Apart from this, the seven-branched candelabrum, whether of the Tabernacle or the Temple, is not referred to at all. The Book of Revelations, in the striking verses describing the descent of the Heavenly Jerusalem, states clearly: "As for the Temple, I did not see any inside it; this is because the Lord, the all-powerful God, is its Temple and so is the Lamb" (21:22). This apocalyptic vision describes no eschatological Temple descending from heaven and, consequently, no sacred objects, hence no menorah as part of Christian messianic hope.

In Judaism, the menorah became a religious and political symbol already in the Late Hasmonean period, long before its appearance in Christianity. In the relief on the Arch of Titus, it bears a double meaning: on the one hand, it is a symbol of Roman victory, on the other of defeat and loss of autonomy for the Jewish people. For this reason, the menorah was not depicted on the coins of the Bar Kokhba Revolt. It reappears, however, with heightened intensity as a symbol of Jewish identity in catacombs, on funerary objects, and on sarcophagi, starting in the 3rd century. From then on, the menorah became the most important Jewish symbol, which it remains until the present day (see articles by D. Barag, L. Habas, A. Meshori, and B. Narkiss in this volume).

2
The menorah between the shewbread table and incense altar
Miniature from a 12th-century Octateuch
Serail Library, Topkapi, Istanbul

To understand the background of the menorah's appearance in Byzantine manuscripts, it has to be placed in the context of Greek patristics and, more generally, in the theological meaning of works of art in a Christian context. The menorah does not appear in Byzantine iconography before the 6th century. It is first mentioned in the text of the *Christian Topography*, a treatise of cosmography and geography written by Constantine of Antioch – also known as Cosmas Indicopleustes.[2] The main purpose of his writings was to try and convince his readers that the world had been made according to the model of the Tabernacle, which he envisioned as a cube surmounted by a dome divided into two spheres – the two "states" of mankind.[3] This model, in the opinion of the author, does not allow allegations of the world being either spherical or flat. His theory, he states, is the only "Christian" one, as it is predicated exclusively on sacred typology and the use of models based on the biblical text – which is the justification of a work of art.

Unfortunately, the only remaining illuminated manuscripts of the *Christian Topography* are three late copies produced in the 9th–11th century.[4] The copies present quite the same iconography, and next to the illustrations the author frequently states "this is the drawing of . . . ," or "here, we draw. . . ." By means of this addition, he intends to emphasize the importance of the drawings as a visual translation of the text.

The menorah appearing in Paragraph 33 of Book V is drawn in accordance with the biblical description. The miniature appears directly under the text that reads: "Here is the seven-branched candlestick; standing at the south of the Tabernacle, it was the replica of the luminaries, for, as stated by the sage Solomon, the luminaries move to the south and throw their light on earth, northwise. The lamps are seven in order to bring to mind the seven days of the week, for it is with the weeks that the revolution of time itself begins, of months and year. Moses commanded to kindle the lamps on one side only: the table, standing on the north, they projected their light from south to north. . . . We draw the candlestick and the table" (fig. 1). The menorah is depicted on the right side of the miniature, standing on a three-legged base. It is accompanied by several legends: "seven-branched candelabrum" appears between the legs of the base, the word "rod" above it, "wrought chalice" on the right, "almond flower" and "bud" on the left, and "three branches" along the right and left branches. This drawing obviously attempts to remain very close to the biblical description. On the other hand, there is no doubt that the three-legged base is based upon a Jewish prototype (see article by D. Sperber in this volume).[5] One detail corresponds neither to the biblical text nor to any known visual source: over the top bar of the menorah (itself part of the Jewish visual prototype), sit six little birds, three to the right and three to the left of the central bud, with flames emerging from their beaks. The birds are probably based upon ceramic lamps of paleo-Christian origin, which could have been the clearest model for the "lamps" of the menorah, as these are not described in the biblical account. Such lamps, however, are rare. The use of birds on the top of the menorah may be an attempt at a typological interpretation. Isaiah 11:1–3 states: "But a shoot shall grow out of the stump of Jesse, a twig shall sprout from his stock. The spirit of the Lord shall alight upon him: A spirit of wisdom and insight, a spirit of counsel and valor, a spirit of devotion and reverence for the Lord. He shall sense the truth by his reverence for the Lord: He shall not judge by what his eyes behold, nor decide by what his ears perceive." In Chrisitian patristics, the "shoot shall grow out of the stump of Jesse" refers to Jesus. Thus, the number of branches of the menorah and the seven spirits of the Lord were unified in one biblical symbol, invested with a deep christological interpretation. The depiction of the menorah becomes a typological image of Jesus.

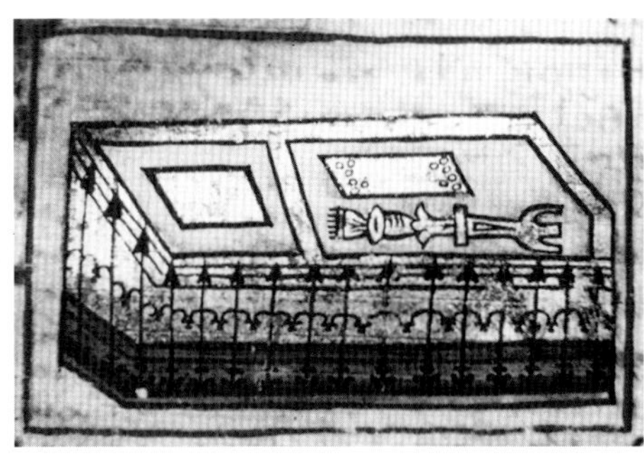

3
The menorah and ark in a plan of the Tabernacle
Miniature from a 12th-century Octateuch
Serail Library, Topkapi, Istanbul

The menorah is depicted once again in the *Topography*, in the miniature showing a plan of the Tabernacle (p. 70). Inside a two-sided perspective of the outer court, which is surrounded by columns and curtains, a bird's-eye-view of the two precincts of the Tabernacle is carefully drawn. On the right we see the Holy, with the shewbread table, the menorah, Aaron's rod, the jar of manna, the tablets of the law, and, probably, the copper snake; on the left, in the second precinct, the ark stands alone. Although Constantine of Antioch cites here the full text of the Epistle to Hebrews, this text does not conform to the miniature in its details: the Epistle, in contrast to the description in Exodus, places the incense altar within the Holy of Holies, next to the ark. In addition, it contains a full list of the objects that were kept within the ark, which in the miniature were "removed" from the ark and placed along with the menorah and the shewbread table. The display of the objects from the ark is known from Jewish art,[6] where it bears profound symbolic meaning. These objects are depicted on the opening pages of Sephardi Bibles from the 13th century onward (see article by B. Narkiss in this volume). The first traces of this Jewish prototype can be found in fragments from the Cairo Genizah, which predate the copies of the *Topography*. A model common to both the Jewish and Christian depictions could probably be traced, but even if there is a definite similarity between the symbolism and its visual translation in both versions, the menorah depicted in the miniature of the Tabernacle plan in the *Christian Topography* differs sharply from the Jewish model: It stands on narrow legs, which form a tripod, above which three short buds rise in a column; these are surmounted by a triangle topped by seven vertical, lightly drawn lines. This formal model no longer bears any resemblance to the biblical text, imitating, rather, certain Byzantine liturgical objects, which can be seen in depictions from the 14th century.

4
The menorah, Moses, and Aaron beside the ark
Miniature from a 12th-century Octateuch
Serail Library, Topkapi, Istanbul

The Byzantine Octateuchs,[7] stemming from the same 6th-century archetype as the copies of the *Topography* and following a similar scheme, represent the menorah in what at first glance seems to be the same manner. Closer examination, however, reveals several differences. In the miniature depicting the menorah standing between the shewbread table and the incense altar (fig. 2), the depiction of base, buds, flowers, and cups resembles that appearing in the *Topography*. However, on top of the horizontal bar that crosses the upper part of the menorah, there are no birds with flames emerging from their beaks, but rather seven fleurs-de-lis, one in the middle and three on either side. In the miniature depicting the plan of the Tabernacle (fig. 3), the menorah and shewbread table are included, but not the incense altar; as for the ark, it appears on its own in a separate section. The menorah, depicted with the seven finely drawn lines on top like the Byzantine liturgical objects, lies on its side; in addition, none of the "objects removed from the ark" are shown.

The Octateuchs contain yet another miniature (fig. 4), which presents the menorah in an unusual context. The miniature depicts a detailed and figurative scene, which shows Moses and Aaron accompanied by sacrificial animals. In the center we see the ark drawn in brown with a golden frame. Over it, the cherubim are depicted as tetramorphs (the symbols of the Evangelists in the Gospels – man, lion, ox, and eagle) in accordance with the Christian interpretation. Opposite Moses and Aaron is a precisely drawn menorah, with a fleur-de-lis budding from each of its seven branches. Over the ark, as if hovering in thin air, a ciborium is painted in blue and gold, topped by a dome. Doves descend upon the cherubim from the heavens, and from the blue skies emerges an outstretched hand from which rays of light shine forth. The meaning of this composition is christological in essence. It represents the replacement of the Old Law by the New, which is symbolized by the ciborium – the Church. Here, the menorah has no typological meaning by itself; rather, it is presented as one of the main components of the Tabernacle, bearing no additional connotations.

5
Mary with the infant Jesus in her arms atop a menorah
Miniature from the 12th century
Izmir, formerly the Evangelist School of Smyrna

A third type of miniature depicting the menorah appears only in the remaining fragments of the *Smyrna Physiologus* (fig. 5), of a later date, which includes the text of the *Topography*.[8] It shows a haloed Mary seated on a cushioned throne, holding the infant Jesus, as is customary for the Byzantine Theotokos. What is unique about this miniature is that Mary sits on top of a menorah, on the highest point of the central branch. The seven branches are all smooth, with no flowers, buds, or cups, but at each end, the branch divides into three flaming torches. In Byzantine liturgy, hymnology, and patrology, Mary was equated with the Tabernacle, the Temple, and all the sacred objects. As a receptacle for the incarnated body of Jesus, she was identified with the ark made of pure gold, the shewbread table, and the seven-branched candelabrum.[9] In this representation of the menorah, the Trinity is expressed by the division of the branches into three. The miniature thus represents yet another stage in the slow typological development of the biblical menorah into a Christian symbol.

The final step in the evolution of the Byzantine menorah is not found in illuminated manuscripts, but rather in the cycles of frescoes in 14th-century churches. In numerous examples – in

6

Wall painting depicting the dedication of the Tabernacle
Decani, Yugoslavia, 14th century

Karje Djami in Constantinople, Decani Gracanica in Yugoslavia (fig. 6), Curtea de Arges in Romania, Mt. Athos, and St. Catherine's monastery in Sinai, the scheme is the same: a scene of the consecration of the Tabernacle in which Moses and Aaron are replaced by the Emperor and the Patriarch.[10] The figures hold liturgical objects over a table covered with a heavy embroidered cloth. On the cloth, and on each of the objects, there is a medallion bearing the portrait and title of Mary. In these scenes, the menorah resembles its depictions in the plans of the Tabernacle in the Topography and the Octateuchs, but the number of branches is no longer constant, varying instead between three and five, and only in rare instances seven. On each menorah, sometimes clearly visible, sometimes barely recognizable, is a medallion of Mary, haloed and with the first letters of her Greek title on each side of her head.

Here, the story of the Byzantine menorah draws to a close. As a sanctuary appurtenance, it is depicted in accordance with the biblical description and appears in conjunction with cosmographic theories. Later, it takes on the symbolism of Mary as the incarnation of eschatological prophecy and slowly comes to be depicted as a liturgical object, related to the Tabernacle and seen as an archetype of the Christian altar. History, symbolism, theology, eschatological typology, it moves gracefully from one to another, leaving the original Jewish meaning and model far behind.

1 Cyril of Alexandria, PG 77, col. 217; H. L. Kessler, "Medieval Art as Argument," *Iconography at the Crossroads* (Princeton, 1993), 59–70.

2 The author, who lived in the mid-6th century, simply signed his treatise "a Christian." The name Cosmas Indicopleustes appears only in copies of his works produced in the 11th century. W. Wolska-Conus, *Cosmas Indicopleustes, Topographie Chrétienne* (Paris, 1968); idem, "Stephanos d'Athénes et Stephanos d'Alexandrie. Essai d'identification et de biographie," *Revue des Etudes Byzantines* 47 (1989): 28–30; "La Topographie Chrétienne de Cosmas Indicopleustes," *Revue des Etudes Byzantines* 48 (1990): 155–191.

3 E. Revel-Neher, "Some Remarks on the Iconographical Sources of the Christian Topography of Cosmas Indicopleustes," *Kairos* 32/33 (1990/91): 78–95.

4 In the Vatican Library (Vat. GR. 699); in the library of the St. Catherine Monastery, Sinai (Sin. 1186); and the Laurenziana Library in Florence (Laur. Plut. IX.28).

5 The Jewish archetype for the legs of the menorah appears early on in Jewish art, though it is not mentioned in the biblical description; see Shula Laderman, *The Jewish Sources to the Theory and Iconography of Cosmas Indicopleustes' Christian Topography*, MA thesis (Jerusalem 1990) (Hebrew).

6 E. Revel-Neher, "La double page du Codex Amiatinus et ses rapports avec les plans du Tabernacle dans l'Art Juif et dans l'Art Byzantin," *Journal of Jewish Art* 9 (1982): 6–17.

7 A group of manuscripts: Rome, Vat. Gr. 746; Vat. Gr. 747; Istanbul, Serail Cod. 8; Athos, Vatopedi 602. See K. Weitzmann, M. Bernabo, *The Byzantine Octateuchs* (Princeton, in press). This biblical unit is composed, according to the order of the Septuagint, of the Pentateuch, Joshua, Judges and Ruth.

8 It contains the Octateuch and other literary texts, cited according to the argumentation of the Physiologus.

9 John of Damascus, *On the Divine Images*, trans. D. Anderson (London, 1950), I, 12–13; H. L. Kessler, "Pictures Fertile with Truth," in *Studies in Pictorial Narrative* (London, 1994), 81.

10 J. Mateos, *Le Typicon de la grande Eglise* (Rome, 1963).

Bianca Kühnel

The Menorah and the Cross

The Seven-Branched Candelabrum in the Church

Perhaps it was only to be expected that the menorah, the seven-branched candelabrum, would make its way into Christian art[1] as one of the many Jewish elements that Christianity took over and made its own. It is not surprising, for example, that illuminated manuscripts of the Bible feature the menorah along with the other appurtenances of the Tabernacle or the Temple, even though the details of the depiction do not always agree with those recounted in the text. The illustration on the opening page of the Book of Leviticus in a Carolingian manuscript (c. 870), in the Church of San Paolo Fuori le Mura in Rome, describes the erection of the Tabernacle and the anointing of the priests.[2] Though the menorah receives particular emphasis – it is large and situated on the main axis of the composition, together with the Ark of the Covenant – its appearance is justified by the context. The menorah, the Ark of the Covenant, and the Tabernacle were assigned a prominent place – in a symmetric composition, with no narrative context – because the opening page, on which the illustration appears, was supposed to represent the entire book. However, the appearance of large, three-dimensional candelabra in churches – sometimes as high as the building itself – as reported in a source that describes a candelabrum that once stood in Durham Cathedral, which has not survived)[3] – is a surprising phenomenon, surpassing whatever one could expect given the nature of the relationship between Christian visual art and Jewish sources. Despite the many depictions of the seven-branched candelabrum in Christian visual art, which appear in various textual contexts, it seems that the menorah's most interesting, significant, and original artistic expression in Christian art is the three-dimensional candelabrum, which served as part of the church liturgical furnishings. The design and ornamentation of these candelabra, as well as the inscriptions that sometimes accompany them, reveal their theological background and document the stages in the development of this motif over the centuries.

Most probably, the seven-branched candelabrum first became part of the standard church furnishings in the Carolingian period, around the time of the above-mentioned illustration on the opening page of Leviticus in the *San Paolo Fuori le Mura Bible*. The emphasis given to the menorah in this pictorial representation and its metamorphosis into a three-dimensional church candelabrum have the same background and motivation, namely, the Carolingian perception of the empire and the church.

Charlemagne, assisted by scholars whom he gathered about himself, made considerable use of Jewish sources in order to consolidate his rule. The Carolingian dynasty, having usurped the throne illegally, tried to seek legitimization in the kingship of David and Solomon; it also sought to associate the dynasty with the Roman Empire, by crowning Charlemagne as Emperor of Rome in a ceremony held at Rome on Christmas Day, 800. Two days before the coronation, Charlemagne received the keys to the Holy Sepulcher and to the city of Jerusalem and Mount Zion, together with a relic of the Cross, from two messengers of the Patriarch of Jerusalem, sent especially for the occasion. Thus, Jerusalem was coupled with Rome, in a well-planned maneuver intended to create a dual ideological basis for the Frankish empire: the biblical kingdom and the Roman Empire. The link with the kings of Israel was expressed in several other ways during the Carolingian period: Charlemagne is referred to in contemporary sources as both the new David and the new Solomon; his court biographer Einhard is called Bezalel; the rector of the Carolingian court church, Hildebald, is likened to Aaron; and the palace church at Aix-la-Chapelle, Charlemagne's capital, is compared in the contemporary chronicles to Solomon's Temple.

These ideological and symbolic expressions were accompanied by practical measures. The octagonal palace church in Aix-la-Chapelle derived its ground plan from the shape of the Dome of the Rock in

Jerusalem, which Christians saw as representing the Temple, a connection which does not neccessarily exclude additional sources of inspiration for the Palatine Chapel mentioned in previous research. Such influences reached Europe owing to the increased number of pilgrims to the holy places during Charlemagne's reign, despite the Muslim rule over the Holy Land. The construction of monasteries and pilgrim hospices, as well as the dispatching of various emissaries to Jerusalem, clearly indicate that Charlemagne considered himself the custodian of the Christian holy places. From pilgrims' itineraries, particularly that of the Frankish monk Bernard, we learn that the Temple Mount and Solomon's Temple were not only included among the holy places visited by contemporary pilgrims but in fact occupied a very prominent position. Moreover, Bernard's description suggests that he was fully acquainted with the magnificent building of the Dome of the Rock, which he calls *synagoga saracenorum*. The Carolingians' attitude to Jerusalem and the Temple Mount was undoubtedly a preliminary stage, preparing the ground for the Crusaders' "baptism" of the Muslim structures on the Temple Mount in the 12th century.[4]

1
Candelabrum of the Essen Cathedral (height: 3.30 m) ca. 1000

Against the background of the Carolingian attitude to the Bible in general and to the kingship of David and Solomon in particular, the seven-branched candelabrum may be seen as yet another expression of the general trend of adopting the most characteristic national and religious symbols of the people of Israel. This thesis is reinforced by the study of the three-dimensional candelabra of the Carolingian period.

We know of two such candelabra from written sources only, as neither has survived. One stood in the Church of the Redeemer at Aniane (built in 779) and the other in the Church of the Redeemer at Fulda (built after 822), during the period of the Hrabanus Maurus as Abbot of the Fulda Monastery. The sources that refer to the two candelabra also mention Solomon's Temple and Bezalel in the same context, thus documenting an awareness of this affinity among both the creators and the beholders of the candelabra. In both cases (Aniane and Fulda), the sources mention the proximity of an Ark of the Covenant, further reinforcing the link between the Tabernacle and Temple, on the one hand, and the Carolingian church, on the other. The source referring to Aniane describes the church altar as the Ark of the Covenant, while at Fulda the term is applied to a reliquary.[5] The association between the Ark of the Covenant and the altar is clearly, although differently, expressed in the small Carolingian church of St. Germigny-des-Prés, where the ark is represented in mosaic in the apse, precisely above the church's altar.[6]

These examples document an iconographic environment that conveyed clear messages as to the role of the church within the Carolingian imperial idea: the church, as both institution and building, was the third factor in the self-perception of the Carolingian rulers as Christian emperors. Just as the crown of the Roman Empire had been placed on the heads of Charlemagne and his successors by the Pope, the biblical heritage could enter the Carolingian court only through the agency of the church. Carolingian art adapted the views of the New Testament and of ancient Christian exegesis – which presented the Christian church as a new, improved, eternal version of the wilderness Tabernacle and of the Temple in Jerusalem and saw the Christian believers as *verus Israel* ("the true Israel") – to the demands of its imperial patrons. The New Testament books most relevant to this view are the Epistle to Hebrews and the Revelation to John. As one might expect from these sources, the attitude of Carolingian art to the sacred objects of the Tabernacle and the Temple was indeed one of superiority; the emphasis, however, was not on antagonism but on continuity. Carolingian artists were adept at finding new, original, visual formulas to express these ideas, and they clearly worked in close and fruitful cooperation with court scholars, in an effort to serve the political ambitions of the Carolingian dynasty. The candelabrum in the church is one of the fruits of these efforts: it was intended to define the church as the Tabernacle in the wilderness, as Solomon's Temple – but an improved, eternal version, located in paradise.

Some of the visual formulas that emerged during the Carolingian period were continued and developed in later periods. The three-dimensional candelabrum belongs to this category. Judging from the relatively large number of written reports, as well as actual surviving candelabra from later periods, one might even argue that the three-dimensional candelabrum became part of the regular church furnishings in the Middle Ages, the Renaissance, and the Baroque. While the Carolingian period was decisive in regard to the emergence of the candelabrum motif in the church, the 11th and 12th centuries were the richest periods in its development, not only quantitatively but mainly because of the variety of iconographic contexts added to the Christian candelabrum.

2
Candelabrum of the Milan Cathedral
ca. 1200

The secret of the menorah's attraction for Christianity lay not only in the fact that it was the Temple object par excellence, but also in its seven-branched shape. The symbolism of the number seven, originating in the Ancient East, was adopted and developed by Christianity, giving rise to an idea of cosmic perfection based on two components: the trinity and the four elements, which were parallel to the four cardinal directions, the four seasons, and the four ages of man, as well as the four rivers of paradise and the four evangelists. The number three also possessed various meanings: the three components of man and his soul (*sensus, ratio, intellectus*), the three stages of history (*ante legem, sub legem, sub gratia*), and so on. In addition, the total number seven had symbolic significance of its own, expressed through the motif of the lamp: according to the Revelation (1:12), seven lampstands symbolized the seven Christian communities that made up the Christian church as a whole, and thus, the seven-branched candelabrum became one of the prime symbols of the church. Seven was also the number of levels of the Holy Spirit, as follows from the Latin version of Isaiah 11:2, which refers to the "shoot from the stump of Jesse" (*virga de radice jesse*), upon which the spirit of the Lord would rest: the spirit of wisdom, thought, counsel, power, knowledge, faith, and fear. The association of the seven-branched candelabrum and the seven levels of the Holy Spirit may already be found in the writings of the Church Fathers,[7] and it continued to be used in medieval exegesis[8], finding visual expression in the art of the period. One of the earliest and most explicit depictions of the candelabrum as a tree trunk bearing seven doves (the visual representation of the seven levels of the Holy Spirit) on each of its seven branches appears in medieval copies of the Christian Topography of Cosmas Indicopleustes.[9]

The three-dimensional candelabrum reflects the complex of exegesis and symbolism that was associated with the menorah from the earliest days of Christianity. The candelabrum standing today in the Essen Cathedral, Germany, which is 3.30 meters high (fig. 1), was made during the time of Mathilde, granddaughter of Emperor Otto the Great and an abbess during the years 971–1011. The general shape of the candelabrum conforms to the biblical description of Exodus 25:31–36. The branches are fashioned from alternating spherical and polygonal balls made up of stylized leaves, which heighten the similarity of the candelabrum to a tree trunk. The base of the candelabrum is a square platform, upon which is a smaller square with a hemisphere in the middle, supporting the lampstand itself. At the ends of the square base four anthropomorphic figures signify, according to the identifying inscriptions, the four winds (only two of the figures survived). The form of the base, combined with the personifications, place the candelabrum at the center of the universe and lend it eschatological significance, based on Ezekiel 37:910; Matthew 24:31; Mark 13:27, and on the exegesis of the Church Fathers, particularly that of Augustine. Very possibly, the Essen candelabrum was originally made as a funerary lamp for the Abbess Mathilde, which would explain the eschatological allusions. But the candelabrum may also have taken on some of the contexts that used to accompany the cross. Medieval sources referring to the Essen candelabrum indicate that it stood by the altar with the cross, which was generally positioned in the center of the church (*in medio ecclesiae*). This information supports the thesis that the candelabrum was seen as a parallel to the cross. The location in the center of the church, and the universe, the association with the four cardinal points, the role in the Resurrection – all these features are shared by the cross and the candelabrum. The similarity of the menorah to a tree trunk also recalls the interpretation of the cross as the Tree of Life. As far as the candelabrum is concerned, the comparison with the Tree of Life may indeed derive from its association with the shoot from the stump of Jesse and the seven levels of the Holy Spirit; but this does not rule out the association with the cross as the Tree of Life. Moreover, there are Christian candelabra (such as the bronze lamp of the Braunschweig Cathedral, made in 1179–1180, which stands 4.80 meters high) decorated with precious and semiprecious stones, like a very common type of cross known as *crux gemmata,* which emphasizes the motif of victory over death. It is also known that many candelabra were used in connection with burial, whether specially made for the purpose or otherwise. Thus, for example, the inscription on the candelabrum in St. Severin's Church, Cologne, states that it was made as a funerary lamp for Archbishop Anno II in 1075.[10] The use of the candelabrum in this context therefore also supports the parallel with the cross.

In the course of the 12th century, a significant change occurred in the shape of the three-dimensional candelabrum, indicating a shift of emphasis in its Christian interpretation and further confirming the affinity with the cross. The candelabrum was designed so that its branches no longer terminated at the same height, but decreased in length from the center outward. At the same time, they became thinner and more flexible. These new shapes enhanced the likeness of the candelabrum to a tree, thus emphasizing its association with the stump of Jesse, as has indeed been noted by modern scholars, but also underlining the affinity with the cross in its aspect as the Tree of Life. One of the most beautiful medieval candelabra of this type (made c. 1200) is still standing in the Milan Cathedral (fig. 2). It is accompanied by a typological iconographic plan focusing on salvation, thus reiterating the eschatological meaning of the candelabrum and the affinity with the cross. The iconographic plan includes depictions of the four rivers of paradise, the zodiac, the struggle between the virtues and the vices, the original sin and the expulsion from Eden, Noah's ark and the binding of Isaac, Moses by the burning bush and the crossing of the Red Sea, the coronation of Esther, and David's victory over Goliath. Most of these scenes figure prominently among the decorative schemes of medieval three-dimensional crosses. Moreover, as in the case of crosses, the base of the Milan candelabrum also features parts of dragons' bodies, probably in an apotropaic role. The inclusion of dragons and hybrid creatures, such as centaurs and sphinxes, is a regular feature in the ornamentation of candelabra, as well as crosses. Examples are the candelabra from the cathedrals of Prague (1140–1150) and Reims (first half of the 12th century, now in the city museum).

The identification of the candelabrum and the cross became more explicit toward the end of the Middle Ages and during the Renaissance, when the cross was directly incorporated into the structure of the candelabrum. A fine example is the candelabrum in the church of St. Leonard at Léau Zoutleeuw, Belgium, dating to 1483.[11] Three of its branches bear figures of Mary, John the Evangelist, and Mary Magdalene, all figures that regularly accompany the crucifixion scene. In addition, the upper part of the central branch in the candelabrum is in the shape of a cross.

In conclusion: Christianity adopted the menorah, the seven-branched candelabrum, making it into one of its most prominent symbols. This phenomenon may be attributed to the menorah's shape, its related meanings, and, in particular, the national importance it assumed in Judaism after the destruction of the Temple. The first expressions of the candelabrum in Christian art were most probably connected with depictions of the Tabernacle and the Temple, as part of the endeavor to stress the superiority of the church. These visual depictions were both based on primary Christian sources and fostered by the political interests of the Carolingian dynasty. During the 12th century, the eschatological aspect of the candelabrum came to the fore, and at the same time, its identification in form and content with the cross received particular emphasis. At this stage, the "Christianization" of the Jewish menorah reached completion, and any signs associating the candelabrum with its original historical environment, the Tabernacle in the desert or the Temple in Jerusalem, were entirely obliterated.

1 For material basic to any study of the seven-branched candelabrum in Christian art, see P. Bloch, "Siebenarmige Leuchter in christlichen Kirchen," *Wallraf-Richartz Jahrbuch* 23 (1961): 55–190; idem, "Seven-Branched Candelabra in Christian Churches," *Journal of Jewish Art* 1(1974): 44–49.

2 H. L. Kessler, "Through the Temple Veil: The Holy Image in Judaism and Christianity," *Kairos* 32/33 (1990;/1): 57ff.

3 Bloch (above, n. 1), 183, no. 11.

4 G. Kühnel, "Aachen, Byzanz und die frühislamische Architektur im Heiligen Land," in *Studien zur byzantinischen Kunstgeschichte. Festschrift für H. Hallensleben* (Amsterdam, 1995), 39–58.

5 J.v. Schlosser, *Schriftquellen zur geschichte der karolingischen Kunst* (Vienna, 1892), nos. 574–390.

6 P. Bloch, "Das Apsismosaik von Germigny-des-Près: Karl der Grosse und der Alte Bund," in *Karl der Grosse, Lebenswerk und Nachleben*, Vol. 3: *Kunstgeschichte* (Düsseldorf, 1965), 234–261.

7 Clemens of Alexandria, *Stromata* V, 6 ch. 34, 9; 35, 1–2.

8 Rupert of Deutz, in *Exodum Commentariorum* 4, 8, pls. 167, 705f.

9 Florence, Biblioteca Laurenziana, Plut. 9/28; Bloch (above, n. 1) fig. 47, p. 72; and Sinai, St Catherine, MS 1186 (see article by E. Revel-Neher in this volume, fig.1).

10 For further examples of the funerary use of the candelabrum see Bloch (above, no. 1), 120.

11 S. Colon-Gevaert, *Histoire des arts du métal en Belgique* (Brussels, 1951), 256f, pls. 55, 56.

Avraham Ronen

The Temple Menorah in Renaissance Art

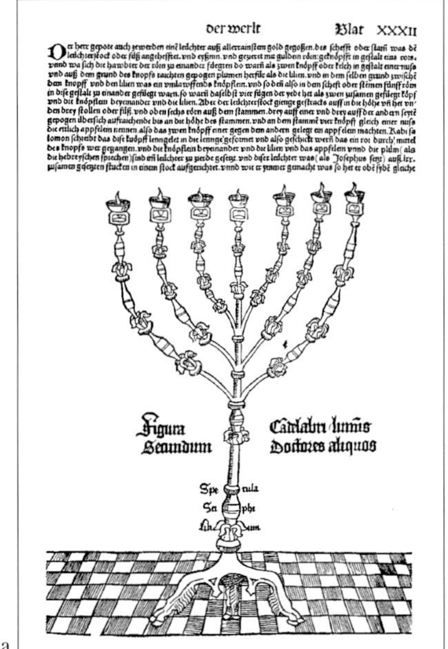

a

1

Hartmann Schedel,
Liber Chronicarum
(Book of Chronicles),
1493
a
Menorah "according
to the scholars"
b
Menorah "according
to Rabbi Moses"

The seven-branched candelabrum, or menorah, described in the Book of Exodus (25:31–38, 37:17–24) and referred to by Flavius Josephus (*Antiquities*, III, 144–146) appears, along with the other implements of the Tabernacle in the desert, in illuminated Latin manuscripts of the Scriptures, beginning with the 7th-century illuminated Bible, the *Codex Amiatinus*, in the Laurenziana Library in Florence. This tradition continued into the Middle Ages and the 15th century in the illuminations on the front pages of Bibles. A typical example of the survival of the medieval tradition of illumination in the 15th century is the Spanish miniature in the *Alba Bible* (Madrid), representing the open Tent of Meeting and, inside it, the menorah and other implements, the high priest Aaron, and a scene of sacrifice (see article by B. Narkiss in this volume).[1]

In the printed Bibles and biblical commentaries of the second half of the 15th century, similar illustrations are found. The woodcuts in the printed editions of the *Postilla Super Biblia* (Commentaries on the Bible) by Nicolaus de Lyra, published in Nuremberg in 1481, are also of this type.[2] The best-known and most detailed graphic representations of the Tabernacle implements, directly influenced by those in De Lyra's book, appear in the *Liber Chronicarum* (Book of Chronicles) by the renowned German humanist Hartmann Schedel, which was published in Nuremberg in Latin and German in 1493. In the chapter relating the wanderings of the Israelites in the desert, the giving of the Law, and the building of the Tabernacle, five pages were devoted to detailed written and pictorial descriptions of the sacred objects of the Tabernacle, based on the descriptions in the biblical text and, to some extent, Josephus' *Antiquities*. The woodcuts illustrating the text include two hypothetical graphic reconstructions of the "lampstand for lighting" (fig. 1a–b): one "according to the scholars," and the other "according to Rabbi Moses [Maimonides]" (the text also mentions "Rabbi Solomon" (Rashi).[3]

In addition to literary sources and miniatures in early 15th-century manuscripts, the depictions of the menorah in Renaissance art were also influenced by three-dimensional bronze candelabra – "reconstructions" of the Temple menorah that stood in churches throughout Europe in the Middle Ages and in later periods. The earliest example is the candelabrum in the cathedral of Essen, dating from about the year 1000.[4]

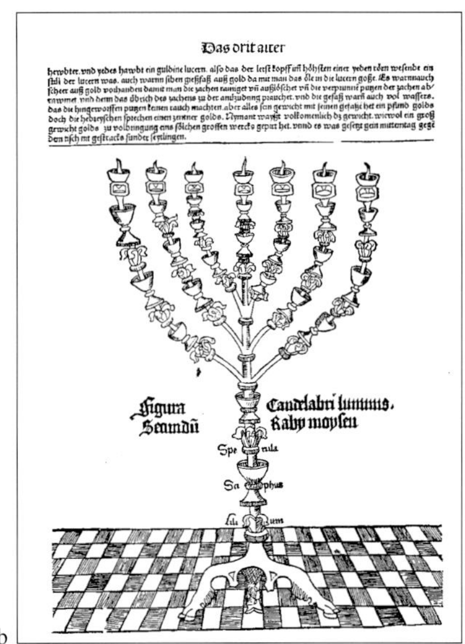

b

At the end of the 15th century, there was an increasing tendency (the beginnings of which are already discernible in medieval Christian thought) to seek a more accurate interpretation of the Holy Scriptures through a careful examination of the sources, which obviously necessitated a knowledge of the Hebrew language. The depiction of biblical stories and characters in works of art began to be less naive and more geared toward producing as accurate as possible a reconstruction of the historical past. In the paintings of that period, Hebrew inscriptions began to appear, and the costumes of the characters were "in the ancient style" (*all'antica*), as opposed to contemporary 15th-century dress. The attempt to provide an authentic rendering of the biblical stories and characters also pertained to the depictions of the Temple and its implements, as well as the costume of the high priest.

According to the Gospels, several episodes in the life of Jesus took place within the Temple, which was also the scene of events in the lives of Jesus' forefathers and of the parents of John the Baptist, as described in the Apocrypha. These events were therefore depicted in Christian art as taking place in the interior of the Temple.[5] The scenes most frequently depicted were the Expulsion of Jehohiachin (Jesus' maternal grandfather) from the Temple; the Annunciation (of the future birth of a son) to Zechariah (father of John the Baptist); the Marriage of the Virgin; Jesus' Circumcision; the Presentation of the Infant Jesus in the Temple; the Disputation between the Twelve-Year-Old Jesus and the Pharisees; Jesus and the Woman Taken in Adultery; and the Expulsion of the Money Changers from the Temple. In many of these renderings, the Temple is depicted as a Christian church or chapel, without any of the implements of the Temple, though in some 15th-century German paintings, the Tablets of the Law are included.

2
Vittore Carpaccio, *The Marriage of the Virgin*, 1504
Pinacoteca di Brera, Milan

At the end of the 15th century and the beginning of the 16th, when the tendency to include authentic details in paintings of biblical scenes had increased, some of the artists derived their representations from book illustrations, such as those of the aforementioned Nicolaus de Lyra and Hartmann Schedel, whose graphic renderings of the implements of the Temple were considered to represent the up-to-date results of the study of these objects by scholars and humanists.

One of these artists was the Venetian Vittore Carpaccio (1455–1525). His painting, *The Marriage of the Virgin*, one of a series of paintings for the Scuola degli Albanesi attached to the Church of S. Maurizio in Venice (1504), includes some details directly derived from the illustrations of Schedel's *Liber Chronicarum* and De Lyra's *Commentaries on the Bible*, including the costume of the high priest and the depiction of the menorah (fig. 2).[6] In order to lend authenticity to his depiction of the Temple, Carpaccio included two Hebrew inscriptions (though both of them are meaningless).[7]

3
Lorenzo Costa, *The Presentation of the Infant Jesus in the Temple*, 1502

About two years before Carpaccio painted his picture, Lorenzo Costa painted his large *The Presentation of the Infant Jesus in the Temple* for a church in Bologna (1502, formerly in the Kaiser Friedrich Museum, Berlin, destroyed in 1945; fig. 3). Like Carpaccio's painting, Costa's included two "authentic" motifs: Hebrew inscriptions (one of which is meaningless)[8] and the Temple menorah. More precisely, on the altar, *two* seven-branched candelabra are depicted. It is difficult to give a definite and convincing explanation of this rare, if not unique, phenomenon in Renaissance art. Perhaps the *two* menorahs are meant to remind us that the candelabrum is also one of the attributes of the Virgin Mary (see article by E. Revel-Neher in this volume). Pairs of candelabra do indeed appear in wall paintings, on gold-glass bases, and in mosaics of the Early Christian and Byzantine periods in the Holy Land and Rome, but it is unlikely that Costa was acquainted with any of these examples.[9] The branches of the menorahs in Costa's painting are not of equal length, but the bases are tripodal, as in the illustrations to the printed books, thus continuing the ancient tradition of the depiction of the menorah in Jewish and Christian art that began in the earliest centuries of the Common Era.

A menorah similar to those appearing in Costa's painting, but with a round base, appears in an engraving by Guilio Bonasone, one of the illustrations to the third book of Achile Bocchi's *Symbolicarum Questionum* from 1574 (fig. 4). In this illustration, the menorah (apparently a symbol of the "Divine Love") is held by Hermes in his mystical, Neoplatonic transformation.[10]

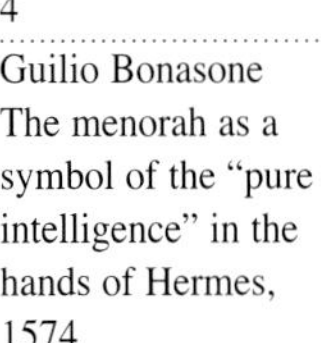

4
Guilio Bonasone
The menorah as a symbol of the "pure intelligence" in the hands of Hermes, 1574

5
Raphael,
The Expulsion of Heliodorus from the Temple (detail),
ca. 1512
The Vatican

One of the most important depictions of the Temple menorah in Renaissance art – if not the most important and beautiful of all – is found in Raphael's famous fresco, *The Expulsion of Heliodorus from the Temple* (fig. 5), painted in about 1512 on the wall of a room in the living-quarters of Pope Julius II in the Vatican (called the *Stanza di Eliodoro*).

The main episode shown in the painting – the expulsion of Heliodorus who had tried to steal the Temple treasures (II Maccabees 3) – is depicted in the right foreground of the work. Inside the Temple, represented as a basilica with a series of vaulted bays, the high priest Onias kneels before the altar, offering a prayer of thanksgiving while facing the lighted menorah on the right. The menorah is shown in foreshortened perspective, with the Ark of the Covenant standing next to it. Although this scene takes place in the distant background of the fresco and is apparently far away from the spectator, Raphael placed it in the geometrical center of the picture. Nevertheless, the menorah has not received much attention in the many studies that have been written about this fresco.[11] Moreover, very few scholars have noticed the fact that Giorgio Vasari (1511–1574), the pioneer of the history of Renaissance art, in his book, *The Lives of the Italian Painters, Sculptors, and Architects* (second edition, 1568), began his account of the fresco (before even mentioning its main subject!) with a description of this scene: "On one of the bare walls, Raphael further did the divine worship, the ark of the Hebrews, and the candlestick." And then: "Apart from these, the High Priest Onias kneels in his priestly garments."[12] Like Carpaccio, Raphael borrowed from the 15th-century wood-cuts mentioned above: the menorah and the high priest's costume indeed resemble the illustrations to the *Liber Chronicarum* and its predecessors.

Giorgio Vasari was also one of the most important Florentine painters of the mid-16th century. His work, *The Presentation of the Infant Jesus in the Temple* (1545, Museo Nazionale di Capodimonte, Naples), painted for the refectory of the Monte Oliveto Monastery in Naples, is heavily influenced by Raphael.[13] Vasari may well have taken the idea of including a depiction of the Temple menorah in the background of the picture from Raphael. And it is perhaps no coincidence that in Vasari's picture the menorah is depicted on the side of the Temple's interior and in a foreshortened perspective similar to that of the menorah in Raphael's painting.

One of the outstanding Florentine painters of the second half of the 16th century was Alessandro Allori (1535–1607). In his painting, *Jesus and the Woman Taken in Adultery* (John 8:2–11), executed in 1577 for the Church of Santo Spirito in Florence, the scene is shown as taking place in the Temple after Jesus had just finished preaching.[14] The seven-branched menorah in the background, standing on a rectangular base, rarely appears in artistic representations of this scene.

The Temple menorah reappears in the 17th century, in Nicholas Poussin's celebrated painting, *Titus Conquering Jerusalem* (1638, Kunsthistorisches Museum, Vienna; fig. 6). The literary source used by Poussin for the representation of this historical event was Flavius Josephus' *Jewish War*, where the seizure of the Temple menorah by the Romans is described (VII, v, 5).

6
Nicholas Poussin, *Titus Conquering Jerusalem* (detail), 1638
Kunsthistorisches Museum, Vienna

Poussin, an outstanding representative of French classicism, aimed at an authentic depiction of historical subjects based on Roman archaeological sources, with which Poussin became well acquainted during his long period of residence in Rome.[15] The details of the battle were inspired by reliefs on Roman sarcophagi and on the two imperial triumphal columns, which stand in Rome until the present day, while the depiction of the seizure of the Temple menorah by the Roman soldiers was based on the famous relief on the Arch of Titus representing his triumphal procession (pp. 190–191).

More than three hundred years after Poussin's picture was painted, the use of this seemingly authentic ancient Roman source resulted in an inauthentic representation of the Temple menorah in the official emblem of the State of Israel (see articles by D. Sperber and A. Meshori in this volume).

1 C. Roth, "Jewish Antecedents of Christian Art," *Journal of the Warburg and Courtauld Institutes* 16 (1953): 24–44, particularly pages 36–37, figs. 9a, 10a; H. Strauss, "The Fate and Form of the Hasmonean Menorah," *Eretz-Israel* 6 (1960): 122–129, and pl. 27:3.

2 Roth (above, n. 1), 38, no. 4; J. M. Fletcher, "Sources of Carpaccio in German Woodcuts," *The Burlington Magazine* CXV:846 (Sept. 1973): 599, n. 5.

3 R. Poertner (ed.), *Die Schedelsche Weltchronik* (1493) (Dortmond, 1978), (fol. XXXI v., XXXII, XXXIII) fol. XXXII r. and v.; Fletcher (above, n. 2), 599, figs. 54–56.

4 For a thorough study see P. Bloch, "Siebenarmige Leuchter in christlichen Kirchen," *Wallraf-Richartz Jahrbuch* 23 (1961): 55–90; see also Strauss (above, n. 1), 127–128, pl. 27: 1–2.

5 A. Stange, *Deutsche Malerei der Gotik*, vol. 5 (Munich-Berlin, 1952), fig. 234; vol. 6 (1954), fig. 249; vol. 10 (1960), figs. 70, 94; vol. 11 (1961), fig. 161.

6 Fletcher (above, n. 2), 599.

7 A. Ronen, "Iscrizioni ebraiche nell'arte italiana del Quattrocento," in *Studi di Storia dell'arte sul Medioevo e il Rinascimento nel centenario della nascita di Mario Salmi*, vol. 2 (Florence, 1992), 610, n. 47.

8 Ronen (above, n. 7), 608; D. Haitowsky, "A New Look at a Lost Painting, The Hebrew Inscription in Lorenzo Costa's Presentation in the Temple," *Artibus et Historiae* 29 (1994), fig. 1.

9 Roth (above, n. 1), figs. 8b, 8d, 9d; R. L. Geller, *Roma Ebraica* (Rome, 1983), figs. 24, 25, 31, 33.

10 E. Wind, *Pagan Mysteries in the Renaissance*[2] (Harmondsworth, 1967), 12, n. 40, 122, fig. 23.

11 L. Dussler, *Raphael, A Critical Catalogue* (London, 1971), 79–80.

12 Giorgio Vasari, *Le Vite de' più eccellenti pittori, scultori, ed architettori*[2], 1568, vita di Raffaello da Urbino.

13 L. Corti, *Vasari, Catalogo completo dei dipinti* (Florence, 1989), n. 32, pl. on p. 53.

14 S. Lecchini Giovannoni, *Alessandro Allori* (Torino, 1991), n. 55, pl. VII.

15 R. Weiss-Blok and S. Rozenberg, *Myth and Power. Masterpieces from Imperial Vienna*, exh. cat., *The Israel Museum* (Jerusalem, 1996), 55, no. 52; R. Verdi, *Nicolas Poussin 1594–1665*, exh. cat., (London, 1995), no. 36.

Iris Fishof

Facing the Menorah
Jewish Art in the Modern Era

The menorah, the seven-branched candelabrum, has long symbolized and expressed the Jewish people's yearning for the splendors of their past and their expectations of future salvation. Over the generations, the form and meaning of this symbol have undergone various metamorphoses. This article is a survey of the various expressions of the menorah in Jewish art over the last four centuries. Throughout this period, the menorah has been a common visual symbol, particularly in synagogue art, but it also appears on a great variety of objects, sometimes branching into other, broader areas, such as ceremonial objects used on specific festivals, especially items for personal use. As a result, the menorah seems to have taken on new levels of meaning, and as the emphasis shifted from the purely religious aspects of the symbol, it ultimately became a symbol of Jewish national identity.

The Menorah in the Synagogue

Since the destruction of the Second Temple, the synagogue has served as a kind of "lesser sanctuary" – a substitute Temple for the Jewish people. Worshipers face Jerusalem; the Torah ark is known in Hebrew as *hekhal* (another word for "sanctuary"); the curtain hanging before it is called a *parokhet* (the word also used for the curtain between the Holy and the Holy of Holies in the Tabernacle and Temple); and the design and ornamentation of many ceremonial objects were inspired by the Temple appurtenances and the high priest's vestments. The menorah, as one of these sacred objects, has played a prominent role in the synagogue – as a wall decoration, on Torah arks, on Torah ark curtains, and on Torah scroll decorations.

1
Torah ark valance
Tyktin, Poland, 1697
Israel Museum
Collection

2
Amulet for the
protection of infants
Italy, 18th century
Israel Museum
Collection

The perception of the synagogue as a "lesser sanctuary" has also led to the depiction of the menorah on the southern wall of the synagogue and the shewbread table on the northern wall, in analogy with their positions in the Tabernacle in the desert and the Temple in Jerusalem. Thus, for example, in the 17th-century wooden synagogue of Gwozdziec, Galicia, the menorah was painted (using the letters of Psalm 67) on the southern wall. Similarly, the menorah and the shewbread table were

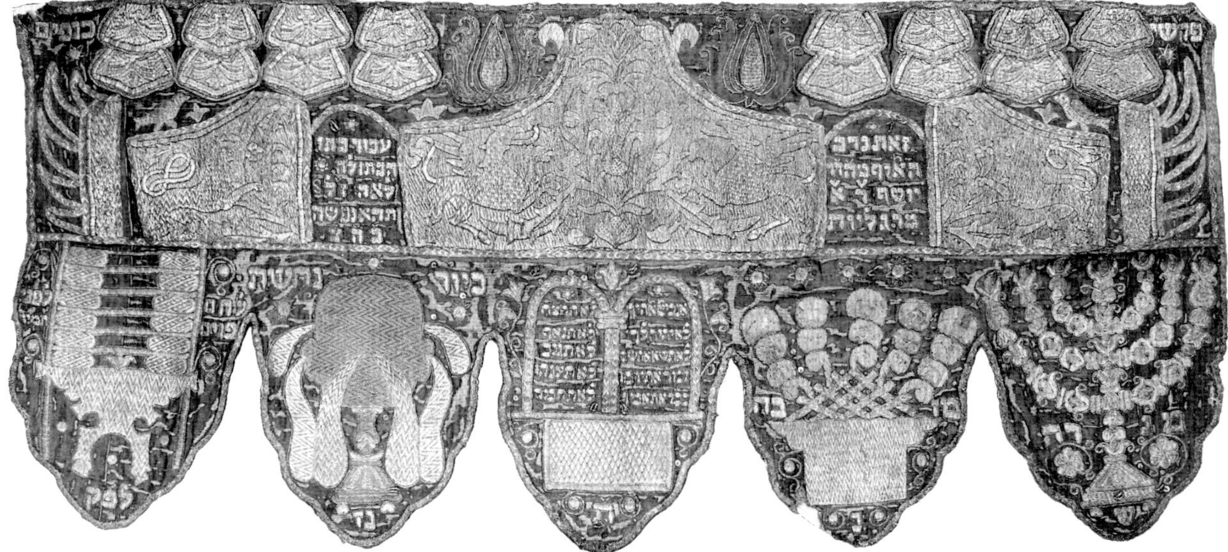

represented on the appropriate walls of the wooden synagogue of Jablonow.[1] The same principle dictated the location of these objects when represented on Torah arks, as in the synagogue of the Rema (Rabbi Moses Isserles) in Cracow, whose double doors, made of an alloy of lead and tin by Jewish artists of Cracow in the 17th century, are now in the collection of the Israel Museum, Jerusalem (p. 64).[2] When the doors were opened, the menorah was revealed on the southern door and the shewbread table on the northern one. The outer surface of the doors was made of wood, decorated with a simple rhomboidal pattern, but their inner surfaces were richly adorned with a wealth of symbols and inscriptions. All that remains today on the doors is a late coat of paint, but some traces of the gold and silver leaf that once covered the patterns are still visible. Here, too, the verses of Psalm 67 were inscribed along the branches of the menorah, as was the tradition. An inscription above the menorah reads: "Let the seven lamps give light at the front of the lampstand" (Numbers 8:2), and along its sides are the final letters of six verses from Psalm 67 and the Hebrew words, "Voice of the Lord," which equal those six letters in numerical value (*gematria*). The artisans who fashioned the doors signed their names, with great erudition, by quoting an appropriate biblical verse in a medallion just below the representation of the shewbread table: "All the artisans who were engaged in the tasks of the sanctuary came, each from the task upon which he was engaged [Exodus 36:4]: the esteemed Zalman and Hayim and Anya(?) Schnitzer and Welwel KS" (two of these artisans also signed similar double ark doors of the "High Synagogue" in Cracow).

3
Torah shield
Eichenstadt, Germany, end of 19th century
Israel Museum Collection, Stieglitz Collection, made possible through a donation by Erica and Ludwig Jesselson, New York, to American Friends of the Israel Museum

Poland was not the only country in which Torah arks were embellished with representations of the menorah and the other sanctuary appurtenances; in fact, the practice may have originated in Italy. For example, the inner sides of the doors of an ark from Saluzzo, Italy, are decorated as follows: the upper halves show the menorah and the revelation at Mount Sinai, while the lower halves bear the altar and the shewbread table.[3]

The menorah, the shewbread table, and other sanctuary appurtenances were frequently embroidered on Torah ark valances in Ashkenazi synagogues (fig. 1). This tradition flourished in particular in 18th-century Bohemia; many examples are housed in the Jewish Museum of Prague. Professional Jewish embroiderers in Bavaria also created ark curtains and valances depicting the sanctuary objects; some of them are in fact known by name: Elkana of Naumberg and Jacob Koppel Gans. The latter embroidered a magnificent ark curtain and valance in 1773 (today in the collection of The Jewish Museum, New York):[4] the sanctuary objects, with the menorah in the center, are shown on the valance, while a larger menorah is portrayed again, in the center of the curtain, with the inscription "a menorah of gold" (p. 105).

Beginning in the 19th century, Torah ark curtains with representations of the menorah began to appear in another cultural environment: the Ottoman Empire. Of particular interest are the Torah ark curtains decorated with metal appliques, mainly from the vicinity of Istanbul and Edirna.[5] In one ark curtain of this group (p. 107), the central motif is of a highly stylized menorah with floral tendrils growing out of its leg. Other Turkish ark curtains bear a menorah composed of the verses of Psalm 67, with the verse "I am ever mindful of the Lord" (*shiwiti* . . .) inscribed above. These curtains are actually embroidered *shiwiti* plaques, with the added value of the menorah serving as a protective charm (see article by E. Juhasz in this volume). The menorah with Psalm 67 is also the central motif in a *shiwiti* ark curtain from Ankara, dated 1826, unique for its colorful chain-stitch embroidery; it, too, combines the menorah's role as a symbol of the Temple with its power as a magical charm.

4
Hanukkah lamp
Italy, 18th century
Israel Museum Collection

Visual representations of the menorah and the other sanctuary appurtenances may be traced even further, by drawing open the ark curtain, so to speak, and examining the decorations of the Torah scrolls inside: There was a custom, albeit not very common, in Germany and in the Ashkenazi Dutch community, of embroidering such representations on Torah mantles, as well.

Particularly prominent among the silver Torah ornaments bearing depictions of the sanctuary appurtenances is a group of Torah finials (*rimmonim*) and Torah crowns from Italy. Most of these objects were created in Venice, which was a major center for the manufacture of Jewish ceremonial objects. Attached to the silver finials and crowns, which were made in repoussé technique in the baroque style, were cast elements, mostly gilt, representing the sanctuary appurtenances. For example, a pair of high, tower-shaped finials from 17th-century Venice has small models of the menorah and other sacred objects screwed onto it. Identical components (probably ready-made in silversmiths' shops) were attached to Torah crowns (p. 104). Interestingly, Italian silversmiths used the same small silver models of the sanctuary objects in *Shaddai* charms, made to be hung over infants' cradles (fig. 2). Here, once again, the menorah evolved from a religious symbol of hope for redemption to a charm believed to be imbued with magical protective powers.

בחנוכה ובפורים אומרים זה
על הנסים ועל הפורקן ועל הגבורות ועל
התשועות ועל הנפלאות ועל הנחמות ועל
המלחמות שעשית לאבותינו בימים ההם ובזמן
הזה:
בחנוכה אומרים זה:
בימי מתתיהו בן יוחנן כהן גדול חשמנאי ובניו
כשעמדה מלכות יון הרשעה על עמך ישראל ל
להשכיחם תורתך ולהעבירם מחקי רצונך ואתה
ברחמיך הרבים עמדת להם בעת צרתם רבת את
ריבם דנת את דינם נקמת את נקמתם מברת

5
The menorah alongside Judith and Holophernes in a manuscript of the *Grace after Meals*
Vienna, 1739

In Germany, during the second half of the 18th century, the menorah began to play a prominent role in another type of ceremonial object, namely, silver Torah shields, especially in Nuremberg, and later, under the inspiration of the latter, in Augsburg and Fürth as well (fig. 3). In these very common Torah shields (dozens of examples of the type are known), the menorah is the dominant decorative motif, often shown above the tablets of the law.[6]

Menorah and Hanukkah Lamp

In the context of the Jewish festivals, one of the most frequent representations of the menorah occurs – not surprisingly – on Hanukkah lamps. The story of the rededication of the Temple in Jerusalem and the miracle of the cruse of oil fired the imaginations of artists and patrons alike, being considered a suitable subject for the backplates of Hanukkah lamps, whether as a symbolic representation of the Temple menorah or as an illustration of Aaron kindling the menorah. Jewish artists in Italy, Germany, Holland, Morocco, and Poland all made Hanukkah lamps whose backplates are decorated with the menorah (fig. 4 and p. 106). Eighteenth-century illuminated manuscripts sometimes include a picture of the seven-branched menorah illustrating the special passage added to the Grace after Meals on Hanukkah; an example may be seen in the Grace after Meals manuscript written by the scribe Aaron Wolf Herlingen of Vienna, in which the additional section is accompanied by a picture of Judith and Holophernes (fig. 5).

As for freestanding Hanukkah lamps for the synagogue, in contrast to the domestic Hanukkah lamps with backplates, their basic design was inspired by that of the Tabernacle menorah described in the Bible.[7] An example is a brass Hanukkah lamp from Poland, dated to the 17th century (fig. 6). In the late 17th century, a type of freestanding silver Hanukkah lamp for private use (smaller than those used in

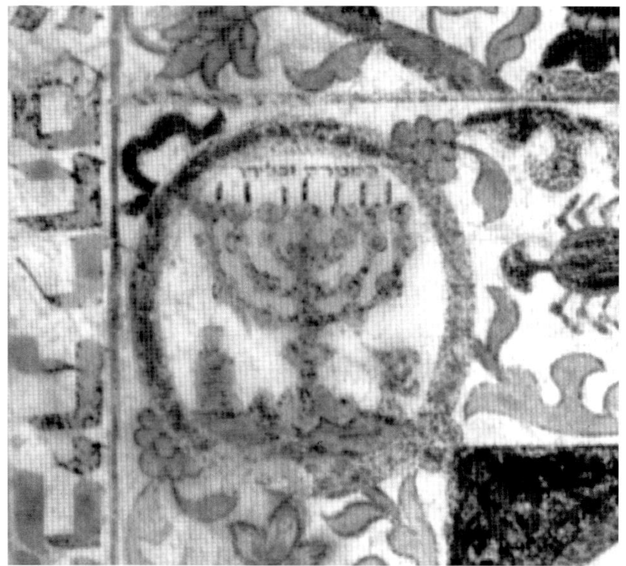

7
Hanukkah lamp inspired by the Tabernacle menorah
Frankfurt am Main, late 17th century
Israel Museum Collection, Stieglitz Collection, made possible through a donation by Erica and Ludwig Jesselson, New York, to American Friends

8
Detail from a ketubbah
Venice, 1740
Israel Museum Collection

synagogues) appeared in Frankfurt am Main, its branches decorated with "knobs and flowers" (*kaftor vaferah*). A typical example of these lamps was made by an artist from Frankfurt named Johann Valentin Schüller (fig. 7).[8]

The menorah was also depicted on objects for use on other festivals, but less frequently. It appears, for example, among the decorations for the booths (*sukkot*) used on the Feast of Tabernacles. The Israel Museum possesses nine painted decorative plaques from the *sukkah* of Rabbi Immanuel Loew (1854–1944), rabbi of the community of Szeged, Hungary. Seven of the plaques describe the seven *ushpizin* (the "guests" who, according to tradition, visit each booth during the Sukkot festival. Another plaque shows a stag supporting a Levites' laver, and the last bears a picture of a magnificent golden menorah, inscribed with the verse: "Let the seven lamps give light at the front of the menorah" (p. 100). The seven lamps of this menorah may symbolize the seven *ushpizin*.

The Menorah on Objects for Personal Use

Representations of the menorah and of the other sanctuary appurtenances may also be found on personal items associated with the Jewish life cycle. For example, many Italian *ketubbot* (marriage contracts), particularly from the vicinity of Venice, feature a pattern of four medallions showing the menorah and its accessories, the Ark of the Covenant and the cherubim, the laver and its stand, and the shewbread table (fig. 8). The function of these illustrations in *ketubbot*, like that of representations of Jerusalem, was most probably to preserve the memory of the destruction of the Temple.[9] In a few cases, the menorah is shown alone, without the other sanctuary objects; an example is a very early *ketubbah* from Rome, dated 1627, which features the menorah at the top of the page, just under a picture of Jerusalem. A unique *ketubbah* with a representation of the menorah, together with other sanctuary implements that are not part of the usual repertoire, comes from Lugo, Italy, and is dated 1821 (p. 68).

The menorah, which once figured centrally in art associated with death and burial, lost its importance in that context in the modern era. In contrast to ancient times, there are almost no examples of the menorah as a symbol on Jewish tombstones in the modern period. Even when a menorah seems to appear on a tombstone, closer examination reveals that the object in question is a Sabbath lamp with three- or five-branches; similar in shape to the menorah. Such candelabra were occasionally depicted on women's tombstones. On the other hand, the seven-branched menorah occurs quite frequently on memorial lamps and *Yahrzeit* plaques, as, for example, a memorial lamp of carved and painted wood from Morocco (p. 98) and a silver memorial lamp from Syria.

6

Synagogue Hanukkah lamp
Poland, 17th century
Israel Museum Collection

Other personal items on which the menorah traditionally appears are *tallit* (prayer shawl) and *tefillin* (phylactery) bags from Algiers, embroidered in metal thread on velvet. A typical pattern in this group shows the menorah, sometimes together with other sanctuary objects, between two spiral columns topped by lions.

In Italy, the menorah made its appearance in heraldry, in the coats of arms of various Jewish families.[10] Some Jewish families in Rome incorporated the menorah in their coats of arms, together with some other component. Thus, a lion with a menorah on its back is the coat of arms of the Tedesco (Ashkenazi) family; a stag with a menorah on its back that of the Castelnuovo family; and two rampant lions, supporting a menorah on either side, that of the Di Segni family. These family insignia decorate Torah scroll and ark ornaments donated by family members to synagogues, as well as *ketubbot*. For example, the Di Segni coat of arms is featured, among other symbols, on a Torah scroll wrapper from 1656 (IMJ 150/52).

Yet another type of object bearing a representation of the menorah is a pair of mortars cast in Verona for Jewish doctors by the De Levis family. One of them, probably made in 1480, was made by the artist Servius de Levis (IMJ 192/26; p.138).[11] The significance of the menorah in this context is difficult to determine; it most probably indicates the religious-national identity of the doctor who owned the mortar, and was not a family emblem. Perhaps this is an early example of the menorah being used as a symbol of national identity in the modern era.

Religious to Secular Symbol

The menorah was one of the main visual symbols embraced by the Zionist movement (see article by R. Arbel in this volume). The Jewish artist Israel Rukhomovsky (1860–1934), for example, used the menorah as an ornamental motif for silver plaques on which he engraved the text of the Zionist anthem *Hatikvah* (p. 196). Bezalel artists also made use of it in many of their creations (see article by S. Steinberg in this volume).

Simultaneously with its adoption as a Zionist, national symbol, the menorah's role as a religious symbol weakened. At this point, however, an interesting phenomenon occurred: relatively small seven-branched candelabra of brass began to appear in Europe, based on the model appearing on the Arch of Titus (pp. 190–191). Thus, at the very time that the religious meaning of the menorah gave way to its role as a national symbol, the menorah became a popular object in many Jewish households.

1 D. Davidovitch, *Wall-Paintings of Synagogues in Poland* (Jerusalem, 1968), 31, 37 (Hebrew).

2 I. Fishof (ed.), *Jewish Art Masterpieces from the Israel Museum* (Jerusalem, 1994), 36.

3 U. Nahon, *Holy Arks and Ritual Appurtenances from Italy in Israel* (Tel Aviv, 1970), 68–71 (Hebrew).

4 N. L. Keeblatt and V. B. Mann, *Treasures of the Jewish Museum* (New York, 1986), 108.

5 E. Juhasz (ed.), *Sephardi Jews in the Ottoman Empire*, exh. cat., Israel Museum (Jerusalem, 1990), 90–92.

6 R. Grafman, *Crowning Glory – Silver Torah Ornaments of the Jewish Museum, New York* (New York, 1996), nos. 21, 23, 29, 30–32, 53–60.

7 M. Narkiss, *Hanukkah Lamps* (Jerusalem, 1939), 71–81 (Hebrew).

8 C. Benjamin, *The Stieglitz Collection, Masterpieces of Jewish Art*, exh. cat. The Israel Museum (Jerusalem, 1987), no. 134.

9 S. Sabar, *Mazal Tov, Illuminated Jewish Marriage Contracts from the Israel Museum Collection* (Jerusalem, 1993), 43–77; I. Fishof, "Above my Chief Joy: Depictions of Jerusalem in Italian Ketubot," *Jewish Art* 9 (1982): 61–75.

10 D. Di Castro, "Gli stemmi degli ebrei romani," in *Arte Ebraica a Roma e nel Lazio*, ed. D. Di Castro (Rome, 1994), 141–169.

11 Benjamin, (above, n. 8), no. 279.

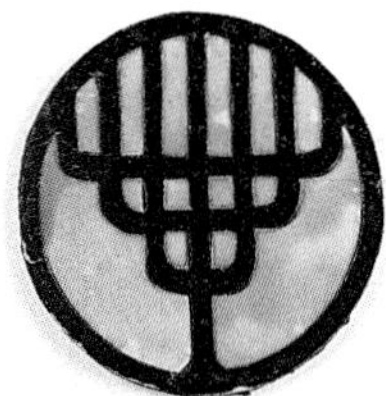

"A Charm Against a Number of Afflictions"

Generations of Jews who viewed the menorah as a symbol bearing a message for the community as a whole also looked to it as a source of magical powers that would protect the individual and guarantee good fortune. Schematic depictions of the menorah appear on glass amulets of the 4th century CE and on jewelry. They are particularly common on *mizrah* and *shiwiti* plaques found in both the home and the synagogue. "Whoever looks at the menorah daily and reflects upon it, it is accounted as though he himself had lit the menorah, and he is assured a place in the world to come . . ." (from a Sephardi prayer book).

The number of branches of the menorah was also counted as one of the menorah's special qualities. Seven was viewed as a magical number, corresponding to the number of planets in the heavens and the number of days of the week. Particular amuletic value was attributed to menorahs drawn in letters, especially the letters of Psalm 67, which has seven verses and forty-nine (7 x 7) words.

The menorah's seven branches also correspond to Herzl's seven golden stars, which signified a seven-hour work day – a remote ideal in the 19th century – adding the aspect of social progress to the menorah's many meanings.

Previous page:
Shivviti amulet
Poland, 18th century
Drilled and engraved silver, 15 x 9.6 cm
Israel Museum Collection, Feuchtwanger Collecion, purchased and donated by Baruch and Ruth Rappaport, Geneva

Amuletic plaque for protection of the house or tomb
Byzantine period, 5th century CE
Limestone, H 31.5 cm
Courtesy of the Institute of Archaeology, The Hebrew University of Jerusalem

Above:
Amuletic pendants for good luck and protection
Byzantine period, 4th–5th century CE
Glass
Israel Museum Collection, gift of Leo Mildenberg; Reifenberg Collection

Right:
Shivviti amulet
Persia, 19th – 20th century
Silver, repoussé and engraved
10.4 x 8.8 cm
Israel Museum Collection

Opposite:
Shivviti plaque made by Zvi Samuel Hakatan
Saqqez, Iranian Kurdistan, 1913
Handwritten in ink on paper, watercolor
96 x 34 cm
Israel Museum Collection, gift of Eliezer Ben-Dov, Teheran

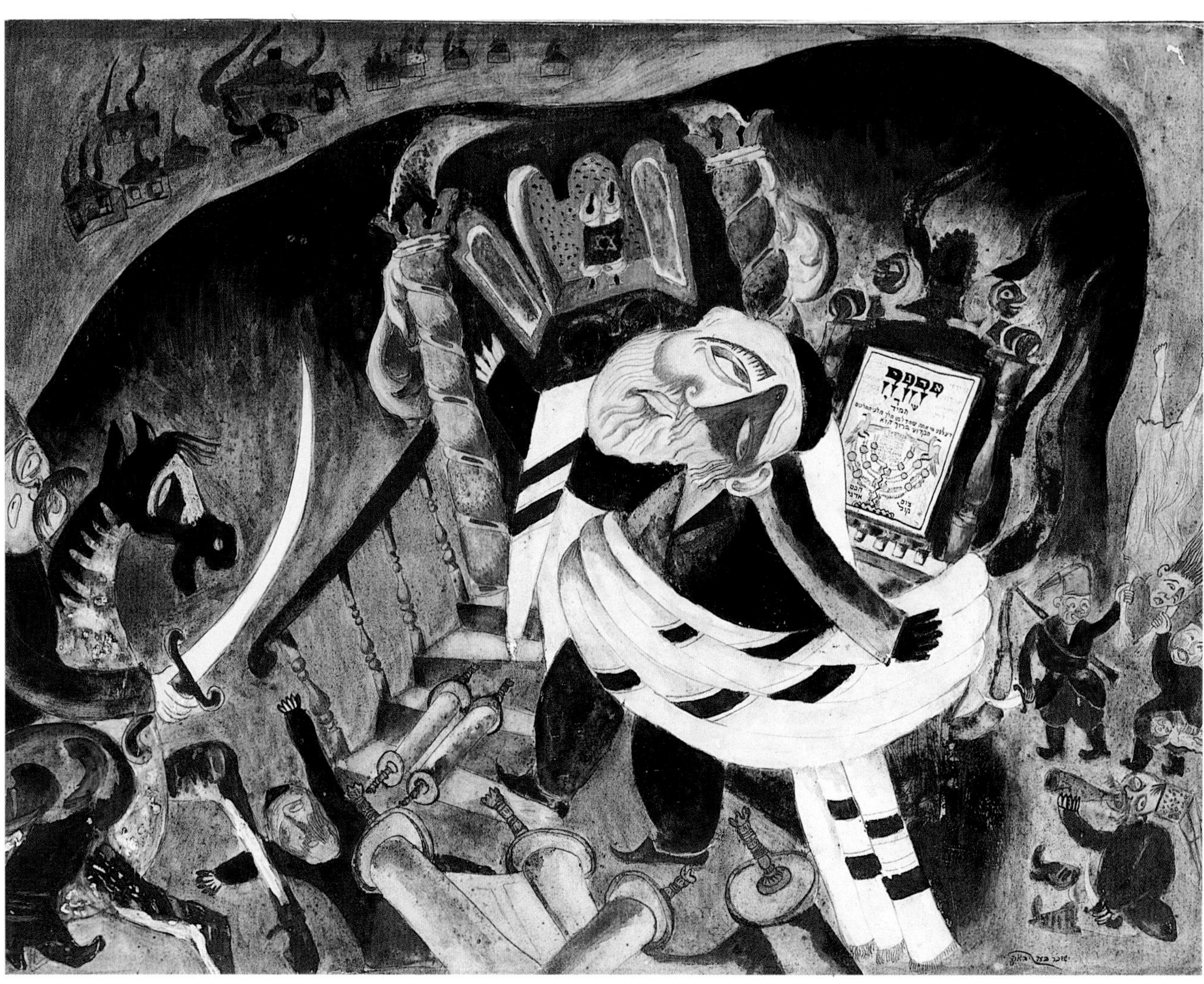

Drawing from the Pogrom series, 1918
Issachar Ryback, Russia, 1897–1935
Pencil, india ink, and watercolor on paper
64 x 49 cm
Collection of Mishkan L'Omanut, Museum of Art, En Harod

Opposite:
Shivviti plaque made by Joel Solomon of Wohart, Germany, 19th century
Handwritten in ink on parchment
14.5 x 11 cm
Israel Museum Collection, bequest of Felix Perla, London

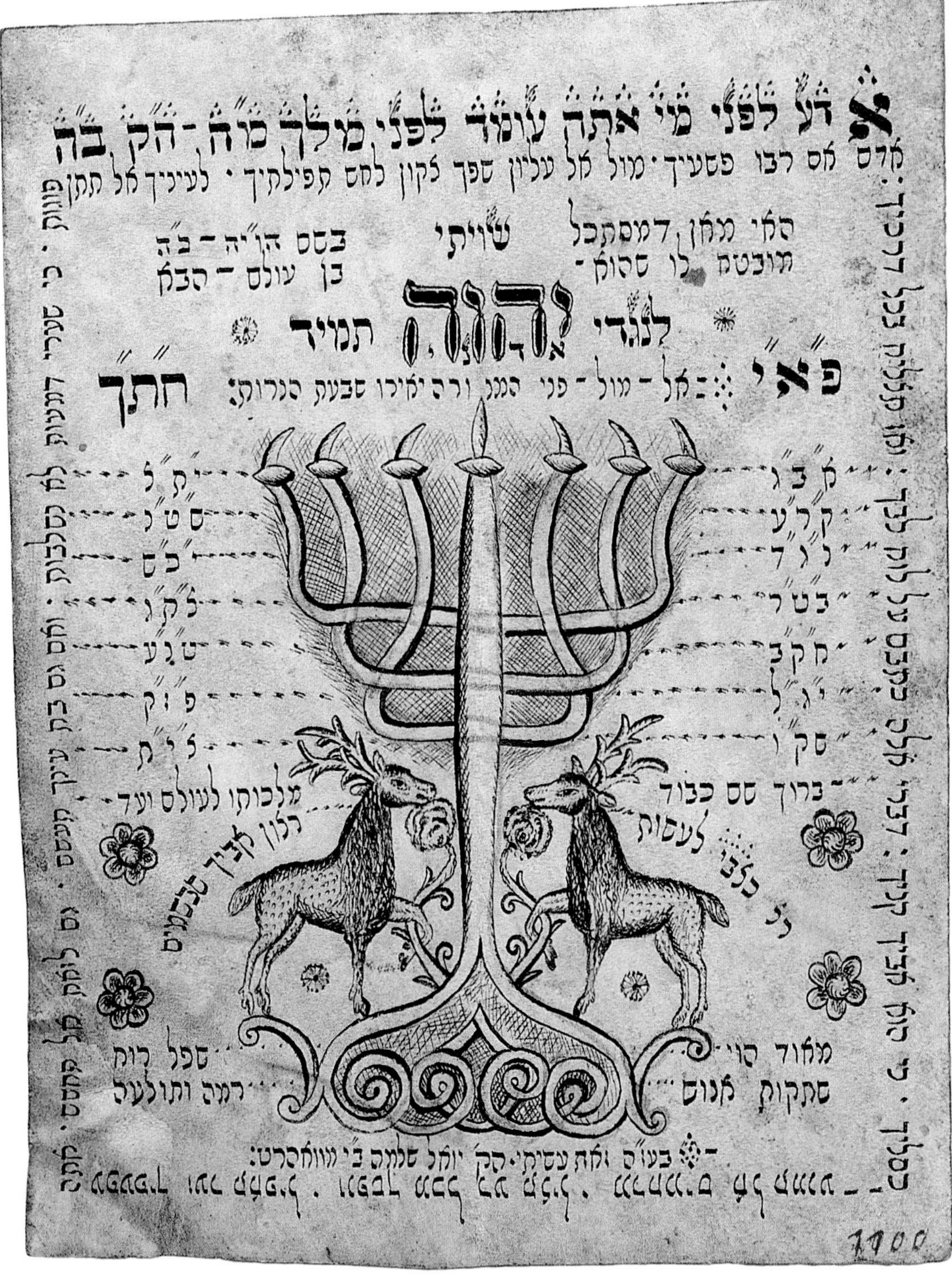
דע לפני מי אתה עומד לפני מלך מה״ה הק״בה
שויתי
לנגדי
תמיד

כתר
תורה
אנכי ה' אלהיך
לא יהיה לך
לא תשא את
זכור את יום
כבד את אביך
לא תרצח
לא תנאף
לא תגנב
לא תענה
לא תחמד
שדי
שדי
שויתי
יהוה
לנגדי
תמיד
כי שם ה אקרא הבו גדל לאלהינו
בשכמלו

Synagogue of the Bucharian community in Jerusalem, 1966

Opposite:
Shivviti curtain for a Torah ark
Istanbul, early 20th century
Wool, chain-stich embroidery in wool thread
208 x 162 cm
Israel Museum Collection

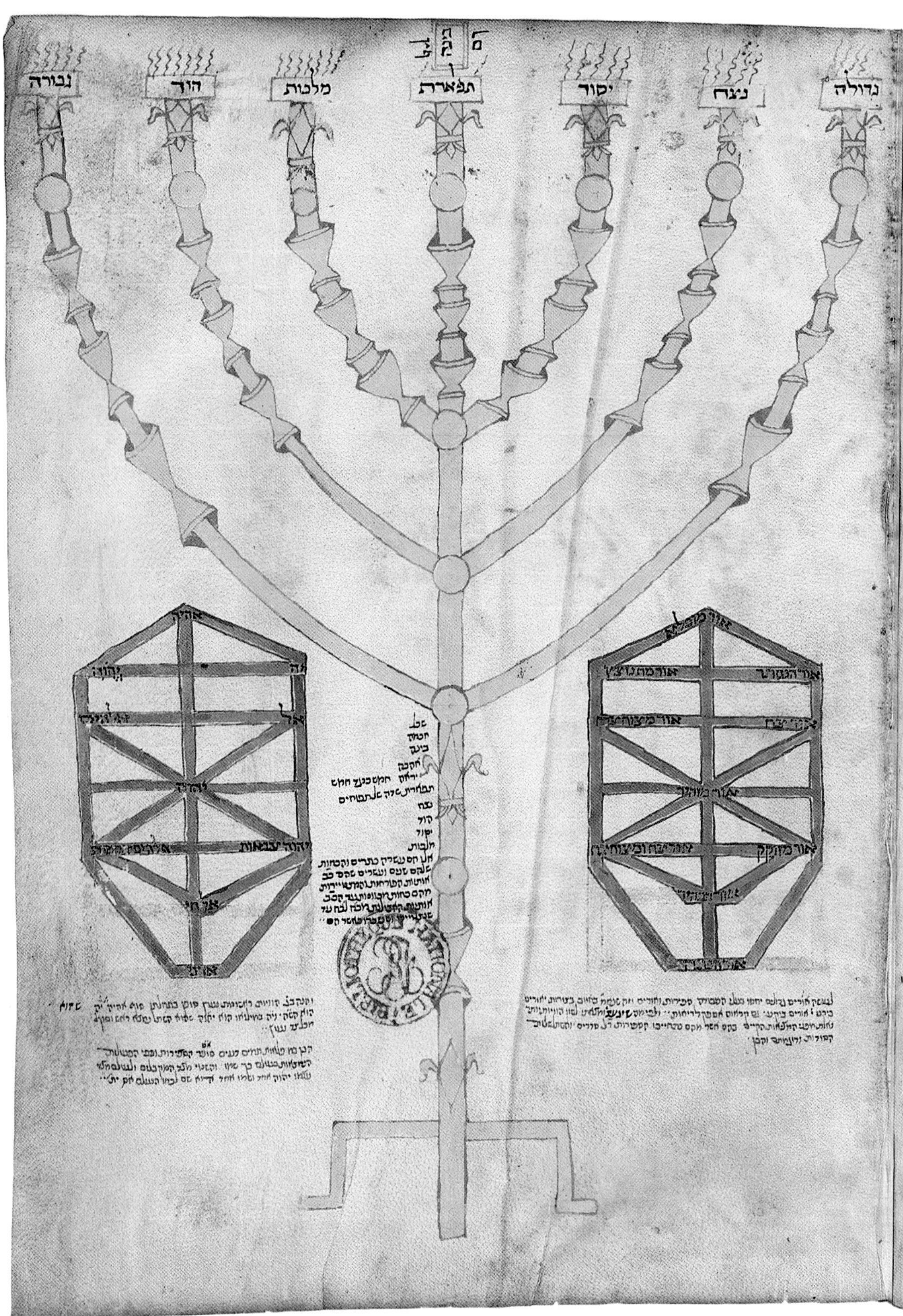

Page from the book *Portals of Light* by Rabbi Joseph Gikatilla
Spain, 1485–1490
Handwritten in ink on parchment, tempera
27 x 20 cm
Bibliothèque Nationale de France, Paris
On either side of the menorah, a sefirotic tree can be seen; beneath one of them the different Names of Light are inscribed and beneath the other the Divine Names.

Moshe Idel

Binah, The Eighth *Sefirah**
The Menorah in Kabbalah

1
Sefirotic tree on an amulet made in Jerusalem
19th century
Israel Museum Collection

The menorah is one of the most ubiquitous of the many symbols with which Kabbalistic literature is replete. Two main symbolic interpretations of the meaning of the menorah in antiquity may be distinguished. Modern scholarship holds that the menorah served in the Bible and in a number of Second Temple texts as a symbol for the Godhead.[1] By contrast, Flavius Josephus (*Antiquities*, III, 144–146) claims that the menorah symbolizes the celestial bodies, namely, the planets and the sun. Both of these interpretations greatly influenced medieval Kabbalah. The astronomical interpretation found its expression in the writings of Rabbi Abraham Abulafia and Rabbi Joseph Gikatilla, among others. In his commentary on the Pentateuch, Abulafia states: "The seven lamps allude to the seven planets, the three lamps on one side corresponding to Saturn, Jupiter, and Mars, and the three lamps on the other side corresponding to the moon, Mercury and Venus, with one lamp between those mentioned. And these seven stars are the gates to the world; God created them as one piece in the menorah" (Sefer Mafteah Hasefirot, MS Milano-Ambrosiana 53, fol. 164b).

Similarly, Gikatilla explains: "The menorah is made completely of pure gold, and the lamps are aligned so as to shed light, just as the seven planets are positioned so as to shed light; and these seven lamps correspond to the seven planets. Hence the intention of these is known – these seven are based upon the three [elements], namely, gold, silver and copper. And thus have we expounded the secret of the menorah" (Sefer Ginat Egoz [Jerusalem, 1989], p. 269).

According to Gikatilla, there are two sets of parallels between the menorah and the material world: the first is between the seven lamps and the planets, and the second is between the materials mentioned (gold, silver, and copper) and the three worlds – the supernal, the intermediate, and the lower world, in that order. These analogies express a perception of the menorah as a microcosm of the entire world (the macrocosm).[2] However, the other interpretation, which sees the menorah and the details of its construction as a symbol of the divine powers known as the *sefirot*, enjoyed far greater influence. Already during the early days of Kabbalah, Rabbi Asher ben David, a Provencal Kabbalist active in the first half of the 13th century, argued that the menorah

> is made entirely – its base and its shaft, its cups, calyxes, and petals – from the bar [of metal] itself, without being joined at any point, and likewise for the six branches. And on each one there is a lamp, and in the middle branch is the seventh lamp, and all the rest of them are facing it, as a symbol that the middle one is the principal one: an allusion to the middle of the seven directions [i.e., the four compass points, together with up, down, and center], that place which is the essence and which sustains them all; thus, the seven directions are alluded to in the menorah, and it is like a cluster. And this is a sign of their being drawn down from the Infinite, which is the light that is the oil that is put in each lamp, and by its means they burn and illuminate, and this is a sign and allusion to the central branch, that sustains all (Perush Shem Hameforash, ed. D. Abrams [Los Angeles, 1996], pp. 224–225).[3]

* A *sefirah* is one of the ten divine manifestations according to Kabbalistic texts.

The menorah serves as a model for both the structure of the *sefirot* and for their activity (fig. 1). From a structural viewpoint, the seven lamps correspond to the seven lower *sefirot*, which are divided into two triads, in the center of which stands *Tiferet* (splendor), the central line connecting them. The oil and the light are the abundance that flows from the Infinite, which is absorbed by the central line that then divides it among the six *sefirot*, or the six spacial directions. As the menorah is all of one piece, it is able to serve as a symbolic solution to one of the most important problems in Kabbalistic theosophic thought: how to explain the absolute unity of the divine powers. Unity within multiplicity was the metaphysical solution adopted, for the most part, by Spanish Kabbalah, for which the menorah became one of the important symbols. But beyond the unity among the seven *sefirot* that are considered as one entity, according to this passage, the menorah also expresses the presence within the sefirotic system of the supernal divine power, the Infinite (*Ein Sof*), from which there follows also a dynamic understanding of the Godhead, which goes beyond a merely static unity. Another Kabbalist, Rabbi Isaac ben Samuel of Acre, wrote in this connection at the beginning of the 14th century: "Therefore it is hammered [of one piece], to allude that the supernal structure is united in a true unity, without any separation or division.

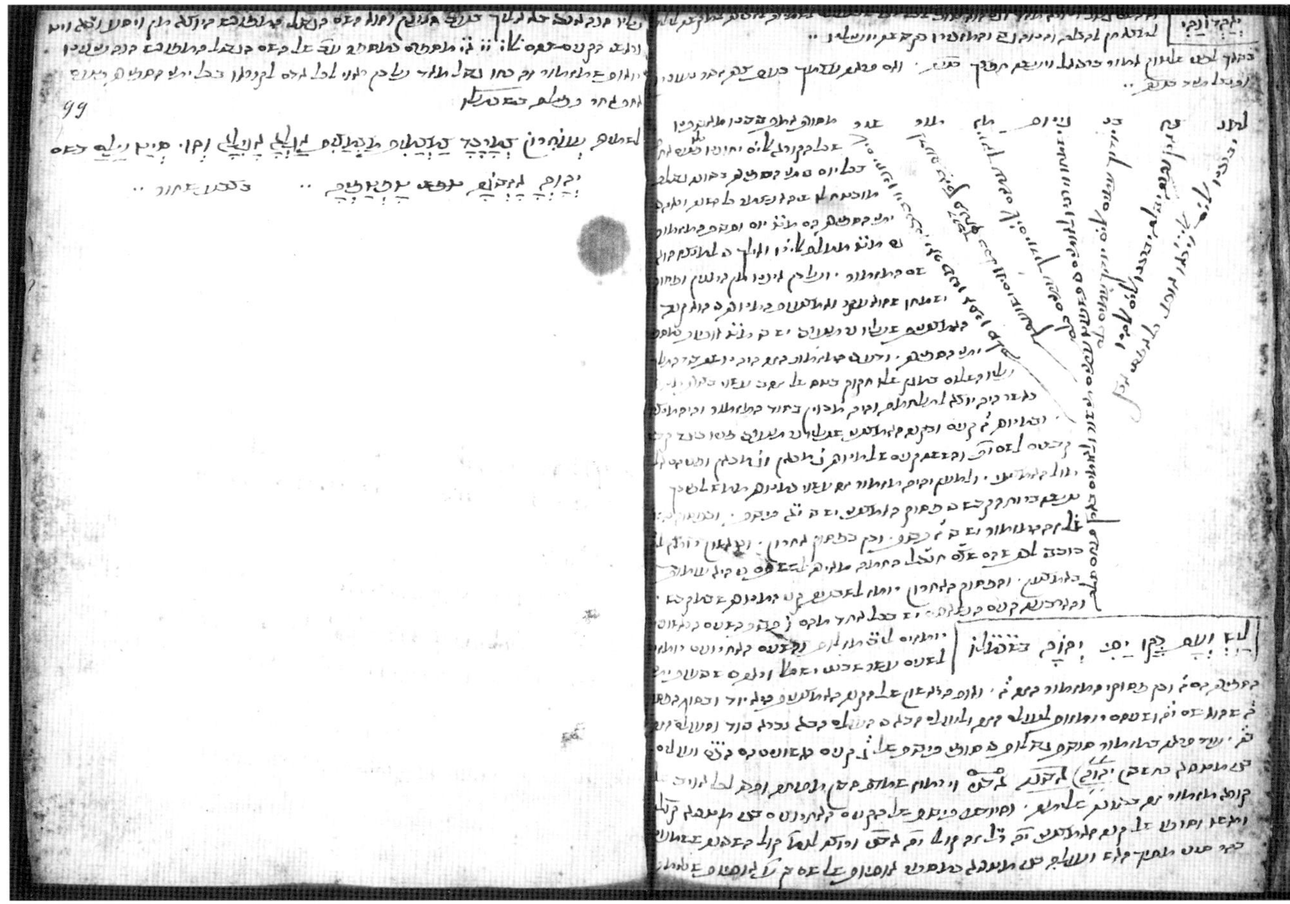

2
Menorah drawn from the verses of Psalm 67 in a manuscript from Spain
Late 14th – early 15th century
National Bavarian Library, Munich

And at the tops of the branches are their souls, for the menorah without its lamps is like a body without a soul, and its soul is the lamp of God . . . And the soul is the oil, and the wick alludes to repentance, and the flame is an allusion to the Supreme Crown, which sheds light upon all those places that are lit up, and there flows from it all kinds of light and blessing" (*Sefer Me'irat Einayim* [Jerusalem, 1993], p. 161).

The supernal structure is identical with the seven lower sefirot, above which is the wick, alluding to the eighth *sefirah,* while the flame symbolizes the highest *sefirah,* from which all Divine abundance originates. Here, as in the interpretation of Rabbi Asher, the Divine Presence is emphasized in a static model, but this time using the relations of body – corresponding to the seven lower *sefirot* – and soul – corresponding to the *sefirot* above them.

According to a later text, written by an anonymous mid-14th century Kabbalist, the menorah itself was the image of God seen by Moses; nevertheless, this Kabbalist finds it difficult to explain the possibility of unity within multiplicity. He writes as follows:

> And Moses found this difficult, that is, that there are forty-nine Gates of Understanding and corresponding to them forty-nine sections of the menorah; and Moses found this aspect of the making of the menorah difficult, namely, that all these forms should be one thing. And even the Shekhinah, which is the diadem, found this thing difficult . . . And what was this thing? The letters MNZPKh,** which are the awesome supernal letters, hidden within the supreme wisdom . . . And this is the image upon which Moses gazed, because it was in the form of the menorah, and it was difficult for him, until it became known to him that all was for the purpose of the unity of the menorah, that is, that all of the forms of the letters would be in the fiftieth gate, which is hidden within [the *sefirah*] of *Binah* (Understanding), like the soul within the body (*Sefer Hatemunah* [Lemberg, 1892], pp. 23b–24a).

According to this anonymous Kabbalist, the menorah is to be identified with the hidden qualities of the eighth *sefirah, Binah* (Understanding), which was associated by the Kabbalists with the Forty-Nine Gates of Understanding received by Moses according to Talmudic lore. This number, however, also corresponds both to the sections of the menorah and to the basic parts of the letters of the Hebrew alphabet, as broken down by this exegete further on in the above quotation. It follows that in his vision Moses saw a menorah that was not only a structure, such as is known to us from the regular descriptions, but also a combination of all the elements of the Hebrew consonants.

One of the most interesting works concerning the menorah is that of Guillaume Postel, who was active in the mid-16th century in Italy and France; Postel composed a Kabbalistic interpretation – in Hebrew, French, Italian and Latin – of the menorah seen by Moses. This work combines cosmic, theosophic, and Christian-messianic elements. Thus, for example, he writes: "The menorah is like a tree within which is arranged the body of universal man; just as the world as a whole was created entirely from the seven planets and the four elements, so was the order of the menorah – from the seven branches which are in one body, and from the four parts, which are the branch, the cup, the calyx, and the petals. For the length of the world was decreed for seven periods, over six thousand years, after having been created in six days, and such is the way of nature (*Perush Lemenorat Moshe*, p. 41).[4]

Here – apparently for the first time – the symbols of the tree and of man are intermingled together with the symbol of the menorah, in order to suggest a structure that symbolizes not only the model for the creation of the world, but also its duration – its length – based upon a seven-fold structure. At the beginning of the work, Postel drew the menorah in a form symbolizing all ten *sefirot*; according to this sketch, the base symbolizes the four creatures of the Divine Chariot. In another interpretation, Postel states that "all of Israel whom God infuses with the holiness of their souls are the lamps of the menorah that are burned by the commandments of the Torah; therefore it was incumbent upon Aaron and the Levitic priests to trim them, for its lamps are the lamps of the configuration, and that is the spirit and the soul" (p. 56).

Unlike the theosophic approaches and those Kabbalistic texts in which the menorah is identified with various divine potentia – the ten *sefirot;* the seven [lower] *sefirot*; the *sefirah* of *Binah* or of *Hesed* (Mercy) – in *Tiqqunei Zohar*, the menorah is identified specifically with the non-divine world. In several discussions, the menorah is identified with the world of the supernal angels. Thus, for example, it is stated there that: "Like the vision which the Lord showed to Moses, so did he make the menorah: This is Metatron, whose letter *Mem* is the menorah, and Nuriel, who is its fire" (*Tiqqunei Zohar* [Jerusalem, 1978], p. 119b).

The elevation of the menorah to the level of an important Kabbalistic symbol contributed to a further development, which can be traced to the beginning in the 14th century – the portrayal of the menorah and its branches by means of the words of Psalm 67 (fig. 2 and pp. 133, 136). This development was based upon the perception of the branches as symbols of the seven lower *sefirot*. In

** MNZPKh. An acronym for the five letters of the Hebrew alphabet – *mem, nun, zadde, peh,* and *kaf* – which have alternative written forms when appearing at the end of a word, to which various mystical qualities are attributed in rabbinic lore (Babylonian Talmud, Shabbat 104a).

many manuscripts – such as Munich 228, fol. 98 and Frankfort am Main 245 8°), different versions of this Kabbalistic exegetical conception appear. This custom also penetrated the literature of practical Kabbalah, in which charms, made of a menorah composed of verses, often appear: "A charm for protection from various troubles; recite this psalm every day in the form of the menorah" (*Sefer Rafael Hamalakh*, p. 62a). It likewise appears in numerous *shiwiti* plaques, along with the verse "I am ever mindful of the Lord's presence" (Psalms 16:8) and frequently together with the forty-two letter Divine Name (see article by E. Juhasz in this volume and pp. 137, 139).

Another interpretation of the menorah, found in medieval and Renaissance mystical and philosophical texts, identifies it with various powers of the soul: thus, for example, the 16th-century preacher Judah Moscato – under the influence of numerous earlier interpretations – states that the menorah symbolizes the seven powers of the soul (see *Sefer Nefutzot Yehudah* [Warsaw, 1880], Sermon 46).

The success of the menorah in serving as a symbol for various kinds of configurations lies in its particular structure, which combines unity and multiplicity in a single form.

1 M. Smith, "The Image of God: Notes on the Hellenization of Judaism, with Especial Reference to Goodenough's Work on Jewish Symbols," *Bulletin of the John Rylands Library* 40 (1958): 473–512.

2 For a similar view, see Rabbi Isaac ibn-Latif's work *Sha'ar Hashamayim;* M. Idel, "The Throne and the Seven-Branched Candlestick: Pico della Mirandola's Hebrew Source," *Journal of the Warburg and Courtauld Institutes* 40 (1977): 290–292.

3 E. Gottleib, *Studies in Kabbalistic Literature*, ed. J. Hacker (Tel Aviv, 1976), 564–565 (Hebrew). Cf. M. Steinschneider, *Hebräische Bibliographie Blätter* 7(1863):116; 10 (1870): 159; 12 (1872): 81, n. 2.

4 F. Secret (ed.), *Guillame Postel, 1510–1581, et son interpretation du candelabre de Moyse* (Nieuwkoop, 1966).

Esther Juhasz

The Amuletic Menorah

The Menorah and Psalm 67

Whoever recites Psalm 67 in the form of the menorah, no evil shall befall him, and he shall succeed in his endeavors.

1
Shivviti
Eastern Europe, 19th century
Israel Museum Collection
Bequest of Felix Perla

One common way of drawing the menorah is through using lines of written words. The most popular text for this "written drawing" is Psalm 67, sometimes referred to as "the Menorah Psalm" or the "May God Be Gracious to Us Psalm." Other texts featured in such drawings of menorahs are Psalms 121 (*Shir Hama'alot*), 122, 124, 128, and others, as well as the prayer *Ana Beko'akh* attributed to Rabbi Nehunyah ben Hakanah. These "letter-drawn menorahs" have mystical and magical connotations and are credited with apotropaic powers.

The relationship between Psalm 67 and the menorah is based on the number seven: the psalm has seven verses (not counting the first, introductory, verse), corresponding to the seven branches of the menorah, and its Hebrew text consists of exactly forty-nine (7 x 7) words. The parallel between the structure of the menorah and that of the psalm has been seen as a mystical substructure, on which further connections and parallels were based, such as the analogy with the seven planets and the seven days of the week, and the connection between the forty-nine letters of the psalm and the forty-nine days of the Counting of the Omer. The most familiar context in which this type of menorah appears is the *siddur* (prayer book). In many prayer books, particularly those including Kabbalistic customs (see below), the menorah constructed from Psalm 67 appears in two contexts: in the Morning Service, as one of the psalms recited (according to the Sephardi rite) in *pesukei dezimra;* or in the prayers accompanying the Counting of the Omer. Sometimes a separate "menorah page," preferably written on parchment, is placed in the prayer book.

The menorah-psalm appears on a variety of objects, most prominent of which are decorated wall plaques, mainly for synagogue use. These plaques are called menorah plaques, owing to the central position of the menorah in their design, or *shiwiti* plaques, after the first word in the Hebrew text of the verse "I am ever mindful of the Lord's presence" (Psalms 16:8), often inscribed above the menorah. Such plaques, which sometimes depict several menorahs, are particularly common in synagogues of the Jewish communities of Iraq, Kurdistan, Syria and North Africa, but they are also found in Ashkenazi synagogues (figs. 1, 5 and pp. 137, 139, 141).

The menorah-psalm combination is also found on *mizrah* plaques (a type of plaque hung on the wall facing Jerusalem and most frequently encountered in European countries; fig. 2); Omer-counting plaques (fig. 3); plaques bearing various benedictions; plaques with illustrations of the holy places of Israel; and others (fig. 4). Similarly, they appear on Torah arks (p. 64), ark curtains (p. 140), and on personal amulets written on parchment or paper or silver pendants or armbands worn as jewelry (the latter found mainly in Iran, pp. 133, 136).

Forms of the Menorah

Sometimes the menorah is drawn in lines and the words of Psalm 67 are written along the seven branches; usually, however, the words themselves form the branches. In terms of shape, the menorah-psalms exhibit several variations: the branches, for example, can be rounded, angular, diagonal,

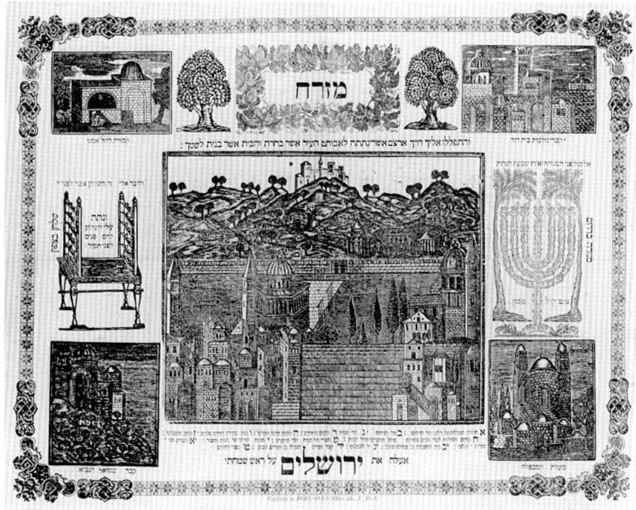

2
Mizrah
Israel Beck Press, Jerusalem
19th century
Israel Museum Collection, gift of Dr. Moshe Spitzer

or wavy. The distribution of the words on the menorah, however, is fixed: the first verse, "For the leader, with instrumental music. A psalm. A song" is inscribed above the menorah as an upper line, its letters divided into seven groups of three letters each, except for the middle group which has only two. Occasionally, these groups of words are placed in the positions of the seven flames of the menorah. The psalm's remaining verses are distributed symmetrically among the six branches of the menorah and the central stem. Sometimes two three-letter words, formed by the last letters of the verses, appear next to the legs of the menorah, accompanied by the words "voice" and "Lord," which in Hebrew equal the numerical value (*gematria*) of these letters.

The menorah generally appears in combination with various verses and texts, written out either in full or in abbreviation (using the first and last letters of the words, or encoded in some way, such as *gematria*). Most prevalent are the various Divine Names: the Tetragrammaton, the Lord, and *Shaddai* (these names are sometimes also combined) and various coded versions of the names, such as one consisting of seventy-two letters and one of forty-two letters, the latter comprising the initial letters of the words of the prayer *Ana Beko'akh*. The texts on these plaques, revolve around several themes: the praise of God and man's place in relation to him, such as "Know before whom you stand, before the King of Kings of Kings" (Avot 3) and "I am ever mindful of the Lord's presence" (this verse was perhaps the most widely used); and hope for redemption, such as "I wait for your deliverance, O Lord!" (Genesis 49:18) or its Aramaic translation, both consisting of just three words. There are also biblical verses referring to the Temple menorah, its preparation, and its kindling, such as "Now this is how the lampstand was made: it was hammered work of gold, hammered from base to petal. According to the pattern that the Lord had shown Moses, so was the lampstand made" (Numbers 8:4) and "let the seven lamps give light at the

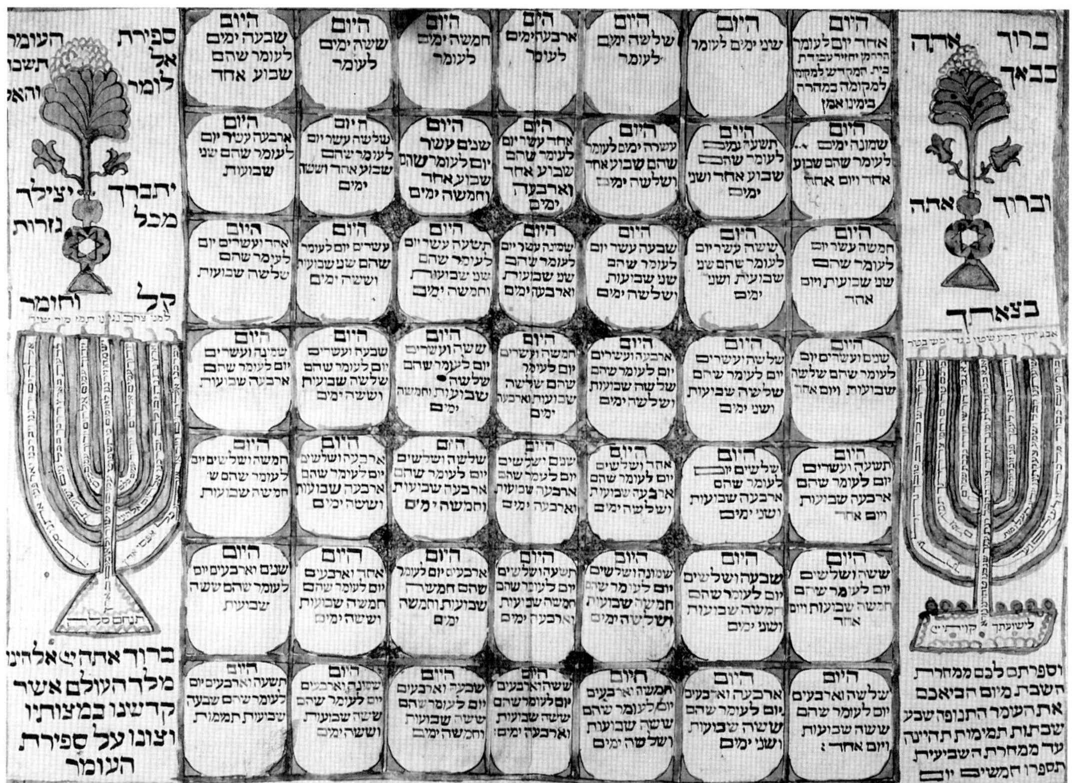

3
Plaque for Counting the Omer
Middle East, 19th century
Israel Museum Collection

front of the lampstand" (Numbers 8:2); similarly, there are verses relating to the menorah, to light, and to God as the source of light and deliverance: "With you is the fountain of life, by your light do we see light" (Psalms 36:10).

Quite frequently, the drawing of the menorah is not the only element in the plaque. At times it is the central motif, and at times several menorahs are depicted. Occasionally, the menorah is one of a group of symbolic, ornamental motifs, such as the Magen David, a pair of outspread hands in the gesture of the priestly benediction, the Tablets of the Law, animal motifs, and so forth. In some plaques, it is surrounded by various Temple implements, such as the tongs, the incense shovels, and the jug of oil. The various combinations of symbols depend on the context, the object on which the menorah is represented and its function, and the iconographic tradition according to which the object was designed.

4
Shivviti
Artist: Hayyim ben Masud Susa
Morocco, 20th century
Israel Museum Collection
Zayde Schulman

The Significance of the Menorah and Its Protective-Mystical Qualities

The combination of Psalm 67 and the menorah motif became a visual-textual symbol heavily charged with hidden meanings. It conceals various secrets, implied by numerical and other associations between the branches of the menorah, its knobs and flowers, and the words and letters of the psalm; these secrets concern temporal cosmological systems (see article by M. Idel in this volume). The mystical qualities of the menorah, with its esoteric associations, were discussed in a book called *Menorat Zahav Tahor* (Lampstand of Pure Gold), attributed to Rabbi Solomon ben Jehiel Luria (known as the Maharshal) and first printed in Prague in 1581. There we read: "The seven verses of this psalm allude to the six ends of the world, that is, east, west, north, south, heaven, earth. And the Holy One, blessed be He, is the Seventh, alluding to the middle branch, which is the body of the menorah. This verse alludes to the seventh day, that is, the Sabbath, whose merit and sanctity extend to the six work days. And it is the Tree of Life that is within the Garden. . . ."[1]

Menorahs of this type are believed to possess magical, apotropaic powers. Individual psalms, as well as the whole book of Psalms, were credited with such powers at an early stage (see, e.g., the book *Shimmush Tehillim* [Use of Psalms], which lists the particular qualities and powers of each psalm).[2] In this case, the psalm is combined with a visual pattern which in itself is reputed to have magical powers, and the combination creates a symbol whose power is greater than the mere sum of its parts.

Tradition links the use of the menorah-psalm as a protective charm with Moses and King David. The mere association of the symbol with such ancient origins, particularly with the venerated figures of Moses and David, reinforces its protective qualities and enhances its power. According to a tradition related in the text accompanying the menorah page in the prayer book, God showed Moses the menorah made up of the verses of the psalm; in addition, the menorah-psalm was engraved on King David's shield, and when he went to war it helped him vanquish his enemies. "For the sages, masters of the Kabbalah, said that the Holy One, blessed be He, showed David, peace be upon him, in the Holy Spirit, the psalm shaped like a menorah; and similarly He showed it to Moses, peace be upon him, as it is written: According to the pattern that the Lord had shown Moses, so was the lampstand made" (*Menorat Zahav Tahor*). "For this psalm was carried by King David, peace be upon him, on his shield, engraved on a sheet of gold fashioned in the shape of the menorah. And when he went to war he would commune with its secret and vanquish his enemies" *(Mahzor Yehiel ben Mattityahu,* Pisa, 1397).[3]

The renowned scholar of Kabbalah, Gershom Scholem, argues that the mystical menorah preceded the Magen David in Jewish magical lore, and the latter links the two symbols together: "It is of interest in this regard that in the late Middle Ages an entirely different tradition began to circulate about the emblem

5
Shivviti
Poland, 18th century
Israel Museum Collection
Bequest of Felix Perla

on King David's shield. Isaac Arama, a famous Spanish Jewish writer in 1470, claimed that Psalm 67 was engraved in the form of a menorah on David's escutcheon. So here we have the noteworthy combination of the menorah with the motif of the Shield of David . . ."[4]

The attribution of mystical qualities to the shape of the menorah lies in the latter's association with the Temple menorah, together with the principle that since the destruction of the Temple, prayers have taken the place of the sacrificial rites. This idea is expressed by David Abudraham (Seville, mid 14th century) in his book *Sefer Abudraham* in which he describes and explains the prayer customs of his time: "And whoever reads it every day, it is as if he were lighting the pure menorah in the Temple and as if he were welcoming the Divine Presence."[5]

The qualities ascribed to the menorah-psalm combination are related in a variety of texts: mystical works about the menorah, prayer books (beside the "menorah page"), texts on practical Kabbalah, and *shivviti* and menorah plaques. One finds an abbreviated formula repeating these qualities which reads: "Whoever looks at the menorah daily and reflects upon it, it is accounted as though he himself had lit the menorah, and he is assured a place in the world to come. Whoever recites Psalm 67 from a text whose words are set out in the form of a menorah, no evil shall befall him, and he shall succeed in his endeavors" (*Bet Oved*).[6] In other words, the symbol's special powers take effect when one looks at the menorah with the proper devotion and recites the psalm while looking at the menorah. The worshiper is thus required actively to associate the text with the shape of the menorah in his mind's eye, or in accordance with the actual pattern before him: "It is good to recite the psalm 'May God be gracious to us' in the shape of the menorah. But if the drawing is not before him, it will suffice to imagine the shape in the mind' (*Prayer Book According to the Rite of the Holy Community of Baghdad and its Environs*).[7] Concentration on the shape of the menorah is a spiritual act, symbolic of lighting the menorah in the Temple; it assures the worshiper of reward in the world to come, but also protects him or her from harm and promises success in this world.

This view is a clear expression of the Kabbalistic perception of ritual as creating a tie between the symbolic and magical aspects of things – a perception in which the concept of intention (*kavvanah*) is of key importance. According to this perception, intention is a necessary component in any prayer; without it, prayer lacks significance and meaning ("Prayer without intention is like a body without a soul," as inscribed on several *shivviti* plaques).[8] In Lurianic Kabbalah, it is intention that enables the worshipper to commune with supernal worlds, and this communion may also influence and protect against the forces of evil; thus the power of the menorah is put into effect through a symbolic act performed with the proper intention.[9]

History of the Menorah-Psalm

In all likelihood, the menorah-psalm combination was first drawn in prayer books, possibly moving on from there to other contexts. Its popularity increased as Kabbalistic rituals entered the prayer book, around the time Lurianic Kabbalah, taught in 16th-century Safed by Rabbi Isaac Luria and disseminated by his disciple Rabbi Hayyim Vital, became widely accepted among Jews.

The earliest letter-drawn menorahs known today appear in a group of 14th- and 15th-century handwritten manuscripts of the *Rome Mahzor* (a prayer book for the entire year, including both weekday and festival prayers, the Passover Haggadah, and so forth, according to the rite of the Roman Jewish community, known also as *Minhag Italiani*). Of these, the earliest dated menorah – though not necessarily the earliest one actually drawn – may be found in a *mahzor* written and illustrated in Pisa in 1397[10] (see article by B. Narkiss in this volume). A menorah page continues to appear in later, printed prayer books, up until the present, according to most rites (Rome, Sephardi, Oriental, and Ashkenazi.)

The earliest texts referring to the combination of Psalm 67 and the menorah are found in works of mystical commentary on liturgical texts, assigning utmost importance to the number of words in the litugical text and dealing with magical numerical relationships and *gematriot* in the context of prayer.[11] However, the earliest dated text that associates the menorah with this particular psalm and ascribes the combination special qualities occurs in *Sefer Abudraham*, from the mid-14th century.

How the menorah spread beyond the prayer book is not known. As we have stated, its qualities were described in widely disseminated works of practical Kabbalah, but it is not known where or when the first large menorah or *shivviti* plaques, of the type hung on synagogue walls, were made. We have almost no amulets or plaques predating the 18th century; most are from the 19th and 20th centuries, and they are still being produced, either printed or written by Torah scribes.

The menorah composed of the letters of Psalm 67 adds a further, mystical-magical dimension to the menorah as a symbol. It places the worshiper or the person gazing at the menorah at a juncture where the past Temple, the future one, and the worshiper himself may meet. A person concentrating on the menorah is considered as if he or she had personally lit the Temple menorah and is thereby associated with the messianic expectation for the rebuilding of the Temple. This association guarantees protection in this world and redemption in the world to come. With the menorah's transformation into a personal amulet, the symbol that it represents passed from the national-collective domain to the private sphere, and thus, the concept of messianic redemption assumed a personal dimension.

---

1 *Menorot Zahav Tahor* (Prague, 1581) unpaginated (copy in the Gershom Scholem Library, with Scholem's handwritten comments).

2 On this book see Joshua Trachtenburg, *Jewish Magic and Superstition* (New York, 1961, first published 1939, 109.

3 *Rome Mahzor*, copied by Meir ben Samuel of Arles, Provence, Pisa 1397, Morning Prayer, fol. 31. The manuscript was formerly in the Sassoon Collection, see *Ohel David* (Oxford and London, 1932) no. 1208. See also L. Avrin, "Micrography as Art," in C. Sirat (ed.), *La Lettre hébraique et sa signification* (Paris, 1981), 55, n. 33.

4 G. Scholem, "The Star of David: History of a Symbol," in *The Messianic Idea in Judaism and Other Essays* (New York, 1971), 269.

5 David Abudraham, *Sefer Abudraham*, Seville, 1340 (Warsaw, 1877), 68.

6 *Bet Oved, Prayer Book for the Days of the Week, for all the Year. According to the Sephardic Rite*, (Leghorn, 1948).

7 *Prayer Book According to the Rite of the Holy Community of Baghdad and its Environs* (Leghorn, 1936). For additional sources see M. Benayahu, *Babylonian Journey*, (Jerusalem, 1955), 113 (Hebrew).

8 *Shulkhan Arukh Ha'ari*, n. p., n. d., fol. 31a.

9 Gershom Scholem, *On the Kabbalah and Its Symbolism* (New York, 1965), 122–128.

10 See above, n. 3.

11 J. Dan, "The Emergence of Mystical Prayer," in *Studies in Jewish Mysticism*, eds. J. Dan and F. Talmage, (Cambridge, Mass, 1982), 87-93 . In a personal communication, Professor Dan suggested that one of these anonymous texts most probably originated among the writings of Hasidei Ashekenaz in the 13th century although no written evidence to that effect has been found.

Religious and National Identity – Sacred and Profane

Already in ancient times, the symbol of the menorah transcended the world of religious ritual and became a means of identifying the Jew within his non-Jewish surroundings in the land of Israel and the Diaspora. In the Byzantine period, identical objects were made for Jews and Christians alike; they are distinguishable only by the symbols they bear – the menorah or the cross.

Over the next one thousand years, the use of the menorah as a symbol of identity was limited primarily to prayer books and synagogues, perhaps due to the Jews' desire (or need) to avoid calling attention to themselves. With the Jewish national reawakening in the 19th century and the establishment of the Zionist movement, the menorah once again became a symbol of Jewish identity. From that point on, however, it would serve as a collective symbol, as opposed to a sign of the Jew as an individual. The menorah is a widespread decorative motif in periodicals and publications of Jewish institutions, as both an expression of identity and a means of propaganda. On posters and everyday objects, it bears a national-Israeli message – from the symbol of the Beitar Jerusalem Football Club to that of the Israel Philharmonic Orchestra.

The selection of the menorah as the State emblem imbued it with additional meaning. As a symbol of national sovereignty, it represented authority and reliability. It is in this manner that it is depicted on Independence Day posters and, even more so, on a variety of consumer goods. Today, the menorah even looks natural on chocolate coins.

In Israeli art, the menorah has mainly been used in the context of the discussion of questions of identity and conscience as they relate to the Israeli experience. In these instances, the menorah serves as the object of discussion and censure.

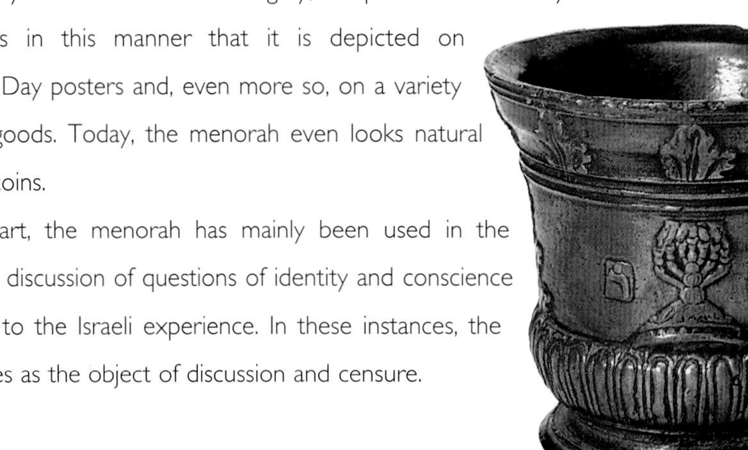

Mortar used by a Jewish physician for grinding drugs
Artist: Servius De Levis (1570–1616)
Verona, Italy, second half of the 16th century
Cast bronze, natural brown patina
H 14 cm
Israel Museum Collection, Stiegletz Collection, through a donation by Erica and Ludwig Jesselson, New York, to American Friends of the Israel Museum

Previous page:
Menorah graffito from the pavement of the main street (the cardo) of Sepphoris
Byzantine period
Courtesy of the Sepphoris Expedition, The Institute of Archaeology, The Hebrew University of Jerusalem

Oil lamps decorated with Jewish and Christian symbols
Byzantine period, 5th–6th century CE
Bronze and pottery
L 8.8–21.5 cm
Institute of Archaeology, The Hebrew University of Jerusalem, the Schloessinger Collection; Reifenberg Collection; Israel Museum Collection, Carmen and Louis Warschaw Collection

Above:
Coins of the Hasmonean king Mattathias Antigonus
40–37 BCE
Bronze, D 15 mm
Israel Museum Collection
During these years, the menorah still stood in the Temple in Jerusalem.

Center:
Contemporary Israeli coin (10 *agorot*)
The menorah motif is based on that appearing on the coins of Antigonus (above).

Below:
Coins from the time of the Umayyad Dynasty
Jerusalem mint, 8th century CE
Bronze, D 15 mm
Israel Museum Collection and collection of Shraga Qedar, Jerusalem
The seven- or five-branched menorah on these Muslim coins is a symbol of Jerusalem.

Opposite:
Assorted stickpins with the menorah motif produced in honor of various Israel Independence Days
Collection of Alain Roth, Herzliya
In some cases, the motif is identical to that year's official poster.

ISRAEL ישראל
קרן קימת לישראל
ישראל
ISRAEL
לישראל
ISRAEL ישראל
קרן קימת לישראל

Postcard of a work by Michael Druks, b. 1940
Part of a children's game produced by The Israel Museum, Jerusalem, the Ruth Youth Wing

Opposite:
Chancel screens decorated with a menorah and a cross from the synagogue at Hammath Gader (above) and the church at Massuot Yitzhaq (below)
Byzantine period, 6th century CE
Marble, W 100 cm; 118 cm
Israel Antiquities Authority Collection

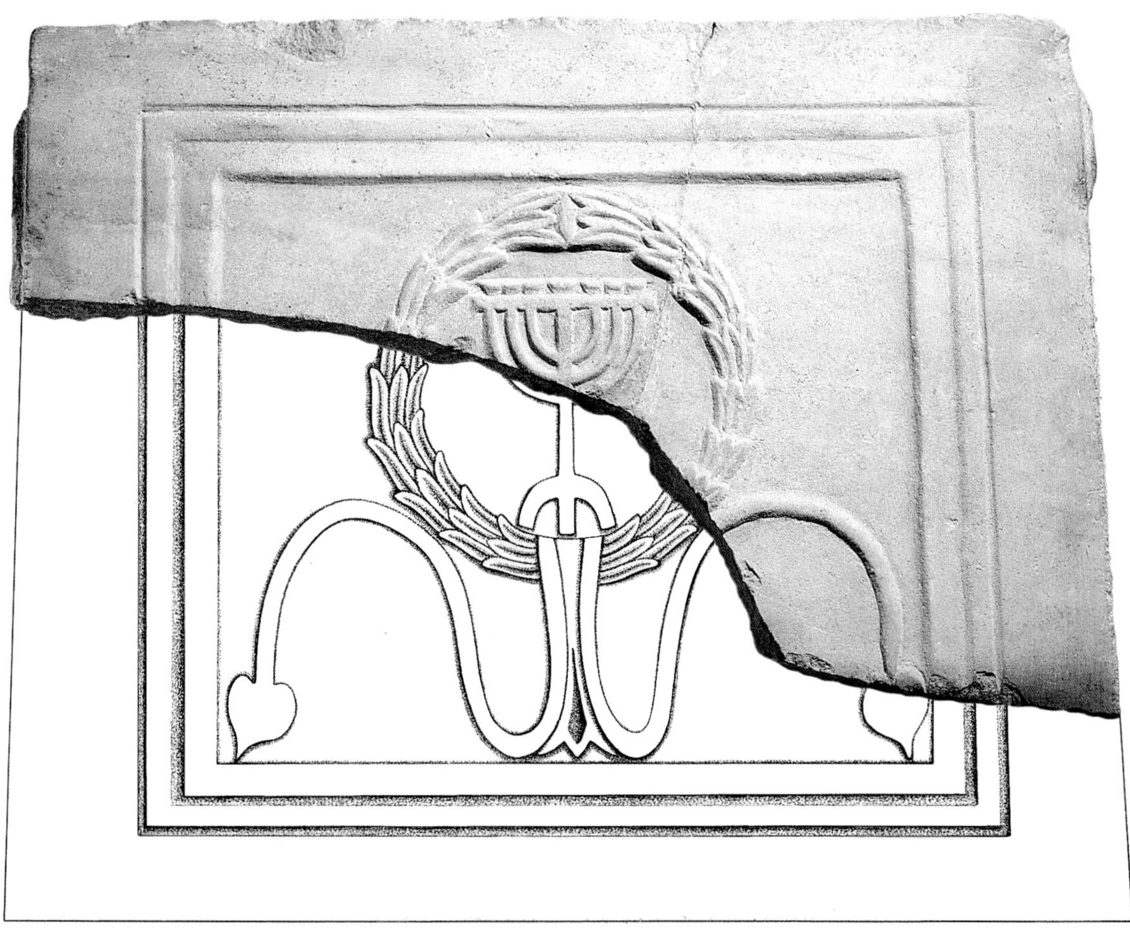

Jewish girl in Herat,
Afganistan, 1973
Courtesy of Musée
de l'Homme, Paris

Suitcase, 1990
David Tartakover,
b. 1944
Collage, 98.7 x 68 cm
Collection of the artist

Left:
Model of pastry traditionally baked in honor of a *brit milah* (circumcision ceremony) or wedding
Lvov?, ca. 1930
Desicated dough, painted
L 34 cm
Goldstein Collection at the Institute of Ethnology, Ukrainian Acadamy of Sciences, Lvov, Ukraine

Right:
Bread stamps with Jewish symbols
Byzantine period
Bronze
H 3.4–5.5 cm
Israel Museum Collection, gift of Leo Mildenberg; Reifenberg Collection

Opposite:
Chocolate coins manufactured by Elite and other companies

כשר פארווע למהדרין
כשר חלב ישראל
ELITE · ISRAEL

Advertisment for Menorah soap manufactured by Shemen, Haifa, ca. 1938
Design: Franz Krausz, b. 1905
70 x 45 cm
Collection of David Tartakover, Tel Aviv

Dress of a Jewish woman hung to dry at the entrance to her house
Ambovar, Ethiopia, 1985
Photo: Joan Roth, New York

MENORA
מנורה

Graffiti at the
Tel Aviv Harbor,
1997
230 x 500 cm
Photo: Hila Zahavi

Opposite:
Souvenir shop on
Allenby Street in
Tel Aviv
Photo: Hila Zahavi

Holder for
The Encyclopaedia of Israel in Pictures,
1952
Metal 20.5 x 26 x 22.4 cm
Collection of David Tartakover, Tel Aviv

Jerusalem, 1998
Belu-Simion Fainaru,
b. 1959
Colored ink on gold
foil
51 x 43.5 cm
Collection of the
artist

Trees of Light and Golden Showers (diptych), 1993
Michal Na'aman, b. 1951
Mixed media on canvas
Each part 25 x 20 cm
Israel Museum Collection, gift of Rita and Arturo Schwarz, Milan

GOLDEN SHOWERS

"Little Israel"
(Srulik), 1968
Dosh (Kariel
Gardosh), b. 1921
Rubber
H 24.3 cm
Collection of David
Tartakover, Tel Aviv

Opposite:
*Uri On, A New
Israeli Hero*
Cover of a comic
book, no. 1, 1987
Michael Netzer
22 x 18 cm
Published by D.N.A.
Israel Comics Ltd.,
Jerusalem
Israel Museum
Collection

אורי-און
רייק
ישראל קומיקס
גליון מס׳
1
ינואר 1987
טבת תשמ״ז
המחיר
2.50 ש״ח
כולל מע״מ
באילת
2.12 ש״ח
גיבור ישראלי חדש
גיליון ראשון מיוחד!
36 עמודים צבעוניים

Abyss, 1995
Israel Rabinovitz,
b. 1954
Iron, stone, and paint
36 x 34 cm
Collection of the
artist

Shlomit Steinberg

Present in Its Absence
The Menorah in Israeli Art

Two of the objects most sacred to the Jewish people were lost over the course of its long history following the destruction of the Second Temple and the loss of national sovereignty: the Ark of the Covenant and the seven-branched candelabrum. It seems appropriate to raise the question as to how early, as well as contemporary, Israeli visual art, which was nurtured by the national awakening and the renewal of independence, has dealt with this loss. Moreover, how have artists and sculptors treated the concrete absence with the help of symbolic depiction? It would be reasonable to expect that the lack of visual knowledge of the appearance of the Temple menorah would awaken and fertilize the imagination of Israeli artists toward an interpretation of their own. This might have occasioned an interesting visualization of the biblical description melded with personal sources of inspiration, but this has not been the case.

In fact, there has been no chronological sequence of artistic creation on the subject of the menorah from the beginnings of Israeli art, marked by the establishment of the Bezalel School of Art and Crafts in 1906, till the present. Though occasional use of this image is discernible, it has usually been part of the private iconography of the few artists who explored this theme. And when they did utilize this image, it held only a limited, secondary place in their work. Another puzzling point: most depictions of the menorah are drawings or prints; few sculptors have dared to fashion a three-dimensional seven-branched candelabrum, and those who did tended to change its form and avoid traditional representation (p. 210).[1] This being the case, the question arises as to why Israeli artists are generally so disinclined to grapple with the subject, and what precisely does the menorah signify for them.[2]

1
Ze'ev Raban and Yaakov Stark
Poster, 1913
Israel Museum Collection

The Bezalel Days

Already in 1897, the seven-branched candelabrum took its place alongside the Magen David (Star of David) as a symbol of the Zionist national reawakening[3] (see article by R. Arbel in this volume). No wonder, then, that in 1906–1929, the early years of the Bezalel School, the first art school in the land of Israel, the menorah was an integral part of the system of chosen symbols (pp. 34–35), which also included the Ark of the Covenant. In contrast with the menorah, however, the Ark of the Covenant failed to become a modern symbol.[4] The fact that Boris Schatz named the new school after Bezalel ben Uri, maker of the Tabernacle and the first biblical master craftsman, expressed the connection between art in the land of Israel and the idea of the building of the Third Temple in Jerusalem. Some of the works of the teachers at Bezalel in the early years express direct connections and identification with the mythical Bezalel ben Uri. He is depicted as a silversmith, in Yemenite or other Oriental dress (like the Damascus metal-craftsmen and Yemenite filigree artists with whom the Bezalel teachers were acquainted), creator of the seven-branched candelabrum – as shown in the frontispiece for a series of postcards produced by Shmuel Ben David and Yaakov Ben Dor, or immersed in making the menorah, against the background of a pair of vignettes of Bezalel buildings – as in the poster by Ze'ev Raban and Yaakov Stark (fig. 1). A formal echo of the menorah in the process of completion by Bezalel ben Uri is the metal seven-branched candelabrum, which was placed on the roof of the Bezalel museum (p. 55), seen both in the postcard and in the poster.

These works reveal how the menorah was perceived by the artists of the Bezalel period: the type they chose for what they considered as the Temple menorah was in most cases the menorah shown on the Arch of Titus in Rome (p. 190–191). This choice emphasized the menorah's historic importance as an object which in their view blended past and present, memorializing past glory and its ultimate destruction, and at the same time, the hope for rebirth in Jerusalem. The Zionist vision of Schatz and his confederates prompted these artists to focus on the process of the actual creation of the menorah. They identified with the primacy of the mission of Bezalel ben Uri and his contemporaries of the Exodus generation. No wonder, then, that when Stark, Raban, and Ben David drew the menorah, they stressed the image of the Hebrew artist who created it. Depicting the menorah was for them a vital expression of the historic rebuilding of the land and revival of the Jewish people.

After the Establishment of the State of Israel

In the atmosphere of the newly reborn State of Israel in 1948, the image of the menorah should have been glorified in Israeli art. After all, the return to Zion and the establishment of the state had quickened the heartbeat of Israeli artists, veteran and newly-arrived. But in those years the trend in Israeli art was modernistic, showing a preference for abstract values in painting and sculpture. The artists of the New Horizons group, led by Yosef Zaritzky, followed the international trends of their time, and took an anti-establishment position, shaking off all symbols of nationalism, heritage, and Zionism.[5] The artists' preoccupation with color and line pushed aside any concern for symbols as a part of the language of painting and sculpture, and the desire to be aligned with world art precluded any association with biblical or Jewish traditional themes.

Another explanation for the absence of the menorah in Israeli art stems from the fact that the seven-branched candelabrum was made the official emblem of the State of Israel. When it came to adorn every government office, was minted on coins, and appeared in the logo of various commercial enterprises, it lost its exalted status and became an everyday object (see article by D. Lapidot in this volume).[6] One of the artists who support this approach is the postmodernist sculptor Philip Rantzer. He grants the menorah a different status than the Magen David, which he frequently uses in his work. The menorah is, in his opinion, too fraught with meaning: historical, religious, and, of course, national; it is too folkloric and does not belong to the lexicon of what is maintained as high art in Israel. The artist David Gerstein also avoids depicting the menorah in his works, seeing it as an iconographic trap for the artist who uses it.

2
Naftali Bezem,
b. 1924
Lamentation Drawings, 1961

In 1961 (the year of the Eichmann trial) the painter Naftali Bezem and the poet Ezra Sussman collaborated on the book *Lamentation Drawings.*[7] One of the drawings appearing in this book has two registers (fig. 2): the upper section depicts a seven-branched candelabrum flanked by lions, one standing on all fours on the right, and the other supporting the menorah with its front paws as if presenting it to an audience. The artist bases this depiction on well-known scenes from the 4th-century Jewish gold-glass bases (see p. 62) discovered in the Roman catacombs, where the images of lions and the menorah symbolize rebirth and redemption. Yet Bezem chose to connect this imagery with the grim context of death and the Holocaust. The menorah and the pair of lions borrowed from the gold-glass bases are presented here in the original context of funerary art. In the background, behind the animals and the menorah, is a small boat, black and empty. Beneath the menorah is a pale circle of light, resembling the reflection of the moon on water. In the lower section of the drawing, an entire family is packed into a mass grave. Beside it are lit Sabbath candlesticks and an open-mouthed fish, symbolizing the mute sacrifice of the Jewish people.[8] Bezem, who since the late

1940s has dealt with the theme of the Holocaust in a highly personal manner, chose to focus here on the aspects of death, sacrifice, and lamentation. Ezra Sussman's poem completes the picture:

Washed by rain and snow, those who came out of the flames. In their ancient beauty.
Every man and his secret, every man and his glory, every man and his blood
In the secret of their community, in the brotherhood of the harvested, in their destruction, full as a pomegranate.
Thirty-two paths of wisdom, two hundred and sixty-five lights of courage
Two hundred and forty-eight lights of benevolence, all the branches of the candelabrum,
All the shedding wings of eagles, were gathered for burial.

According to the poem and the drawing, Bezem seems to have used the division of the drawing to create a separation between the figures in the mass grave and the vision of the lion above them.

The face of the people were calmed before the father in the harvest of flames
The lion in their tranquil faces will be fearful and silent
Fathers and mothers, children and light, and the candlestick stands guard.

Contemporary Art

More than two decades divide Naftali Bezem from Moshe Gershuni's 1982 work, *I Grieve for You, Jonathan My Brother* (fig. 3). Between a black-crested cypress tree and a triangular banner warning of mortal danger bursts a pinkish, phallic wave with a rounded tip, emitting an inscription quoting David's lament on the death of Jonathan (II Samuel I:26). Two gray brushstrokes emerging from the middle of the circle recall the wings on the Israeli Air Force pilot's insignia, seven red vertical lines in the background hint at the seven-branched candelabrum on fire. In his painting Gershuni melds religious and secular, military and national symbols. The picture, made during the Lebanon war and dealing with the parting from a friend (or lover) who has fallen in battle, unites personal mourning with national mourning and private pain with public bereavement. The fire, blood, and pain blend into one shout, against the background of the seven branches of the national menorah. The combination of the menorah with the biblical text imparts an additional, historical dimension to the work, and emphasizes male love and camaraderie.

3
Moshe Gershuni, b. 1936
I Grieve for You, Jonathan My Brother, 1982
Mixed media on paper
Givon Gallery Collection, Tel Aviv

In a 1983 work by Michael Druks, white Sabbath candles forming a seven-branched structure and placed on a cardboard surface create an unusual menorah. Only once did the artist kindle it (p. 158), allowing the melting wax branches to drip their charcoal impression on the pale cardboard. Above the central branch Druks pasted the word *tsafon* (north), recalling the prophetic words "From the north shall disaster break loose" – the year was 1983, and the disaster was the war in Lebanon. Furthermore, the broad context that Druks was trying to stress in this work was death and destruction, which are an inseparable part of Jewish history. His choice of working with a self-destructing material is a powerful metaphor: the knowledge that lighting the candles/sculpture will spell the destruction of the menorah is not only a warning to the holders of the work itself, but also a warning against igniting (metaphorically or literally) national symbols, which may lead to the self-destruction of the State of Israel.

A message similar to Druks' is conveyed by a wood and cloth wall relief by Arnon Ben David. He created the sculpture in 1989, about a year after the outbreak of the Palestinian Intifada and the violence on both sides of the barricades. The name of the work, *State Terror,* is a play on words uniting place and situation: Ben David is hinting, on the one hand, that acts of terror committed against the State of Israel are a fact of life, but on the other hand, that Israel itself is a state in which terror is committed against segments of the population. At the center of the work, the national emblem is drawn in a haphazard fashion: the menorah has nine skewed branches. Ben David deliberately confuses the menorah as state emblem with the Hanukkah lamp and demonstrates his critical stance toward national symbols which in his opinion are being tarnished and which now condone terror within and do not protect against terror from without.

A small diptych painted by Michal Na'aman in 1993 depicts a seven-branched candelabra (pp. 170–171) in the shape of olive branches (left panel) with burning ends. Beside each menorah stands a tree with wolves seated on its outspread branches. The names of the two parts of this work are written beneath the paintings in simple typography: *Trees of Light* and *Golden Showers.*[9] This diptych belongs to a group of works in which the artist grapples with her Jewish identity.[10] This concern, which has preoccupied the artist from the outset, leads her along unconventional paths. In *Trees of Light* and *Golden Showers* Na'aman creates an unusual visual tie between a central motif in Jewish art and a motif mentioned in Freud's writings of case studies. The Jewish psychoanalyst describes how one of his patients had a recurring dream of wolves perched in a tree opposite his bedroom window. To illustrate his dream the man drew a picture of "the wolves' tree," which Freud included in his book. Na'aman has incorporated this drawing into her work. In this diptych the juxtaposition of the tree of wolves and the burning olive tree, which is also a seven-branched candelabrum, is in fact a juxtaposition of two entirely different approaches: the modern discipline of psychoanalysis, which helps decipher the personal "I," and the quotation from religious, traditional, and Jewish historical sources concerned with the collective national "I." Na'aman's multilayered, complex puns fuse the *Trees of Light* concept with the self-illumination that results from psychoanalytic therapy. The idea of *Golden Showers* is borrowed from Israeli banking parlance and tied to the shower of golden coins on Danae in Greek mythology, but also with the image of the seven-branched candelabrum engraved on the gold-finished ten agora coin in Israel today.

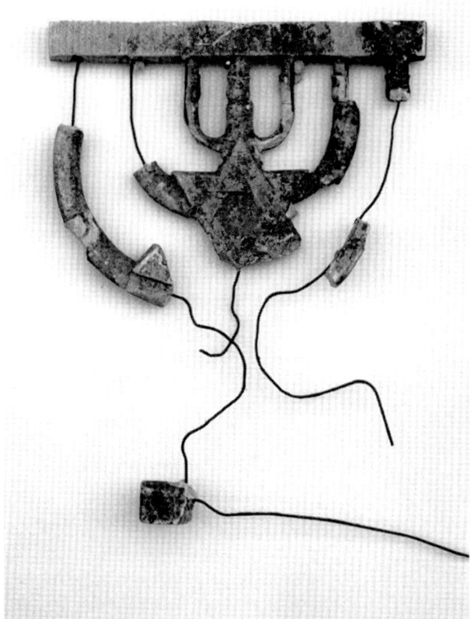

4
Israel Rabinovitz, b. 1954
Fractions on Yom Kippur, 1995–96
Concrete, iron, blue paint
Collection of the artist

The series *Seven Etchings for the Book of Zechariah* created by Igael Tumarkin in 1996–97 presents a personal interpretation of the biblical text. According to the artist, the idea for the work was based on the vivid description in the first chapter of Zechariah: "In the night, I had a vision. I saw a man mounted on a bay horse, standing among the myrtle trees that were in the deep, and behind him were bay, sorrel and white horses" (Zechariah 1:8). For Tumarkin, this vivid, colorful description evoked the visual memory of the massive horses of the Florentine Renaissance painter Paolo Uccello in his painting *The Battle of San Romano* (1447–1454). Uccello's horses appear in all of Tumarkin's etchings. In two of the seven prints they are joined by the seven-branched candelabrum from Zechariah's vision, painted in red. "I see a lampstand all of gold, with a bowl above it. The lamps on it are seven in number, and the lamps above it have seven pipes; and by it are two olive trees, one on the right of the bowl and on its left" (Zechariah 4:2–3). The base of the candelabrum is replaced by an arrow pointed downward, a kind of dynamic rocket ready to shoot toward the heavens (p. 61). Tumarkin chose vibrant red for the menorah instead of the more regal gold. In the second etching, too, he retains the red color and ignores Zechariah's color specifications, thus using the red color to evoke memories of fire and destruction. He was, however, careful to adhere to Zechariah's image of the two olive trees flanking the upper section of the menorah, connecting his prints to his work *Describing the Olive Tree* produced in the 1980s (and now in the Billy Rose Sculpture Garden of the Israel Museum). He also connected them to one of his acts of political protest, in which he laid down a putrid fish next to the tomb of Zechariah in the Kidron valley – implying that in Israeli politics, as the saying goes, "the fish stinks from the head down."

Israel Rabinovitz, unlike most artists of his generation, does not shy away from the heavy symbolism of the menorah, but internalizes it. In one of his works from 1995–96, *Fractions on Yom Kippur* (fig. 4), the menorah appears, composed of wire and broken stones; in *Vines in the Shadow of the Stone* from 1994, a seven-branched palm tree is depicted which resembles an inverted menorah. Sometimes he creates a double meaning when he replaces the date palm, which in his personal iconography stands for locality and the "East," with the image of the menorah, which he connects to the past, to the destruction of the Temple, and to the exile of the people. In *Abyss* from 1995 (p. 174) Rabinovitz places the menorah on top of a water tower, recreating a familiar Israeli landscape and evoking the memory of Independence Days on kibbutzim, where menorahs were lit on top of water towers. The combination of water tower and menorah (water and fire) fuses the Zionist symbol and local associations, transforming the seemingly simple sculpture to a signpost of past and present and emphasizing the dialectic tension inherent in them.

The menorah motif is not common in Israeli art. But in the few cases where it does appear, it expresses a particular stance toward the state, the bearer of this symbol. A review of the image of the menorah over the years reveals a change in artists' view of Zionism and the state. The use of the menorah to express the exultation and fulfillment of the Zionist vision in works from the Bezalel days gradually yielded to the vicissitudes of time and to social and political criticism, which finds expression in the works of the latest generation of artists. The use of familiar national symbols is inherently problematic, but the artist's ability to touch upon the familiar and mundane and infuse it with new meanings is the essence of art and the secret of its magic.

---

1 An example of such depictions is Benno Elkan's seven-branched candelabrum displayed in a park near the Knesset. It is square and deliberately different from the menorah in the Arch of Titus in Rome, which served as the source for the designers of Israel's state emblem.

2 This essay does not attempt to deal with all the Israeli artists who have used the image of the menorah in their works, but only with the works of particular artists of various generations.

3 Y. Zalmona and N. Shilo-Cohen, "Style and Iconography in Bezalel Work," *Schatz's Bezalel, 1906–1929* (Jerusalem, 1983) 203 (Hebrew).

4 The Ark of the Covenant with its winged cherubs designed by Ephraim Moses Lilien appeared on the flag of the Bezalel School, and adorned the ex libris of Boris Schatz.

5 The connection between the establishment of the state and the founding of the New Horizons group of artists may suggest the possibility that with the fulfillment of the Zionist vision, the symbolic light and the menorah lost their importance and were replaced by depictions of natural light and local landscape.

6 This explanation was posited by art historian Avigdor Poseq. The discussions with him, as well as with the artists Philip Rantzer and David Gerstein mentioned in this essay, took place during the summer of 1997.

7 N. Bezem and E. Sussman, *Lamentation Drawings* (Ramat Gan, 1962), 16–17.

8 Ziva Amishai-Maisels dealt in depth with Naftali Bezem's iconography regarding his works on the Holocaust, including this drawing: Z. Amishai-Maisels, *Depiction and Interpretation: The Influence of the Holocaust on the Visual Arts* (Oxford, 1993): 86–88, fig. 226.

9 The expression "golden shower" refers not only to the mythological rain of gold coins through which Zeus manifested himself and made love to the imprisoned princess Danae, but also a common expression connected with urinating on one's lover in (homosexual) sex.

10 I am grateful to Chaya Friedberg for her help in deciphering Michal Na'aman's work. For more on Na'aman's Jewish identity see C. Friedberg, "The Letter 'H' in the Female Gender," *Mishkafayim* 32 (March 1998): 44–47 (Hebrew).

Daphna Lapidot

From the Arch of Titus to Chocolate Coins

The Menorah in Consumer Goods and in Applied Graphics

Dedicated to the late Izzika Gaon,
artist, designer, curator, and friend

1
Seal of the Menorah Group, 1920s

The seven-branched candelabrum, used in the cultic rites of the Temple, was divested of its sanctity even before the establishment of the State of Israel, when it became a device for propaganda, used initially for the promulgation of nationalistic ideas but soon thereafter even for advertising consumer goods. The use of a symbol in advertising is based on its ability to convey the merchant's message to the buyer; the designer is the intermediary in this process. The first designer-intermediary who used a symbol to convey a divine message was Bezalel ben Uri, builder of the Tabernacle menorah. The choice of the form of the menorah as an all-encompassing symbol of sanctity and eternity was a brilliant idea. Apart from its obvious role as a lighting device (in all senses of the word), the tree-like form of the menorah represents the three stages of development inherent in any process: the base of the menorah symbolizes the roots, signifying the past; from the roots the stalk – or stem – emerges, representing the present; and from the stalk branches grow, which signify the future. Thus, like the Tree of Life motif, the very form of the menorah signifies growth, development, renewal, and hope for the future.

Before the Establishment of the State of Israel

3
Playing cards produced by the Arieh company

With the founding of the Zionist movement, the menorah was chosen as the symbol of national identity and became associated with feelings of national pride. The menorah was concurrently enlisted for use in the areas of propaganda and advertising (see R. Arbel's article in this volume). From this point on, it came to symbolize not only Jewish manuscripts, synagogues, and tombs, but also insurance companies and soaps. The sphere of influence of the menorah had spread to the secular domain.

More than ninety years ago, graphic artists had already grasped the effectiveness of a symbol that stood for growth and hope for the future for promoting and marketing products. The history of graphic design in Israel begins in 1906, with the founding of the Bezalel School of Art and Crafts. Within a few years, several commercial firms had already decided to use the menorah as their logo. The Menorah Group, which was established in the 1920s by Bezalel artists Ze'ev Raban, Meir Gur-Arieh, and Shmuel Persoff, specialized in making reliefs, sculptures, household items, and toys from terra-cotta (fig. 1). Photographer Ya'akov Ben-Dov, also of the Bezalel School, chose the menorah as the name and trademark of the motion picture company he founded. In the following years, a change occurred in the field of graphic design, owing to the infiltration of European modernism into the local world of visual images. In 1935, the Association of Hebrew Artists for Applied Graphics in Palestine was established. The topic of advertising, which "until recently had been an unknown concept in Israel, or one that was even frowned upon,"[1] was now a major topic of discussion. The status of the field of applied graphics is reflected accurately, though perhaps somewhat naively, in the association's catalogue: "With the appearance of outstanding works and their growth and distribution in Israel and abroad, the recognition of the value and economic significance of applied graphics has penetrated into economic life and other

2
Logo of the Menorah insurance company, 1930s

areas. . . . Today, our educated audience demands, as in other countries, tasteful packaging for merchandise, a prominent, recognizable trademark, artistic quality, and allure" (ibid.). This new state of affairs made it necessary to formulate catchy visual images that would reflect the Israeli message in all the communications media: journalism, cinema, billboards, and so forth. As part of the campaign to promote the purchase of local products, graphic designers developed a style that combined biblical motifs with modern ones, an approach that was certainly in keeping with Zionist ideology. The Menorah insurance company (fig. 2), for example, built up its image as a company based upon Jewish values, which looked forward to the rebuilding of the nation (unlike the British-based Phoenix insurance company, whose image was based upon universal values and economic strength).

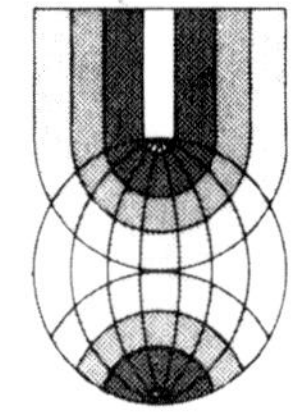

7
Logo of the Beitar Jerusalem Football Club

8
Logo of the Israel Tourist and Travel Agents Association

9
Logo of the World Union for Progressive Judaism

10
Logo of the Movement for Quality of Government in Israel
Design: Dror Ze'evi, 1991

After the Establishment of the State of Israel

The choice of the menorah as the national emblem of the State of Israel led to a distinct change in the way this symbol was regarded (see article by Alec Meshori in this volume). From this point on, the menorah became more than a metaphor for territory – it became the symbol of actual territory. In the military ceremonies celebrating Israel's Independence Day (the new national-secular holiday), the shape of the menorah was formed by parading soldiers and airforce formations, and along Israel's beaches, competitions were held for constructing menorahs in the sand.

The menorah began to be flown above many public buildings in Israel and abroad, and its name was given to new hotels as well as souvenir shops (p. 166). As a souvenir, which by its very nature has no practical function and is cut off from its original meaning, the menorah joined the ranks of jewelry bearing the Magen David, olive wood camels, and bottles of colored sand from Eilat, serving as one of the symbols used to market Israel's image. But the market was also flooded with products decorated with the menorah that were meant for local consumption: from household items, such as carpets and plates, to jewelry, coins, stamps, ex libris, children's games, playing cards, key-rings, and so forth (fig. 3). The menorah also began to appear on the packaging and labels of various products, including wine, *tehina* (sesame paste) (figs. 4, 5), chocolate coins, a record album, and Sabbath and memorial candles (pp. 99, 163). The first of these commercial goods was Shemen soap, which already bore the shape and name of the menorah in the 1930s (fig. 6 and p. 164). But the product that is perhaps most often identified with the State is the "Little Israel" doll – "Srulik" (p. 164), created by the renowned Israeli caricaturist Dosh (Kariel Gardosh). Sporting a menorah on his shirt pocket, Srulik became the unofficial emblem of the Israeli.

Organizations, institutions, and companies adopted the menorah motif in order to lend their activities an "official" air. The menorah became the ultimate symbol of quality, reliability, and continuity.

In posters, one of the most important means of propaganda, the menorah played a prominent role, particularly in propaganda posters intended to convey ideological messages and promote activity related to a particular value or values, as opposed to consumer-related activity. Many of the posters produced on behalf of public organizations or those that marked official events or ceremonies, especially the posters produced in honor of Israel Independence Days, bore the menorah symbol. The menorah was employed as a tool for disseminating ideological messages related to the promotion of the Zionist enterprise, such as support for the forestation of the country, the need for *aliyah* (immigration to Israel), and the importance of industry, agriculture, and construction (pp. 199, 201). In these cases, the designers frequently opted to use the form of the menorah that occurs on ancient coins, mosaics, and sarcophagi. One example is the Independence Day poster of 1954, which features a depiction of the chancel screen

4
Label of a bottle of champagne from France, 1997

5
Can of Aztmaut (Independence) *tehina* (sesame paste)

6
Menorah soap manufactured by Shemen, 1930s

from the synagogue at Ashkelon (6th century CE). This combination expresses the sense of continuity between the nation's past, its present, and its future.

The trademark, unlike the poster, is a word, sign, or shape (or a combination thereof) that an institution or company uses in order to identify its products and on which its advertising and marketing is based. A surprisingly large number of companies, organizations, and institutions, both public and private, incorporated the menorah in their trademark (pp. 36, 185). A well-known example is an earlier logo of the Beitar Jerusalem Football Club (fig. 7), in which a ball serves as the base of the menorah, thus symbolizing Israeli soccer. In the various logos of the Israel Tourist and Travel Agents Association and the World Union for Progressive Judaism (figs. 8, 9), the menorah is part of a globe, an expression of universal values and international relations. In the symbol of the Movement for Quality of Government in Israel (fig. 10), the menorah is flanked by two hands, which represent the concept of guarding and protecting the State. Occasionally, the message is conveyed by specific parts of the menorah, such as the central stem, which assumes various forms. In the symbol of the Yad Lebanim Museum complex in Petah Tikvah (fig. 11), it is depicted as a sword wrapped in an olive branch, simultaneously symbolizing both war and peace. In the logo of The Israel Philharmonic Orchestra, the central stem is in the shape of a tuning-fork (fig. 12).

11
Logo of the Yad Lebanim Museum Complex, Petah Tikvah

12
Logo of The Israel Philharmonic Orchestra
Design: Werner Epstein, 1936

13
Logo of the Israeli Broadcasting Authority
Design: Natan Karp, 1970

14
Logo of the Sport Federation of Israel

15
Medal in honor of Israeli fashion
Design: Roly, 1975

16
Medal: "And there was light"
Design: Ya'akov Agam, 1985

The wealth of formal possibilities inherent in the shape of the menorah made it popular with designers, and the ways in which it was depicted in earlier sources proposed new challenges. The menorah is made up of geometric forms, the most prominent of which is the arch. The upper part of the menorah, consisting of three, up-turned arches traversed by a central stem, creates a striking, symmetrical shape consisting of concentric semicircles. In a medal in honor of Israeli fashion from 1975 (fig. 15), the arches of the menorah become part of the garment. When the arches are turned upside-down, however, they assume the shape of a rainbow – as in the trademarks of the Keshet and Eden Natural Mineral Water companies. Ya'akov Agam, designer of the medal "And there was light" (fig. 16), made double use of this motif: the lines curving upward represent the menorah, while those curving downward create a rainbow. The very shape of the semicircles also drew the attention of designers, enabling many different variations. In the logo of the Israeli Broadcasting Authority (fig. 13), the words written in the form of an arch represent sound waves, while at the same time, they create a full circle together with the branches of the menorah. This emblem evolved into the three concentric circles that symbolize Israel's Channel One; those who recall the original form of this emblem may still be able to identify the menorah motif in it. The new logo of the Mabat news program consists of two almost completely closed circles with the globe in the center. The logo of the Sport Federation of Israel (fig. 14) is also a circle formed from the Hebrew letters *heh* and *samekh* and the branches of the menorah. The circle is a basic, and deeply significant formal motif: "The circle, as a coin, a symbol, a map, or a seal, is one of those images that does not only convey the conceptual message, in other words, the content it represents; it also appears as a formal factor in its own right, which is occasionally filled with different content. Thus the circle creates a kind of different key, a peephole which organizes the storeroom of memory on the basis of its shapes, as opposed to its meanings."[2]

The designers did not always adhere to the formal scheme of the menorah used in the national emblem. The branches are not always of uniform height, nor are they always seven in number. This did not stem from the confusion between the seven-branched candelabrum and the Hanukkah lamp, which has nine branches, but from the designers' confidence that the association with the menorah motif would be sufficient to convey the message. "This lack of precision could be interpreted as [the designers' attempt to] distance themselves from the form and make it a secondary factor, as a result of the internalization of the content and meaning of the symbol both on the collective level and on the individual level."[3] The branches of the menorah are sometimes depicted in the form of a plant – *kaftor vaferah* (calyx and petals), a date palm, an ear of wheat or corn, or the moriah plant (see article by

N. Hareuveni in this volume). At times, the lower part is not rendered at all, and at times it is tripodal or consists of two hexagonal podia placed one on top of the other, as on the Arch of Titus. This lack of consistency may have been the result of the ongoing debate concerning the shape of the early Temple menorah (see article by D. Sperber in this volume).

It is precisely this artistic license that is one of the signs of the process by which the menorah symbol was divested of its traditional meanings. The appearance of this symbol on the shirt of Uri On, the Israeli Superman of the comic strip series (p. 173), is a fascinating example of the shift in the status of the symbol and its transformation into a sign of Israeli identity. On the breast of Uri On, the menorah is a symbol of the Israel of today; it serves to identify Israeli children, while at the same time, it connects them to children from all over the western world. The menorah represents Israeli identity in caricatures as well: Moshik Lin depicts it as part of the skeleton (the ribs) of the Israeli (fig. 17), while Dosh presents the Israeli in suit and tie barbecuing meat over the flames of the menorah (fig. 18). In both cases, the menorah is used to point to the loss of the values associated with the early days of the Jewish State and to the materialism of the contemporary Israeli.

Simultaneously with the erosion of the religious meaning of the symbol and the broadening of its boundaries, a new phenomenon has become apparent in recent years: the return of the Magen David alongside the menorah motif. This has been particularly prominent at sites where acts of terrorism were committed, and could also be seen in the Yitzhak Rabin Plaza in Tel Aviv during the mourning period following his assassination – both in the form of graffiti and shaped from numerous burning memorial candles, converting the menorah itself to a memorial lamp. This phenomenon points to the fact that despite its secularization, the menorah was and remains a symbol of Israeli-Jewish identity.

Logo of the Israphon record company on a record

1 *Commerical Art of Palestine. Catalogue of the Association of Hebrew Artists for Applied Graphics in Palestine,* designed by Franz Kraus (1938) (Hebrew).

2 I. Levy, *The State of Israel Has Been Established! This Meeting Is Concluded! Proclamation of Independence,* 21 Plates by David Tartakover (Israel: Modan Publication Ltd.,1988), 18.

3 B. Donner, *Magen David – Israeli and German Artists Delineate Territories of a Symbol,* exh. cat., Tower of David, Museum of the History of Jerusalem (Jerusalem, 1995), 7 (Hebrew). In her article, Donner claims that the lack of adherence to the official symbol also characterized the many versions of the Israeli flag, on which the proportions between the two stripes and the Magen David were never consistent. Nor were the flag's colors consistent (even though they had been regulated by law).

17
Moshik Lin
From the book *Never on Saturday,* 1981

18
Kariel Gardosh (Dosh)
From the book *Forty! The Story of the State in Caricatures,* Ma'ariv, Tel Aviv, 1988

1
Menorah Hotel
Design: Yoel Aronstam, 1983

2
Department of Religious Culture, Ministry of Education, Culture, and Sport
Design: Zvi Steiner, 1980s

3
Company for the Reconstruction and Development of the Jewish Quarter

4
Inter-Kibbutz Archive and Holiday Institute, Beit-Hashitta
Design: Hashitta Graphic, ca. 1996

5
Bank of Israel
Design: Naomi and Meir Eshel, 1994

6
Matan Gas, Ltd.
Design: David Portal, 1993

7
Israel Government Coins and Medals Corporation, Ltd.
Design: Miriam Kroli, 1958

8
The Rina More National Seminary
Design: Dov Cohen, 1973

9
The General Federation of Labor in Israel
Design: Asher Kalderon, 1970

10
World Zionist Organization
Design: Natan Karp, 1979

11
The Israel Academy of Sciences and Humanities
Design: Zvi Narkiss, 1967

12
Society for Jewish Art
Design: Zvi Steiner, 1983

13
Israel Medical Association, 1950

14
Olympic Committee of Israel
Design: Uri Ben Yehuda, 1980

15
Elitzur, Religious Sports Union
Design: Uri Ben Yehuda, 1982

16
The Center for the Blind in Israel

17
Israel Antiquities Authority
Design: Asher Oron, 1990

18
Income Tax and Property Tax Commission

19
Zionist Council in Israel

20
Shaal, Supporting Services for Travel Agents in Israel, Ltd.

21
Ministry of Defence Publication
Design: Sol Baskin, 1980s

22
The Holy Sites Authority
Design: Raphie Etgar, 1990

23
Eyal, Israel Epilepsy Association
Design: Naomi Porush-Margolin, 1985

24
Academic Center, Cairo
Design: Yakov Enyedi, 1987

25
Jabotinsky Institute in Israel

26
Etz – Making Zionism Happen, The Youth Movement of the Zionist Organization
Design: Arieh Haskin and Moshe Nisan, 1997

27
Logo of the Independence Day Celebrations, 1970
Design: David Neeman, 1970

28
Prize of the Knesset Chairman for Quality of Life
Design: Natan Karp, 1995

29
Beitar Jerusalem Football Club, 1997

1

2

3

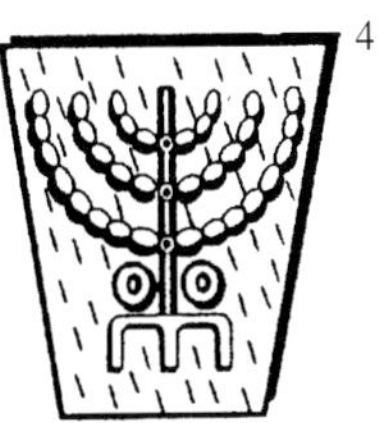
4

5

6

7

8

9

10

11

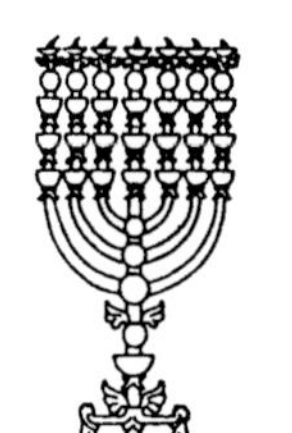
12

13

14

15

16

17

18

19

20

21

22

23

24

25

26

27

28

29

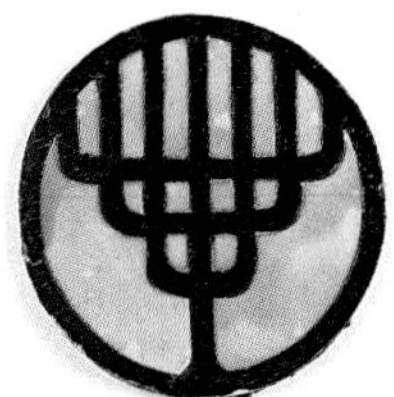

הקונגרס הציוני הכ״ה · ירושלים

25th ZIONIST CONGRESS · JERUSALEM

דפוס מסדה בע"מ

From Destruction to Rebirth

In addition to symbolizing the glory of days gone by, the menorah was also a reminder of the destruction of the Temple and Jerusalem. Its prominent position among the reliefs appearing on the Arch of Titus attests to the great importance the Romans attached to the menorah as an emblem of their victory over Judea, while for the Jewish people, it represented the intensity of their loss. The connection between glory and destruction is one of the factors that led to the adoption of the menorah as the national emblem. This decision added a new layer of meaning to the menorah as a symbol – that of national rebirth.

From the early days of the establishment of a national entity in the land of Israel, the menorah was enlisted as a symbol of the Zionist enterprise and was applied to various aspects of secular, daily life in the country. The applied arts gave concrete expression to the menorah's bridging of past, present, and future, and ancient depictions of the menorah inspired new forms and met new needs. In a sense, the circle was closed, both in the formal sense and in conceptual terms.

The olive tree also has a place among the menorah's many different meanings. The olive trees in Zechariah's vision, which represent not only the source of the oil used to light the menorah but also the religious and national leadership, made their way into the national emblem, in which they express the yearning for peace – an allusion to the olive branch borne by the dove in the biblical story of the Flood.

Through its various layers of meaning and rich connotations, the menorah symbol captures the essence of thousands of years of Jewish history.

Previous page:
Poster for the 25th Zionist Congress, 1960
Design: Kopel Gurwin, 1923–1990
100 x 70 cm
Collection of the Central Zionist Archives, Jerusalem

Qiryat Bialik, 1950s
Walter Zadek,
1900–1992
24 x 24.2 cm
Collection of Alain
Roth, Herzliya

In 71 CE, following the Roman victory over Judea, a triumphal procession was held in Rome in which the spoils taken from the Temple in Jerusalem were paraded through the city. An arch decorated with reliefs depicting the procession was erected in honor of Titus, commander of the Roman forces that fought in Judea, in the Forum.

In the section of the relief shown here, Roman soldiers can be seen carrying the menorah, the shewbread table, and the trumpets taken from the Temple. This relief represents a turning point in the history of art, for it exhibits the new perception of depth characteristic of Roman Impressionist art. Its true importance, however, lies in the fact that its depictions of the sacred appurtenances of the Temple were produced relatively close in time to the seizure of these objects. The menorah featured in the relief stands on a stepped base, which is carved with images of imaginary creatures – despite the religious proscription against such depictions and unlike all other representations of the menorah. This unusual form thus calls into question the credibility of the depiction.

The Temple appurtenances borne in a triumphal procession
Relief on the Arch of Titus, Rome
After 81 CE
Marble
H of relief 204 cm, W 385 cm

Interior of the synagogue at Bergen-Belsen, 1944
Pessach Irsai, 1896–1968
Drawn after the artist's liberation from the camp in 1945
Soft-ground on paper
34 x 49.5 cm
Collection of the Yad Vashem Art Museum, Jerusalem

Proposed poster for Israel's 10th Anniversary, 1958
Design: Pessach Irsai, 1896–1968
Pencil, gouache, and collage on paper
49.4 x 34.2 cm
Collection of David Tartakover, Tel Aviv

Carpet with a portrait of Herzl
Kashan, ca. 1915
Silk
108 x 60.5 cm
Collection of William and Dorothy Gale and Family, Jerusalem

Opposite:
Poster for Israel Independence Day and May Day, 1952
"Israel's Independence is Its Work Force"
Design: The brothers Gabriel and Maxim Shamir
Lithograph
98.5 x 68.5 cm
Collection of the Lavon Institute – Labor Archive, Tel Aviv

ישראל
עצמאות ישראל-
בעצמת הפועל
ה׳ אייר תשי״ב
30·IV·52
1 במאי 1952
ההסתדרות הכללית של העובדים העברים בארץ-ישראל מרכז לתרבות והסברה
שמיר
ליתו׳ "דפנה"

Plaque with notes and lyrics to *Hatikva* in the early version
Artist: Israel Rouchomovsky, 1860–1934
Odessa, Russia, 1899
Silver, engraved, cast, and partly gilt
6.6 x 11.3 cm
Israel Museum Collection
The plaque was produced in honor of the founding of the B'nai Zion movement in Odessa and for the promotion of the Zionist idea.

Poster for the Jewish National Fund, 1950
"A Million Jews in Israel"
69.7 x 50 cm
Collection of the Central Zionist Archives, Jerusalem

Above:
Poster for Israel Independence Day, 1954
Design: Rotchild and Lipman (Rolly)
96 x 65 cm
Collection of David Tartakover, Tel Aviv

Below:
Top of a chancel screen from the synagogue at Ashkelon
Byzantine period, 5th–6th century CE
Marble
W 47 cm
Collection of the Deutsches Evangelisches Institut für Altertumwissenschaft des Heilgen Landes, Jerusalem

Opposite:
Poster for Israel Independence Day, 1979
"And I Will Give Peace and Quiet to Israel"
Design: Assaf Berg, 1937–1997
98 x 67.5 cm
Israel Museum Collection, gift of the Central Office of Information, Publications Center

שלושים ואחת לעצמאות ישראל

ושלום ושקט אתן על-ישראל

Left:
Poster for Israel Independence Day, 1950
Design: Troop
97 x 67 cm
Collection of the Central Zionist Archives, Jerusalem

Right:
Poster for the *Histadrut* (General Federation of Labor in Israel), 1968
Design: The brothers Gabriel and Maxim Shamir
98.4 x 68 cm
Collection of the Central Zionist Archives, Jerusalem

Poster for promoting industry in Israel, 1990
"Industree"
Design: Dan Reisinger, b. 1934
69 x 49 cm
Israel Museum Collection, gift of the artist

Poster for Israel Independence Day, 1973
Design: Assaf Berg, 1937–1997
99 x 68 cm
Collection of David Tartakover, Tel Aviv

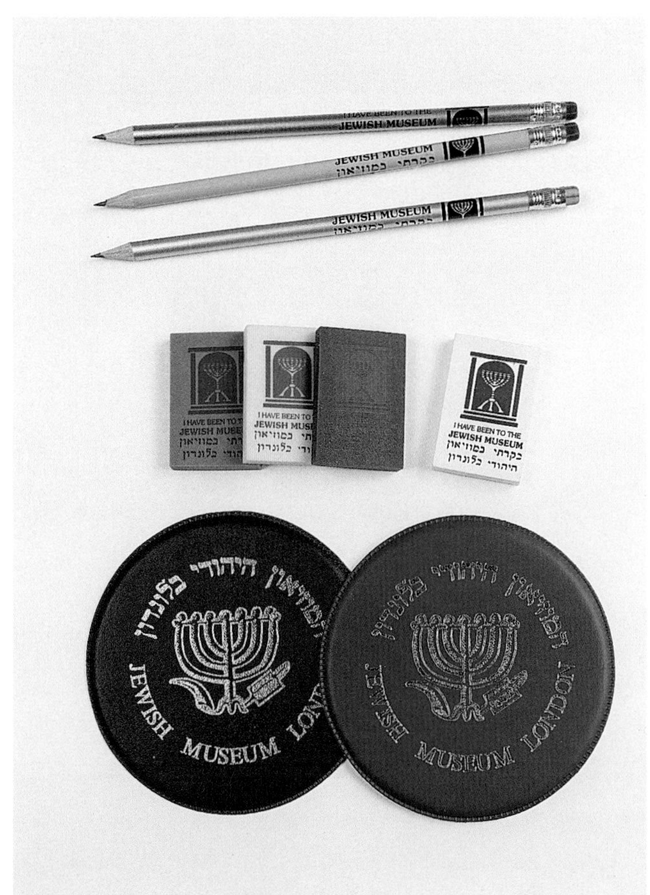

Left:

Pencils, erasers, and coasters – souvenirs of The Jewish Museum, London
Israel Museum Collection, gift of Alain Roth, Herzliya

Right:

Keychain produced by the Maccabi World Union in conjunction with the exhibition "Follow the Menorah and Discover Your Roots"
Pierre Gildesgame Maccabee Sports Museum, Kfar Maccabiah, Ramat Gan
Polyethylene
Collection of Jonathan and Daniel Lewitt, Jerusalem

Proposal for poster for El Al Israel Airlines, 1959
Design: Rafi Mintz, b. 1938
Tempera and collage on paper mounted on cardboard
100 x 70 cm
Collection of Rudi Dayan, Haifa

Rachel Arbel

Menorah and Magen David
Two Zionist Symbols*

The founding fathers of Zionism were well aware of the role symbols play in the consolidation of a national movement. In *The Jewish State* (1896), Theodor Herzl wrote: "We have no flag, but we need one. Wishing to lead many people, we must raise a symbol over their heads." The Zionist movement indeed considered cultivation of the national spirit a major goal; it was pursued deliberately, with intensive use of myths and symbols. Prominent among these were visual symbols, which, within a few years, were widely disseminated and became an integral part of Zionist culture.

Such visual images were concrete representations of basic concepts of the Zionist movement, in particular, the idea of national rebirth, which also possessed a rich verbal symbolism: the ancient, long-suffering nation would cast off the sicknesses that had plagued it, shatter its chains, stand erect, renew its youth, break the bonds of slavery, embrace its freedom, and emerge from darkness to bright light. Such metaphors were translated in the very earliest days of Zionism into visual terms, of which the most common were dawn: the sun rising in the East; the pioneer plowing or sowing; the young woman shattering her chains; the rainbow. Besides these images, frequently used in 19th-century European culture (mainly the Romantic movement and the Jugendstil), Zionism also invoked symbols deriving from specifically Jewish sources. Biblical prophecies of comfort and quotations from the prayer book became an inseparable element of Zionist rhetoric, and such venerable Jewish symbols as the emblems of the twelve tribes and pictures of the holy places in the land of Israel were given a place in Zionist iconography. The seven-branched candelabrum, an extremely ancient and familiar Jewish symbol, was one of these images, but not the most conspicuous or widely used.

Until chosen in 1948 as the heraldic emblem of the State of Israel, the menorah had not represented the Zionist movement – that had been the role of the Magen David (the Star, literally, Shield, of David) since the movement's inception. The choice of the Magen David was taken for granted; it was adopted without arguments, doubts, or official decisions. By the late 19th century the Magen David had become the most familiar Jewish symbol. It proudly adorned the tops of the magnificent synagogues being built all over Europe; it was the sign that the Jews chose to identify themselves to their environment. The choice of the Magen David answered the basic and immediate needs of the Zionist movement for a representative symbol. Nevertheless, by embracing the Magen David for that purpose, the Zionist movement actually gave it a new, different meaning. Western and Central European Jews, eager to acquire equal rights and take their place in society while maintaining their religious identity, had become particularly attached to the Magen David. They chose it as a symbol that would identify them as a group, differing in religious faith and cultural heritage from its environment. As far as they were concerned, the Magen David was a "symbol of Judaism" as against the cross, the "symbol of Christianity." It was the Zionists, in their endeavor to confirm the existence of a Jewish national identity, who made the Magen David the emblem of the national movement of the Jewish people and of that movement's goals.

1
Title page of the monthly periodical *La Renaissance juive*
Cairo, 11 December 1912
Central Zionist Archives, Jerusalem

* This article is based on materials collected for the Beth Hatefutsoth exhibition "Blue and White in Color: The 100th Anniversary of the First Zionist Congress, 1897–1996."

2
Cover of *Ost und West,* Berlin, 1904
Artist: Ephraim Moses Lilien
Mehlman Library, Tel Aviv University

Even if the Magen David occupied the central place in Zionist iconography, the menorah, though by no means as central or common, did not disappear – it was too old and famous for that. The menorah brought to the Zionist world of symbols content and meanings that the Magen David could not supply. Gershom Scholem, in a highly ironic article, described "the brilliant and empty career of the Magen David in the nineteenth century" as "a sign of Jewish decay." The Magen David, he wrote, "expresses no 'idea,' awakens no primeval associations which have become entwined with the roots of our experiences, and it does not spontaneously comprise any spiritual reality." The Zionists had chosen it as a symbol because "it possessed two qualities which had to recommend it to men in search of a new symbol. In the first place, it was known to everyone because of its general dissemination through the centuries. . . . Secondly, in contemporary consciousness it lacked any clear connection with religious conceptions and associations. This fault became a virtue: rather than calling to mind past glory, it addressed hopes for the future, for redemption."[1]

Such deficiencies of the Magen David were precisely the merits of the menorah: it was heavily charged with myths from the past and rich in associations from the deepest levels of Jewish cultural tradition. Although official Zionism tried to keep its distance from explicit religious associations, these were still an inseparable part of the cultural world of most Zionists. Thus, the menorah, too, was enlisted in the service of Zionism, and like other traditional Jewish symbols, it was subjected to a process of adaptation and secularization.

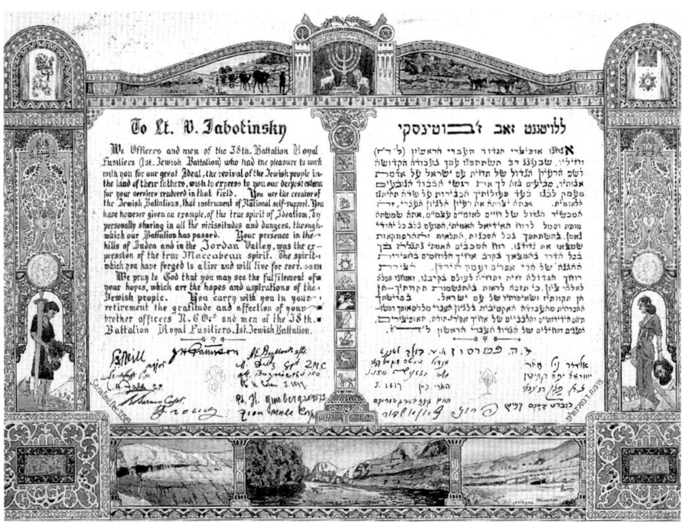
To Lt. V. Jabotinsky

We Officers and men of the 38th. Battalion Royal Fusiliers (1st. Jewish Battalion) who had the pleasure to work with you for our great Ideal, the revival of the Jewish people in the land of their fathers, wish to express to you our deepest estem for your services rendered in that field. You are the creator of the Jewish Battalions, that instrument of National self-support. You have however given an example, of the true spirit of Idealism, by personally sharing in all the vicissitudes and dangers, through which our Battalion has passed. Your presence in the hills of Judea and in the Jordan Valley, was the expression of the true Maccabean spirit. The spirit which you have forged is alive and will live for ever.

We pray to God that you may see the fulfilement of your hopes, which are the hopes and aspirations of the Jewish people. You carry with you in your retirement the gratitude and affection of your brother officers N.C.O.s and men of the 38th. Battalion Royal Fusiliers. 1st. Jewish Battalion.

3
Certificate of appreciation presented to Ze'ev (Vladimir) Jabotinsky by the 38th Battalion of Royal Fusiliers
Sarafant, 3 Dec. 1919
Artist: Meir Gur-Arie
The Jabotinsky Institute in Israel, Tel Aviv

In the first decades of the movement's existence, the menorah figured primarily in an ornamental capacity, together with other symbols. A characteristic example is the title page illustration in a periodical entitled *La Renaissance juive,* published in Cairo in 1912 and devoted to culture and art (fig. 1). The center of the field is taken up by motifs signifying national renewal and renaissance: the rising sun, Noah's ark resting on Mount Ararat. These are flanked by the Tablets of the Law, menorahs, Stars of David, and lions. The "Zionist" menorah is not accompanied by the usual, time-honored motifs: the incense shovel, the *lulav* (palm branch), and the *shofar* (ram's horn). These belonged to the religious-cultic context, which was of no interest to Zionism. The menorah, combined with the Tablets of the Law and the Magen David, symbolized Jewish ties with the land of Israel and with the historical past. Thus, while the Tablets of the Law represent the role of the Torah and of Jewish law in the molding of Jewish identity, and the Magen David symbolizes the modern Jewish-national entity, entering its claim for equal rights among the nations, the menorah stood for the past, the golden age of the Temple. The Temple, originally a cultic center, had become a symbol of lost Jewish sovereignty.

The menorah frequently appears either intertwined with the Magen David or standing opposite or next to it. Although the combination is usually attributed to the Zionist artist E. M. Lilien, this coupling of the two symbols was probably conceived by more than one person. Lilien used the combination as the emblem of the Zionist publishing house Jüdischer Verlag and in the illustration on the title page of the Zionist-oriented periodical *Ost und West,* edited by Martin Buber and published in Berlin. In the 1904 volume of *Ost und West*, Lilien filled the entire cover of the book with a carpet-like interconnected pattern featuring both symbols (fig. 2). A menorah and a Magen David, interwoven or side by side, repeatedly figure as illustrations on Zionist postcards, delegates' cards to conferences and congresses, and Jewish National Fund stamps.

The menorah and Magen David pairing may be elucidated through a comparison with other Zionist symbols that also appeared in pairs, hinting at opposite, complementary ideas. Such couplings may already be found on delegates' cards for the early Zionist congresses: one side shows a pioneer plowing and sowing, the other, Jews praying at the Western Wall. The pioneer, taking his fate into his hands and returning to the land, represents national renewal. His choice is contrasted with that of the praying Jews, who symbolize the impotence of the Diaspora and a focus on the past. Yet these opposites are complementary and interdependent: the pioneer relies on tradition, on generations of Jews who yearned for Zion, and draws his strength from them, while the traditional Jew has no hope and future without the pioneer. Similarly, another common pairing – old and young – symbolized contrast and continuity, the link between past and future. This use of emblematic images that were both contradictory and complementary reflects the attempt of Zionist propaganda to mitigate the revolutionary shock of national revival, to make room both for those who were eager to change the face of Jewish culture and society and for those who wished to preserve the old frameworks and traditions.

4

Title page of *Tagar* (Struggle), bi-weekly magazine of Zionists-Revisionists and Brith Trumpeldor (Beitar) in the Far East
Shanghai,
15 Feb. 1948
The Jabotinsky Institute in Israel
Tel Aviv

The menorah/Magen David pairing also represents complementary opposites: the Magen David, lacking roots in a remote historical past or in national myths, symbolizes Jewish national identity, as embodied in a political movement which, in the spirit of 19th-century nationalism, was struggling for sovereignty and equal rights. The menorah, by contrast, was heavily charged with historical memory and ancient myths. No longer generally associated with its role as a ritual object in the Temple, it nevertheless had eschatological associations. Significantly, the religious-Zionist Mizrahi movement, which in its early days refused to attach any messianic significance to Zionism, avoided using the menorah as a symbol, preferring the Tablets of the Law, which expressed devotion to Torah and *halakhah*. And so, one finds that a stamp acknowledging a donation to the Orthodox *Torah Va'avodah* educational system features the Tablets of the Law, while a stamp issued by the Yiddish school system of the socialist Poalei Zion movement shows an intertwined menorah and Magen David.

The menorah and the Magen David were sometimes combined, sometimes shown separately as parallel and equal symbols. A *Yizkor* book published in 1917 in memory of members of Hashomer – the first of many memorial volumes associated with the Zionist endeavor – shows a Magen David draped in black, together with a falling menorah with smoke rising from its extinguished lights. The two images appear here in an equal capacity, each symbolizing the nation mourning its dead heroes.

Around the same time, the menorah was associated with Jewish power and heroism in the emblems of the Jewish Legion. It was one of the components in the insignia of the American Jewish Legion (founded in 1917 by Jewish volunteers from the USA and Canada), together with a Magen David; and it was the sole heraldic insignia of the 38th Battalion of the Royal Fusiliers, which was made up of Jewish volunteers from Great Britain. Ze'ev Jabotinsky, founder of the battalion, relates in his memoirs how he proposed that the soldiers' caps should bear "a seven-branched menorah with the Hebrew inscription *kadimah*, which means both 'forward' and 'to the East.'"[2] This was also the insignia of the combined battalions of Jewish volunteers consolidated in 1919 under the name "The First Judean Regiment" – a name which, like the host of verbal and visual images that accompanied the establishment of the various units of the Jewish Legion, presented these military units as expressions of the Hebrew renaissance: the new Jew was a heroic warrior, like his ancestors, and like them he was setting out to conquer his homeland and defend it (fig. 3).

How did the menorah, which symbolizes the sacred service in the Temple, come to be chosen to represent Jewish heroism? Jabotinsky does not explain his choice in the above source, but the answer may be found in a different context. A few years after the establishment of the Jewish Legion, the menorah was chosen as the emblem of the Beitar movement, whose founder and first leader was Jabotinsky (fig. 4). In *Habetari: A Little Encyclopedia for Beitar Members*, published in Lwow in 1935, we read: "The insignia of Beitar is the menorah. When Judas Maccabeus liberated the Jews from the Syrian yoke, the menorah was kindled in the Temple as a symbol of freedom for the Jewish people. When Ze'ev Jabotinsky created the Jewish Legion, he gave it the menorah for its insignia. The menorah was a symbol of the liberation of the land. The menorah reminds the Beitar member of his duties: to fight for the liberation of the land of Israel and the freedom of the people of Israel; to fight for the establishment of a free Jewish state in the land of Israel."

5
Certificate detailing the activities and achievements of the Anglo-Palestine Company, Jerusalem, 1910
Artist: Jacob Stark
Central Zionist Archives, Jerusalem

Thus the menorah had become a symbol of Jewish heroism, of the national struggle for freedom. Zionism, which had enlisted the Hanukkah festival and its symbols in the service of its ideals, invested both the Hanukkah lamp and the seven-branched menorah with a new, secular-national, meaning: the Hanukkah lamp no longer represented the miracle of the cruse of oil, symbolic of divine intervention to renew the sacred service in the Temple; the menorah was no longer "just" a cultic utensil. Both came to represent the might and heroism of the Maccabees, whose struggle was interpreted in Zionist lore in a purely national sense, worthy of emulation by Zionists.

One Zionist body which embraced the menorah was the Bezalel School of Art and Crafts. Although the menorah was not the official emblem of the institution, it was mounted on the roof of the Bezalel building in Jerusalem and thus became its representative symbol. The menorah was also the central element in official publications, such as a poster advertising a Bezalel exhibition in 1913 – rather than the Ark of the Covenant, which appeared on the school flag. A sketch by Ze'ev Raban for the title page of a utopian novel by Bezalel's founder, Boris Schatz, *Jerusalem Rebuilt* (1924), features the biblical craftsman Bezalel, creator of the menorah in the Tabernacle, with Schatz on the roof of the Bezalel building in Jerusalem; a menorah hovers above them (p. 55). Beneath the title of the book is a quotation from the *Pesikta*: "In the future Jerusalem shall be a beacon to the nations of the world and they shall follow its light." Here the menorah of the Bezalel School symbolized not only the yearning for the golden age of biblical times and Schatz's vision of the renaissance of Jewish creativity in the ancestral homeland, but also the Zionist hope, in the spirit of Ahad Ha'am, that the Jewish enterprise in the land of Israel would become a spiritual and cultural center for the Jewish people and for the whole world (see article by S. Steinberg in this volume).[3]

The menorah as a source of light, like the rising sun, symbolizing Zionist renewal and hope, appears frequently in a variety of contexts. One such menorah is featured on a Jewish National Fund medallion which appeared in innumerable publications. On one side were a map of the land of Israel and a child putting money into a JNF (Jewish National Fund) box. The other side showed a lighted menorah, above which was a six-pointed star. Rays of light from the star and from the flames create a bright halo around the menorah. The lower part is decorated with a wreath made out of the biblical "Seven Species" of the land, symbolizing abundance and blessing. The Bezalel artist Jacob Stark also used the menorah to represent prosperity as a central motif in the elaborate certificate he designed for the Zionist bank, the

Anglo-Palestine Company, in 1910 (fig. 5). On each branch of the menorah one of the bank's spheres of monetary and economic activity was inscribed; the use of the menorah lent these activities a distinct eschatological meaning.

The menorah as a symbol for the spiritual richness of the Zionist endeavor received lyrical treatment in a poem by Abraham Shlonsky, entitled *Shabbat* (1927).[4] The pioneers' work "on roofs, on roads, on the sands of my homeland" is the new sacred service; as such, it is entitled to receive the divine grace emanating from the menorah. Here the religious-eschatological symbol was called upon to reinforce and vindicate Zionist activity, in fact, to sanctify it. Inspired by Zechariah's prophetic vision of redemption, in which the menorah plays a central role, the symbol returns to its roots in Shlonsky's poem: an emblem of the sacred service in the Temple and also of spiritual redemption, it now comes to symbolize Zionist hopes for the redemption of humankind and of the nation:

For there are seven days to the week
And seven branches to the menorah,
And whoever has kindled the menorah in his soul
Shall pour oil by its light.
O pour the oil and see, how much song
Has been sprinkled from your golden goblet –
On roofs, on roads, on the sands of my homeland.
It is Your hand, my Sovereign, that has poured this . . .

In the undeclared rivalry of the Magen David and the menorah for the right to represent the Zionist movement, the menorah slowly but surely asserted its power. The various interpretations and associations that were linked with the menorah during the first half of the 20th century endowed this ancient object with an undeniably Zionist aura. When the movement achieved its goal and the State of Israel was declared, the two symbols divided the honors of statehood between them: the Magen David on the nation's flag and the menorah on its coat of arms. And by choosing the depiction of the gold candelabrum taken from Titus' Arch for the emblem (pp. 190–191), yet another interpretive layer was added: at one time an image of destruction and exile, a sacred vessel taken from the Temple into Roman "captivity," the menorah had now come to symbolize national sovereignty and the Jewish people's return to its land.

---

1 Gershom Scholem, "The Star of David: History of a Symbol," in *The Messianic Idea in Judaism and Other Essays* (New York, 1971), 257–81; quotes on pp. 259, 280–81.

2 Ze'ev Jabotinsky, *Megillat Hagedud*, 1919.

3 *Bezalel 1906–1929*, ed. Nurit Shilo-Cohen (The Israel Museum, Jerusalem, 1983).

4 Abraham Shlonsky, *Leabba-Imma – Zeror Shirim* (Tel Aviv, 1927).

Knesset (Israeli parliament) menorah, 1948–56
Benno Elkan, 1877–1960
Bronze, ca. 4 x 5 m

The large seven-branched candelabrum that stands in the Wohl Rose Garden opposite the Knesset gates is a gift of the British Members of Parliament to their colleagues in the Israeli Knesset, a token of their esteem for the Zionist enterprise. The creator of the menorah, Benno Elkan, was a German-born Jewish artist who lived and worked in London. This menorah is one of several that he made for synagogues and Jewish communities throughout the world. The menorah was first erected in downtown Jerusalem, near the site of the former Knesset building. From there it was transferred to its permanent location within the government complex.

The seven branches of this bronze menorah are covered with twenty-nine reliefs depicting key events and figures in Jewish history and tradition, beginning with Abraham, through the Babylonian exile and the Warsaw Ghetto revolt, and culminating in the Jewish pioneers in the land of Israel. The menorah's reliefs also relate to important spiritual figures and leaders, principles of belief and morality, and such themes as reality and myth, exile and destruction, hope and redemption.

Lenders to the Exhibition

Alan and Roni Baharaff, Tel Aviv

Arnon Ben-David, Tel Aviv and New York

Chaya Benjamin, Jerusalem

Aldo Bises, Rome

Rudi Dayan, Haifa

Avinoam Denin, Jerusalem

Itzhak Einhorn, Tel Aviv

Adina and Avner Elkayam, Aviva Askarov, and the late Naomi Dayan

Ruth Eshel, Kibbutz Sha'ar Hagolan

Belu-Simion Fainaru, Haifa

William and Dorothy Gale and Family, Jerusalem

The Gross Family Collection, Tel Aviv

Kes Takuya Hadana, Beth Shemesh

David Jeselsohn, Zurich

Daphna Lapidot, Mevaseret Zion

Illy Levinson, Jerusalem

Jonathan and Daniel Lewitt, Jerusalem

Willy Lindwer, Amsterdam

Ya'akov Meshorer, Jerusalem

Yehuda Mizrahi, Jerusalem

Shlomo Moussaieff, London

Shifra and Moshe Na'amat, Tel Aviv

Shraga Qedar, Jerusalem

Israel Rabinovitz, Jerusalem

Esther Reifenberg, Jerusalem

Yeremiyahu Rimon, Haifa

Alain Roth, Herzliya

Eva Sznajderman, Moza Ilit

Ora Shwartz-Be'eri, Jerusalem, and Nurit Shwartz, Hadera

Judy and Michael Steinhardt, New York

David Tartakover, Tel Aviv

Micaela Vitale, Rome

Georges Weil, Israel

Anonymous loan

Archive of the Jabotinsky Institute in Israel, Tel Aviv

Artists' House, Jerusalem

Bibliothèque Nationale de France, Paris

Central Office of Information, Publications Center

Central Zionist Archives, Jerusalem

Deutsches Evangelisches Institut für Altertumswissenschaft des Heiligen Landes, Jerusalem

École Biblique, St. Etienne Monastery, Jerusalem

Elite Industries Ltd., Ramat Gan

Etz Hayyim, Amsterdam

Har'el Printers and Publishers, Jaffa

Institute of Archaeology, The Hebrew University of Jerusalem

Israel Antiquities Authority

Israel Government Coins and Medal Corporation, Ltd., Jerusalem

Israeli Broadcasting Authority, Jerusalem

The Jewish Museum, New York

The Jewish National and University Library, Jerusalem

Lavon Institute – Labor Archive, Tel Aviv

Mishkan L'Omanut, Museum of Art, Ein-Harod

Musée Royal de Mariemont, Belgium, through Solomon Gil, Brussels

Museum für Spatantike und Byzantinische Kunst, Berlin

National Library of Russia, St. Petersburg

Soprintendenza Archeologica delle Province di Napoli e Casesta, Naples

Soprintendenza Archeologica di Roma, Museo Nazionale Romano, Rome

Staff Officer for Archaeology, Judea and Samaria

The State Archives, Jerusalem

The Katz Research Institute for Hebrew Literature, Tel Aviv University

Yad Vashem Art Museum, Jerusalem

Photographs and Drawings

Photographs

Most of the photographs are © the Israel Museum, Jerusalem/ by David Harris. All other photographs are © the following:

Alinari, Florence: pp. 51:3, 52:4, 124:5
Hillel Burger: p. 73 below
Paul Huber: Zurich p. 70
Nogah Hareuveni: pp. 38–42
Boaz Wohl: p. 109 right
Hila Zahavi: pp. 166–167
Avraham Hay: p. 110
David Harris: pp. 19, 69
Erich Lessing, Vienna: pp. 125:6, 190–191
Phototech, Gabriel Mila, Paris: pp. 113–115
Garo Nalbandian: p. 210
Israel Rabinovitz: p. 178:4
Joan Roth, New York: p. 165

Central Zionist Archives, Jerusalem/ by Reuven Milon: pp. 16. 197, 200
The Jewish National and University Library, Jerusalem: p. 30
Beth Hatefutsoth, The Nahum Goldmann Museum of the Jewish Diaspora, Tel Aviv: pp. 205–208
Beth Hatefutsoth, The Nahum Goldmann Museum of the Jewish Diaspora, Tel Aviv/ by Avraham Hay: p. 162 left
The Government Press Office: p. 141
Musée de l'Homme, Paris: p. 160
The Jewish Museum, New York/ by John Parnell: p. 105
The Israel Museum, Jerusalem: pp. 126:2, 130
The Israel Museum, Jerusalem/ by Avi Ganor: pp. 126:1, 127:3, 116:7, 154
The Israel Museum, Jerusalem/ by Avraham Hay: pp. 155, 159
The Israel Museum, Jerusalem/ by Yoram Lehmann: pp. 62, 64, 95, 99
The Israel Museum, Jerusalem/ by Reuven Milon: pp. 149–150
The Israel Museum, Jerusalem/ by Meidad Suchowalski: pp. 138, 189, 202, 204
The Israel Museum, Jerusalem/ by Nahum Slapak: pp. 32, 36, 65, 68, 97, 101, 140, 158
Kaiser Friedrich Museum, Berlin: p. 123:3
Institute of Archaeology, The Hebrew University of Jerusalem Sepphoris Expedition/ by Gabi Laron: p. 153
Institute of Microfilmed Hebrew Manuscripts, The Jewish National and University Library, Jerusalem: pp. 81:2, 78:1, 144
The Center for Jewish Art, The Hebrew University of Jerusalem: pp. 82:3–4, 83:5–6
The Center for Jewish Art, The Hebrew University of Jerusalem/ by Ze'ev Radovan: p. 89:5
Sotheby's, Tel Aviv: p. 84
Biblioteca Nacional, Lisbon: p. 57
Bibliothèque Nationale de France, Paris: pp. 33, 66, 142
National Library of Russia, St. Petersburg: p. 63
Staff Officer for Archaeology, Judea and Samaria: p. 67

Photographs from books

P. 36 based on Dan Reisinger, *Symbols* (Tel Aviv) p. 34: 1-8
Pp. 43–47 based on *Eretz-Israel* 18 (1985): 256–267, figs. 1a–b, 2, 5–9 (Hebrew); p. 45:7 courtesy of the authors
P. 50:1 based on B. Mazar, *Beth She'arim*, vol.1 (Jerusalem, 1944), 87 (Hebrew)
P. 71:1 based on L. Y. Rahmani, "The Tomb of Jason," *'Atiqot* 4 (1964): 11:7 (Hebrew)
P. 74:4 based on B. Mazar, *Beth She'arim*, vol.1, 156:29
P. 75:5 based on N. Avigad, *Beth She'arim*, vol. 3 (Jerusalem, 1971), 198:130 (Hebrew)
P. 72:3 based on E. R. Goodenough, *Jewish Symbols in the Greco-Roman Period*, Bollingen Foundation, New York, vol. 11 (New York, 1964), pl. 3
P. 76:2 based on Goodenough, vol. 3 (New York, 1953), ill. 739
P. 77:3–4 based on Goodenough, vol. 3, ills. 806, 817
P. 78:6 based on Fratelli Palombi (ed.), *Arte Ebraica a Roma e nel Lazio* (Rome, 1994), ill. 34. Photo: German Institute of Archaeology, Rome
P. 79:7a based on Palombi (ed.), ill. 28. Photo: Sam Wagenaar Fund
P. 79:7b based on Goodenough, vol. 3, ill. 721
P. 83.6 based on Goodenough, vol. 3, ill. 789

Drawings

Pnina Arad: pp. 50:2, 69, 71:2, 111:4
Florica Vanier: p, 73 below